Awadh in Revolt
1857–1858

A STUDY OF POPULAR RESISTANCE

Other books by the same author

The Penguin Gandhi Reader (1993)
Spectre of Violence: The Kanpur Massacres in 1957 (1998)
Trade and Politics in the Indian Ocean World: Essays in Honour of Ashin Das Gupta (1998)

Awadh in Revolt
1857–1858
A STUDY OF POPULAR RESISTANCE

Rudrangshu Mukherjee

Anthem Press

Anthem Press is an imprint of
Wimbledon Publishing Company
PO Box 9779,
SW19 7QA

This edition first published by
Wimbledon Publishing Company 2002

This edition © Permanent Black 2002 is reprinted by arrangement with
the original publisher and is only for sale outside South Asia

All rights reserved.
No part of this publication may be reproduced,
stored in a retrieval system, or transmitted, in any form
or by any means, without the prior permission in writing of
Wimbledon Publishing Company, or as expressly permitted
by law, or under terms agreed with the appropriate
reprographics rights organization.

British Library Cataloguing in Publication Data
Data available

ISBN 1 84331 075 9

1 3 5 7 9 10 8 6 4 2

For Asok Sen

'We shall not cease from exploration
And the end of all our exploring
Will be to arrive where we started
And to know the place for the first time.'

INTRODUCTION TO THE PAPERBACK EDITION

This book was born under a cusp. It was published in 1984 but the text was completed in early 1983. It thus missed the full impact of the most important intervention in modern Indian historiography, the shift in thinking initiated by *Subaltern Studies* and Ranajit Guha's *Elementary Aspects of Peasant Insurgency in Colonial India* (1983). My text could do no more than include a passing reference to the first volume of *Subaltern Studies*, published in 1982. There were themes in my book which could have been enriched from the perspective opened up by Guha and his colleagues, and most of the recent writings on 1857—as neglected a field now as it was in the late 1970s and early 1980s—have followed lines suggested in the writings of Guha and others in the Subaltern Studies collective. This introduction will look at some of these developments.

There were two formative intellectual influences on my text. One was immediate and obvious. This came directly from the writings of Eric Stokes on the revolt of 1857. These marked, as the preface to the first edition indicated, the starting points of my enquiry, and some of Stokes's conclusions were also the targets of my critique. The other influence was the history-from-below approach of E.P. Thompson, Christopher Hill, George Rudé and Rodney Hilton. I drew inspiration from the writings of these historians and tried to use some of their methods. This seemed valid at the time. But as I read more of the writings of some of the scholars of the Subaltern Studies collective and reflected on the implications of their work, I recognised that they were pushing me to think beyond history-from-below and some of the other accepted shibboleths of radical historiography.

Soon after the appearance of *Awadh in Revolt* came the publication of Eric Stokes's posthumous book *The Peasant Armed*.[1] This was not a finished work and it did not have the section that Stokes wanted to write on Awadh. The general thrust of Stokes's analysis as revealed in his earlier articles[2] was strengthened by the pieces Bayly had put together in *The Peasant Armed*. Stokes urged that it was more important to look at local differentiae in the revolt than seek linkages and connections. Until the

---

[1] Eric Stokes, *The Peasant Armed: The Indian Revolt of 1857*, edited by C.A. Bayly (Oxford, 1986).
[2] These articles are available in Eric Stokes, *The Peasant and the Raj: Studies in Agrarian Society and Peasant Rebellion in Colonial India* (Cambridge, 1978).

local differences were set out district by district, historians would be 'striking matches in the dark'.[3] This was based on an overall scepticism about the possibilities of generalisations in history. 'Historical truth,' Stokes averred, 'marches only briefly to tunes of sounding generality.'[4] My book tried to show the inadequacies of such a disaggregated view of the rebellion. There is no need here to rehearse those arguments. But it is important to recall the fact that Stokes's book gave a pivotal role to the peasantry.

All the great issues of interpretation of 1857, Stokes said, turned on the assessment of peasant action. The peasantry formed the vital link between military mutiny and rural turbulence. 'In a real sense,' he wrote, 'the revolt was essentially the revolt of a peasant army breaking loose from its foreign masters.'[5] But this assignation of a central role to peasants was not matched by any gesture towards making peasants masters of their own destiny. Peasants were invariably the objects of one thing or the other— land-revenue policy or some other policy on the part of the colonial state or the local landlord or usurer. The actions of peasants in the great rebellion were not informed by any consciousness: their actions were determined by local magnates, dominant peasants, or worse by designing men, all of whom turned instinctively against their 'natural enemies' once the structure of the colonial state had collapsed under the onslaughts of the native soldiery.[6]

It was precisely here that Guha's *Elementary Aspects*[7] taught us to look and to think anew about peasants in revolt. Guha located the peasantry in colonial India within a relationship of power, in a relationship of domination and subordination. On one side were the dominators— the triumvirate of *sarkar*, *sahukar* and zamindar—and on the other the subordinated peasantry. Implicit in this pairing or opposition of power was the autonomous subjectivity of the dominated, the peasants. For if the peasants were not autonomous and undominated, the dominators, in the very exercise of their domination, would suppress and obliterate the dominated. Domination would thus be left without its Other. The peasantry thus had to be given its own autonomous domain. Guha argued that this domain could be located in what was opposed to domination, i.e. resistance. It was in resistance that the peasantry became conscious of the dominator and of its own autonomous identity.[8]

[3] *Peasant Armed*, p. 225. On page 14 he wrote, 'The nature of the rural uprising in Upper India needs to be looked at more narrowly and its local differentiae observed.'
[4] Ibid., p. 14.
[5] Ibid.
[6] Ibid., pp. 214–25.
[7] Ranajit Guha, *Elementary Aspects of Peasant Insurgency in Colonial India* (Delhi, 1983).
[8] Ibid., Introduction.

Introduction to the Paperback Edition ix

When peasants revolted, the dominators were forced to recognise them. Insurgent peasants forced their way into the historical archives created and preserved by dominators. By reading this archive against its grain, the historian would gain access not only to the actions of peasants but also to the consciousness that informed those actions. Peasants had too much at stake to take to arms in a fit of absentmindedness. The archive of the dominator preserved, in a mirror image, the consciousness of the dominated who were powerless to record their own actions, perceptions and knowledge.[9] Guha's aim was not to depict the struggle of peasants as a series of specific encounters but in its general form. He sought to isolate the ideological invariants of peasant consciousness: he called them 'elementary aspects'. There were six such: negation, ambiguity, modality, solidarity, transmission and territoriality. To illustrate these aspects, Guha drew on an enormous amount of historical material, which inevitably meant from the events of 1857, in which the peasants had played such a crucial and important part.

Peasants, Guha wrote, could recognise themselves and form their own identity through an act of negation of their superiors. This negative consciousness was expressed first through discrimination—peasants selected the targets of their violence—and then extension—peasants extended their violence to all that was associated with their enemies. In 1857, *banias* and *mahajans* were the victims of attacks and were ousted from land. Guha cited examples from Muzaffarnagar and Hamirpur. In 1857 peasants destroyed and plundered the properties of Europeans and did relatively less damage to those of natives. The violence was extended by the logic of association, in the words of one British official, to everything 'with which we are connected', prisons, record rooms, factories, the telegraph, railways stations, the courts and so on were all targets of attack.[10] The other form of the expression of negation was inversion. Peasants asserted their resistance by appropriating for themselves the signs of authority that belonged to the dominator. They sought to invert the terms of domination and subordination. Rebellion violated the established codes of deference. In 1857 the sepoys, in station after station, became more and more insolent towards their superior white officers before they finally took to arms. British women taken as prisoners after the massacre at Satichaura Ghat in Kanpur were made to grind corn. Mahomed Ali Khan, an influential person in Kanpur known as the Nunneh Nawab and as a friend of the British, had his horse taken

---

[9]Ibid.; also see R. Guha, 'The Prose of Counter-insurgency, ' in R. Guha (ed.), *Subaltern Studies II* (Delhi, 1983).

[10]See Guha, *Elementary Aspects*, pp. 20–5.

away and was given a mule belonging to a servant. Dominators became the objects of humiliation and abuse which were normally directed towards the dominated.[11]

This inversion of the codes of dominance and subordination during insurgency often meant that rulers were liable to misread the signs of rebellion as crime. This gave to insurgency a degree of ambiguity, the second of the aspects Guha analysed. But crime and insurgency 'derive from two different codes of violence': 'unlike crime, peasant rebellions are necessarily and invariably public and communal events ... the criminal may be said to stand in the same relation to the insurgent as does what is conspiratorial (or secretive) to what is public (or open) or what is individualistic (or small-group) to what is communal (or mass) in character.'[12] Unable to recognise the distinction between crime and rebellion and the moment when the former becomes the latter, officials in 1857 labelled all rebels as dacoits—as if the two words were synonymous. Guha gave examples of this confusion and ambiguity.[13] There was a warning in Guha's text to stop the historian from thinking like a *daroga*.

Destruction was the principal modality or form of peasant insurgency. Guha identified four forms of destruction: wrecking, burning, eating and looting; the violence was also public, collective and total.[14] The public and collective character of the revolt of 1857 is obvious from the reports available of *panchayats* and discussions that preceded the call to arms.[15] In Kanpur, the rebels met before the uprising to discuss things, and General Wheeler in the entrenchment was actually informed that the attack on the entrenchment was about to begin. Even the decision to massacre the British on the river was taken collectively.[16] Wrecking, burning and looting were extensive in 1857. The British and those seen as their friends had their property and their insignias of authority destroyed and plundered. A representative description was cited by Guha from Mark Thornhill's account of the sack of Mathura: 'The plunder of the revenue office was followed by that of the English houses. In this amusement the villagers spent what remained of the day. The houses contained little that they valued; that little they carried off, the rest they broke to pieces. In the morning they returned and

[11]For inversion see ibid., pp. 28ff; sepoy insolence is well documented, Guha gives instances on p. 39. The Kanpur examples are from Rudrangshu Mukherjee, *Spectre of Violence: The 1857 Kanpur Massacres* (Delhi, 1998), chapter entitled 'The Event'.
[12]*Elementary Aspects*, p. 79.
[13]Ibid., pp. 101ff.
[14]Ibid., ch. 4.
[15]Ibid., pp. 118–19.
[16]Mukherjee, *Spectre of Violence*, pp. 49–51 and 70–1.

continued the work of destruction.'[17] Fire was the principal instrument of destruction. Recalling a series of fires that destroyed a cantonment, a bungalow and a telegraph office, at Ranigunj and Barrackpore, W.H. Carey wrote in retrospect, 'the Fire King began to demonstrate an inkling of what was in store for almost every station in the North Western Provinces.' In the summer of 1857, across the plains of north India, it was arson that destroyed record rooms, session courts, bungalows, post offices, and so on.[18] The public character of the insurgency was also expressed in the setting up of a rebel authority with power to impose laws, sanctions and punishments. In 1857, as is well known, this meant harking back to the pre-British order.

Solidarity, Guha wrote, was the categorical imprint of rebel consciousness. Its quality could vary but no rebellion was without it. Solidarity to the rebel cause in 1857 showed itself in the steadfast refusal of common people to collaborate with British authorities. When the magistrate of Saharanpur entered the village of Manuckpur to arrest its headman, he found the village 'all but deserted' despite a large reward for the apprehension of the headman.[19] In Awadh, as I had shown, villagers withheld supplies to the advancing British army.[20] Even after their victory the British, in the course of their enquiry into the events, found it difficult to establish facts and find names of rebels because the people refused to come forward with evidence.[21]

One indicator of the strength of this solidarity was the speed with which the message of rebellion was transmitted, leaving the rulers bewildered. This touches upon the two best-known features of the revolt of 1857: the circulation of the *chapati*, and rumours. Nobody has been able to explain the significance of the circulating chapati. There is no trace left in the records of the meaning attached to it by the peasants of 1857. The British did not know what to make of it, but after the event some bureaucrats and scholars used it as a convenient peg on which to hang their conspiracy theory. T. Rice Holmes, in fact, compared the chapatis to the 'fiery cross that summoned the clans-men of Roderick to battle.' They misread, as Guha points out, a symbol as an index and the chapati became the transmitter of the message of conspiracy and revolt. But there were local administrators in 1857 who were not willing to endow the chapati any such significance. For them, in the words of Guha, 'the chapati was more of a red herring than a fiery cross.' Guha,

---

[17] *Elementary Aspects*, pp. 138–9.
[18] Ibid., pp. 140–1.
[19] Ibid., pp. 206–7.
[20] Mukherjee, *Awadh in Revolt*, ch. 4.
[21] Guha, *Elementary Aspects*, pp. 213–14; and Mukherjee, *Spectre of Violence*, p. 109.

however, brought to the chapati phenomenon a new angle. He showed, via William Crooke's observations of rural life in northern India, that during an epidemic some ritually consecrated object was circulated to push the disease outside the boundaries of a village or a locality. This technique was called *chalawa* which means, according to Crooke, 'passing on the malady'. North India had witnessed a cholera epidemic and the chapati could have been the traditional chalawa. But the chapati could have meant different things to different people. Guha summed up thus:

> The symbolic agent of an epidemic in the countryside it [the chapati] took on an added meaning as the carrier of an imminent but undefined political holocaust ... As an omen it looked ahead of events, and in an atmosphere charged with growing unrest in agrarian communities and army barracks it transmitted the rebellion in anticipation by sounding a tocsin for all to hear but none to understand why.[22]

Guha analysed rumours as both a 'universal and necessary carrier of insurgency in any pre-industrial, pre-literate society'. The power of rumours is acknowledged in the efforts the authorities put in to suppress and control their circulation. But rumours had more to them than the alarm engendered among those who had most to lose from a popular uprising. It helped spread the message of rebellion: it was a trigger and a mobiliser, a necessary instrument of rebel transmission. Rumours, by definition, are anonymous and verbal. The latter feature gives to rumours functional immediacy which allows it to seize upon important issues in periods of social tension. Rumours have a socialising process embedded in them since the passing on of a rumour, in the words of one authority, 'involves a desire on the part of the transmitter to affect other people's behaviour, to bring their perspectives in line with his own, or, at the very minimum, to share a valuable piece of information.' It is to this 'comradeship response' that rumours owe their remarkable speed. Characteristically, rumours originate and circulate where people assemble in large numbers. Kaye, in the context of 1857, described rumours as 'the lies of the Bazaar'. As any student of the great rebellion knows, Kaye drew on material linking the rumours in circulation in the bazaars with the spreading disaffection among the sepoys. Rumours can never be pinned down, they are by nature ambiguous. Kaye mentioned the vernacular saying 'It is in the air'. This, according to Guha, is what makes rumours 'a mobile and explosive agent of insurgency'. Rumours are open because they are anonymous and unverifiable; they are transitive

---

[22]For Guha's discussion on the chapati, see ibid., pp. 238–46; all quotations in this paragraph are from these pages.

Introduction to the Paperback Edition xiii

and free; their circulation is unpremeditated and therefore liable to improvisation. In 1857, rumours about greased cartridges soon spread to include edible items like flour and ghee, and then to a general conspiracy to defile and convert the entire population of India. Thus rumours brought sepoys and civilians together by a common suspicion.[23]

Together with chapatis and rumours, prophecies circulated in 1857. The most important of the prophecies was the one that said British power would be destroyed on the centenary of the battle of Plassey. Rumours were the carriers of such prophecies. It made rebels the agents of forces outside and independent of themselves. Rebels saw their destiny as a function of others' wills and actions. Drawing on Marx, Guha described such attitudes as a 'product of self-alienation', a characteristic false consciousness of the period which made the rebel look upon his own act of resistance as a manifestation of another's will.[24]

Peasant rebellions were invariably confined to a particular locality. This led Guha to look at territoriality as the final aspect of peasant insurgency. Territoriality was not always a limiting factor in rebel mobilisation. Guha illustrated this by drawing on the events of the great rebellion of 1857. The mutiny of the sepoys spread swiftly beyond the cantonments and acquired local bases. These bases became the targets of British counterinsurgency campaigns. The locality of the rebellion was defined by the domain of the local enemies—the sarkar and the sahukar. Official buildings, and all that was seen to be associated with British power in an area, became targets, as did the property of the moneylender. Thus the limits of the rebellion's geographical space were determined by a principle of exclusion, by the rebels' perception of the spread of their enemies' authority and power. It was also informed by a notion of ethnic space. In north India, where the revolt was concentrated, large populations belonging to the same caste lived in contiguous areas and had perpetuated this territorial arrangement through ritual and kinship. In 1857, ethnic groups articulated their solidarity through rebellion. Various Rajput clans rose en masse. Guha illustrated this with the example of the Bundelas, the Mewatis, the Gujars, and so on. From Awadh, one could add the names of the Bais, the Bachgotis, and others. Most of the villages were single-caste settlements and 'these village-based primordial ties were the principal means of rebel mobilisation ... A local insurrection, whatever its immediate cause, tended invariably to adapt itself to the existing pattern of ethnic solidarity in a given area.'

[23]Guha discusses rumours in ibid., pp. 251–68; all quotations in this paragraph are from these pages.
[24]Ibid., pp. 268–77.

But Guha was also quick to note that the territoriality of a revolt was not always marked by a coincidence of its domain and a caste region. A locality larger than a village—a *pargana*, or a district—could be the site of the uprising, with more than one caste taking to arms. Guha made a detailed analysis of the revolt of Meghar Singh in Ghazipur to make this point. Drawing from Awadh one could say that an entire principality could be the site of the revolt and powerful Rajput *talukdars* could leave their villages and their *ilaqa* and go with their men to fight under the banner of Birjis Qadr in Lucknow.[25]

Guha's analysis of some aspects of the revolt of 1857 firmly situated the rebellion as a project of power. It served also to free the subject from the coils of causality. All previous work on the subject, including Stokes's and my own on Awadh, had tried to understand the uprising in terms of its background or its context. Guha tried to emphasise *how* the rebels had acted was as significant, if not more significant, than *why* they had acted. They were not always objects of this or that policy. It was invariably assumed that the act of rebellion would become comprehensible if the material context was fully laid out. Guha, on the other hand, looked at the actions of the rebels rather than at the context of their actions. He saw them as conscious agents working to overturn a power structure that they considered alien, exploitative and oppressive. This insight brought a new dimension to the study of the great uprising.

For the historian of 1857, Guha's emphasis on peasants as conscious agents in the making of their own history focussed attention on the fact that the sepoys who had mutinied were of peasant stock. The peasant origins of the sepoy army had been noted but not elaborated in chapter 3 of *Awadh in Revolt*. I had drawn attention to the importance of Awadh, especially Baiswara, as a recruitment ground for sepoys. Subsequent research on the sepoy army by Seema Alavi tends to confirm these suggestions.[26] The peasant origins of the sepoys facilitated the swift merging of sepoys with peasants after the mutinies. But the specific contribution of the sepoy element to the uprising needs to be reiterated. The sepoys were in a unique position. Apart from the princes and talukdars, they were the only people to have been been proximate to state power. As sons of the peasantry, they had left the village for the world: now, during the revolt, they were bringing the world back to the village. As peasants, they had seen peasants as mere objects of officialdom; as sepoys they could

[25]Guha's analysis of territoriality and the revolt of 1857 will be found in ibid., pp. 308–32; this paragraph is a bald summary of his rich analysis; the quoted lines will be found on pp. 316–17.

[26]S. Alavi, *The Sepoys and the Company: Tradition and Transition in Northern India 1770–1830* (Delhi, 1995).

identify the state as the real object of hatred. The sepoys' proximity to state power had a dual aspect. On the one hand, they could identify the state as the enemy. On the other, the same exposure and experience, especially the many battles they had fought in India on behalf of the British, had forced on them the realisation that, in the conduct of war, leadership, discipline and structures of command were crucial. The return of the sepoys to their villages as an armed peasantry was thus informed by a new consciousness. The invoking of the traditional leadership could be a product of that consciousness. It is significant that in 1857 dethroned kings or dispossessed princes—Bahadur Shah, Nana Sahib, Rani Lakshmibai, Birjis Qadr and so on—that is, those who previously established claims to leadership and command, were chosen to give the uprising legitimacy. An older and legitimate political order had lost out to the British or had had their power usurped by the British in the late eighteenth and early nineteenth centuries; the sepoys, in their quest for legitimacy, leadership and command, were reviving that order and fighting a war on its behalf and in its name.[27] Further, as Alavi points out, the re-emergence of these centres of power meant that for the sepoys 'the Company ceased to be the most attractive employer in India and patrons amongst the rebel leaders were able to hold to them [the sepoys] the material, political and ritual inducements which the Company had once monopolised.'[28] Thus the former princes who emerged as leaders, often under popular pressure, were dependent on the sepoys for their fighting power and survival. But the sepoys too were tied to the princes for their livelihood and survival. Such ties gave the rebellion its strength and solidarity.

Stokes suggested—in a remarkable reconstruction of the military dimension of the revolt from the sepoy army's perspective—that by moving towards Delhi, Lucknow and Kanpur—in other words to fight under the regional leaders—in the initial and crucial phase of the revolt, the sepoys gave up what could have been their tactical strength, a war of movement.[29] The successful attacks on these centres by the British, especially Delhi, led to a collapse in organisation. The sepoy regiments had lost their white officers and had not replaced them with native ones. This, not lack of courage, explains the overall lack of success.[30] The harking back to the kings and princes was thus not without a drawback. But as Tapti Roy, in her study of the revolt in Bundelkhand, has noted pertinently, soldiers in mutiny, whatever their origins, do not stop being soldiers after they have mutinied. An army by definition is an arm of

---

[27] This paragraph is based on what I wrote in *Spectre of Violence*, pp. 65–6.
[28] Alavi, *Sepoys and the Company*, p. 296.
[29] Stokes, *Peasant Armed*, ch. 2.
[30] Ibid., p. 98.

the state and a rebel army stakes its legitimacy by declaring its loyalty to a political authority.[31] Rebel sepoys in 1857 did so by announcing that they were fighting for the Mughal emperor or for Birjis Qadr or Nana Sahib and so on. This declaration of allegiance and loyalty often closed options for the princes and many of them were forced to accept the mantle of leadership under tremendous popular pressure.[32]

This harking back to an older political order reintroduced the question of the ideology of the revolt, which had been a subject of discussion in *Awadh in Revolt*. Some historians have seen patriotism as the driving force behind the rebellion. They have argued that the rebels were motivated by something more than a desire to bring back the eighteenth-century Mughal order and princely power. There was a discernible attachment to a wider entity that went beyond the confines of class, caste, community and village. That overarching entity could be *din* or *dharma*.[33] Rajat Ray has given this argument a sharper edge by suggesting that the consistent invocation to Hindus and Mussalmans in all the proclamations that came out of the rebel camps was a precursor to 'the Indian nation' which the Congress leaders invoked in the 1920s.[34] The only difficulty in this interpretation is that the actions and motives of rebels come to be seen through the filter of terms and concepts which were perhaps unknown to them.

To the 'non-question'[35] of whether the revolt was retrograde or forward looking, Chris Bayly in his book on empire and information has introduced a new dimension.[36] He has shown that just as the British used a variety of communication channels and information-gathering networks to facilitate their counterinsurgency operations, the rebels too showed a remarkable degree of awareness about the importance of communication in the success of a rebellion. As is well known, one of the first things they did was cut the telegraph wires. In some places they even cut off postal communications along the Grand Trunk Road. The road, in fact, became the site for a battle to keep the *dak* running. Rebel

---

[31]Tapti Roy, *The Politics of a Popular Uprising: Bundelkhand in 1857* (Delhi, 1994), pp. 44–5.

[32]For an analysis of how this worked in the case of Nana Sahib, see Mukherjee, *Spectre of Violence*, pp. 63–4; and for the Rani of Jhansi, see Roy, *Bundelkhand*, pp. 103–4.

[33]See Rajat Ray, 'Race, Religion and the Realm: The Political Theory of the "Reigning Indian Crusade", 1857', in N. Gupta and M. Hasan (eds), *India's Colonial Encounter: Essays in Memory of Eric Stokes* (Delhi, 1993), pp. 133–82; and C.A. Bayly, 'Patriotism and Ethical Government, c. 1780–1860' in *Origins of Nationality in South Asia: Patriotism and Ethical Government in the Making of Modern India* (Delhi, 1998), pp. 86ff.

[34]Ray, 'Race, Religion and Realm', p. 166.

[35]The very apt epithet is Tapti Roy's: *Bundelkhand*, p. 258.

[36]C.A. Bayly, *Information and Empire: Intelligence-Gathering and Social Communication in India, 1780–1870* (Cambridge, 1996).

Introduction to the Paperback Edition xvii

leaders also used the customary mode of placards near mosques. There were also proclamations; and rebels even used forms of modern media. There were anti-British newspapers and 'the whole panoply of written indigenous communication—*akhbarats, charitas, parwanas, roznamachas* and the like—were employed to spread the message of revolt and the restoration of the authority of the King of Awadh.' The rebel court in Lucknow kept meticulous records and had its own team of writers and *munshis*. The rebel leadership in Awadh used the printing press: 'the most important proclamation of early August 1857 was lithographed.' Rebels also had their own counter-intelligence system and they restored the *harkara* system.[37] Rebels by no means abhorred modern methods of communication.

The year of the rebellion also saw a sudden blooming of Indian medicine and astrology, forms of knowledge that the British had sought to marginalise on account of their interest in spreading English education and Western science. One Pandit Hari Chander reportedly incited rebels with his 'knowledge of the stars and the occult sciences'. Native doctors came in to dress the wounds of soldiers. The revolt thus became a battleground of ideas.[38] But the ideas of those who lost are not adequately documented in the available archives.[39] There was in 1857, one could say invoking Foucault, 'an insurrection of subjugated knowledges'.[40] These were popular knowledges disqualified from the hierarchy of knowledges and sciences. Their reappearance and articulation constituted a critique of British rule and of the intellectual apparatus it imposed on Indians to justify and perpetuate its domination.[41] This battle of ideas was inevitably one-sided because a fully embodied intellectual system was attacked by 'a local..[and] a differential knowledge incapable of unanimity.'[42] But an awareness of this conflict is important because it disrupts a process of appropriation by which the uprising of 1857 is made a part of the grand narrative of Indian nationalism and the making of a modern Indian state.

---

[37] The facts and the quotations are taken from ibid., pp. 320–4.

[38] Ibid., pp. 329–30.

[39] There is the possibility that this perspective might be factually enhanced from Urdu and Persian sources. A step has been taken in this direction by the History Department of Aligarh Muslim University. Some of their initial findings were put together in an issue of *Social Scientist*, vol. 26, nos. 1–4 (Jan–April, 1998), devoted to the revolt of 1857.

[40] M. Foucault, 'Two Lectures' in *Power/Knowledge: Selected Interviews and Other Writings, 1972–1977*, edited by Colin Gordon (New York, 1980), p. 81. Bayly (p. 330) uses the phrase but does not work out the implications.

[41] Ibid., p. 82.

[42] Ibid.

PREFACE

The events of 1857 aroused passions both among participants and observers to a level unsurpassed before or since in the relations between Britain and India. For historians the revolt of 1857 has been a cornucopia.[1] Ever since the days of Kaye, whose work still commands magisterial authority, through the jingoism of V.D. Savarkar[2] and the spate of scholarly monographs in the centenary year, the rebellion has been a popular subject for general accounts. However, such accounts have been constricted in their scope in the sense that they have been concerned mainly with characterizing the events of 1857: mutiny, war of independence, feudal uprising, what have you. There has been very little effort to move away from such a concern with labels to questions of social composition and material background. Perhaps the only exception is the work of S.B. Chaudhuri who analyses the areas of 'civil' rebellion in 1857.[3] But in the battle of books that ensued in the centenary year, even that author was drawn into the rather sterile debate on nomenclature.[4] This concern with the character of the revolt, wherein the terms of reference are always 'mutiny', 'first freedom struggle' or 'feudal uprising', has led to a kind of 'mental cramp':[5] a great deal has been written but the significant questions have neither been asked nor answered.

---

[1] For an annotated bibliography of what has been written on 1857 in English, see J.M. Ladendorf, *The Revolt in India, 1857-58: an annotated bibliography of English language materials* (Switzerland, 1966); also see S.B. Chaudhuri, *English Historical Writings on the Indian Mutiny, 1857-1859* (Calcutta, 1979) and K.K. Sengupta, *Recent Writings on the Revolt of 1857: A Survey* (Delhi, 1975).

[2] V.D. Savarkar, *The Indian War of Independence, 1857* (London, 1909).

[3] S.B. Chaudhuri, *Civil Rebellion in the Indian Mutinies, 1857-59* (Calcutta, 1957).

[4] S.B. Chaudhuri, *Theories of the Indian Mutiny* (Calcutta, 1965).

[5] This phrase is Eric Stokes' in 'Traditional Resistance Movements and Afro-Asian nationalism: the context of the 1857 Mutiny-Rebellion', *Past and Present*, 'No. 48. Aug. 1970; reprinted in E. Stokes. *The Peasant and the Raj: studies in agrarian society and peasant rebellion in colonial India*. (Cambridge, 1978), pp. 129.

Preface

The first major break with this historiographic tradition came with three seminal essays by the late Eric Stokes.[6] In these essays Stokes focused on the upper and central Doab and showed how the impact of British land-revenue policy was connected with 'rural political affiliation in the hour of crisis'.[7] The basic approach of this book is essentially similar: it is a detailed study of an area to explore the interaction between the material environment affected by colonial policy and the events of the revolt. In a way, Awadh was the most obvious area for such a study: all historians agree that the revolt was most fierce and lasted longest in Awadh. Yet no one, Stokes included, has investigated the rising in this area along the lines mentioned above. Awadh seemed a remarkably fertile and virgin territory for any historian of the 1857 uprising.[8]

The archival material I have used induced considerable modification in my approach. The hitherto unused data on the actual course of events and the extent of mass participation were both voluminous and significant. In the light of this material I have often found it necessary to fall back on the narrative method before interpreting the events I have described. Today, when historians who had once stressed the study of *structures* are emphasizing the relevance of narrative history,[9] perhaps this way of presenting facts and arguments requires no apology.

The choice of the word 'popular' in the title and in the text is deliberate. The revolt in Awadh pertained to the *people as a whole* and was carried on by the people; hence the adjective is

---

[6]'Nawab Walidad Khan and the 1857 Struggle in Bulandshahr District', *Bengal Past and Present* (Diamond Jubilee Number, 1967); 'Rural revolt in the Great Rebellion of 1857 in India: a study of the Saharanpur and Muzaffarnagar districts', *The Historical Journal*, xii, 4 (1969); and 'Traditional elites in the Great Rebellion of 1857: some aspects of the rural revolt in the upper and central Doab', in E. Leach and S.N. Mukherjee (ed.), *Elites in South Asia* (Cambridge, 1970). All three are reprinted in *Peasant and the Raj*.

[7]Stokes, *Peasant and the Raj*, p. 14.

[8]The only modern work, apart from nineteenth century first-hand accounts, which focusses on Awadh is J. Pemble, *The Raj, the Indian Mutiny and the Kingdom of Oudh, 1801-1859* (Sussex, 1977). This is a very disappointing work: see my review in *The Indian Historical Review*, iv, No. 1, July 1977, pp. 192-5.

[9]L. Stone, 'The Revival of Narrative: Reflections on a New Old History', *Past and Present*, No. 85, Nov. 1979, pp. 3-24; also see E.J. Hobsbawm, 'The Revival of Narrative: Some Comments', ibid., No. 86, Feb. 1980, pp. 3-8.

appropriate. If one were to accept J. H. Hexter's division of historians into 'lumpers' and 'splitters',[10] then the present book is an exercise in 'lumping' rather than 'splitting'. I have emphasized linkages and connections rather than divisions. Yet the fractures in the rebellion have not been altogether ignored. In my narrative I have often let the sources speak for themselves; hence the preponderance of citations and quotations. This is meant to forestall any accusation that I have read too much into my sources in order to prove my case.

In exploring the popular character of the uprising I have tried to draw attention to certain hitherto unnoticed aspects of the rising. Certain features of the immediately pre-annexation agrarian scene are shown to be causally linked to the specific characteristics of the revolt in this area — the fact that the general populace, especially talukdars and peasants, fought together against a common foe. I have argued that forms of practical co-operation between various strata of rural society were in-built within the functioning of Awadh rural society. This is not to gloss over conflict and exploitation in a society dominated by aristocratic clan heads. It is to emphasize a certain 'commonality' of interests and mutual dependence which might not only have acted as instruments of legitimation in an essentially paternalistic world but also provided the basis for common and united action at this tumultuous conjuncture.[11] This world was disrupted by the first British revenue prescriptions which dispossessed the talukdars and exposed the peasants to overassessment. The dispossession of talukdars meant not only the loss of power and status but also the loss of control over surplus from which such power and status grew. It also meant a threat to a certain life-style

[10] J.H. Hexter, 'The Historical Method of Christopher Hill', *Times Literary Supplement*, 24 Oct. 1975, reprinted in J.H. Hexter, *On Historians* (London, 1979), pp. 227-51.

[11] See R. Hilton, *Bond Men Made Free: Medieval Peasant Movements and the English Rising of 1381* (London, 1973) for an analysis of how domination and co-operation could coexist in feudal England; in particular see the very suggestive sentence on p. 30: '... a peasantry dominated by aristocratic clans is not necessarily devoid of forms of practical co-operation among the peasants which would provide the basis for a common self-consciousness'. Also see E. Genovese, *Roll, Jordan Roll: The World the Slaves Made* (New York, 1974), pp. 3-7 for an analysis of the world of paternalism where exploitation/oppression and dependence or even reciprocity can coexist.

Preface xxi

that held together, however loosely and tenuously, talukdar retainer and peasant. I have tried to emphasize this amalgam as being at the root of the rural disaffection, instead of trying to seek an ever elusive 'prime' or 'paramount' motive.[12]

A word is in order here about my treatment of the first British revenue settlement, commonly known as the Summary Settlement of 1856-7. This particular revenue settlement and the revolt have been studied in a recent work by T.R. Metcalf.[13] His account is also based on some of the sources used here. But neither the revolt (or the 'mutiny'[14] as Metcalf prefers to call it) nor the 1856-7 settlement are his chief conern; consequently even when the same sources are used he asks very different questions and does not find it necessary to delve into as much detail as I do. For example my treatment of the Summary Settlement of 1856-7 in Chapter Two, while using the same sources as Metcalf's section on the topic, reveals the facts of extensive dispossession and overassessment, virtually ignored by Metcalf. These facts are central to my argument, for it was through these that the traditional rural world of Awadh was disrupted and the foundations laid for extensive disaffection.

Again, Metcalf is concerned with the revolt in so far as it affected British policy towards the talukdars and the latters' subsequent history. Hence sepoys, peasants and the general populace are not of any major relevance to his study whereas my primary aim is to explore the popular character of the revolt. It was a remarkable feature of the uprising in Awadh that the people as a whole rose in arms against the British raj. It would have been easier for a more sophisticated history if there were instances of a talukdar-peasant tension within the folds of the rebellion. Such instances are rare in Awadh; rather the combined fighting of talukdar, peasant and sepoy elements demands greater attention. I find the answer to such a remarkable and perhaps unprecedented unity in Awadh in the shared traditions of

[12] Even as perceptive a historian as Eric Stokes wrote with reference to such terms. See *Peasant and the Raj*, pp. 135 and 170.

[13] T.R. Metcalf, *Land, Landlords and the British Raj: Northern India in the Nineteenth Century* (London, 1979).

[14] I have sought to avoid the somewhat futile controversy over labels by using the words rebels and insurgents more or less interchangeably; the terms 'rebellion', 'uprising' and 'revolt' have been used equally interchangeably.

commonality in rural Awadh as well as in the commonly perceived threat from the raj to that traditional world. The sepoys form a crucial copula in the rebellion. I have tried to show the links the sepoys had with Awadh and how their mutinies had an underlying unity in terms of motives as well as in types of action. The sepoy mutinies quickly demolished British authority in Awadh — epitomized in the cantonments strewn over the province — and made possible a more general uprising where it became wellnigh impossible and unnecessary to distinguish between sepoy and peasant.

In discussing the transformation of a 'mutiny' into a general uprising I attempt to shed some new light on how the talukdars and peasants took up arms, on the ways in which the rebels sought to fight the British, and on questions of leadership and social composition. I propose a new understanding about the organization of the rebellion and its aims. The revolt may have been sparked off by mutinies in the sepoy lines but a considerable degree of organization and administration went into maintaining the struggle. Propaganda and rumour cleverly circulated and, buttressed by an appeal to religious feelings, spurred men on to fight an alien order. Prince, talukdar, peasant and sepoy, their many worlds and their many histories were brought together in 1857. This made for a certain complexity in the history of the revolt. I try to study the many overlapping strands, the emotive intensity, and the interconnections underlying the struggle.

ACKNOWLEDGEMENTS

This book has been long in the making and in a sense has travelled a complete circle. It was begun as a research project in 1976-7 when I was a Junior Research Fellow at the Centre for Studies in Social Sciences, Calcutta, and finally completed in its present form in 1981-2 when I was Fellow in History at the Centre. In between the book had its dress rehearsal as an Oxford D.Phil. thesis. I am extremely grateful to the Inlaks Foundation for its generosity when I was an Inlaks Scholar at St Edmund Hall, Oxford. I will remember my days at Teddy Hall as being among my happiest. I wish especially to recall here the kindness and consideration of Bruce Mitchell and Ken Seghers. Susanta Ghosh at the Centre for Studies in Social Sciences provided all the freedom and facilities for research as well as a lot of affection and encouragement.

I am beholden to the staff of the National Archives of India, the UP State Archives and the India Office Library and Records. Anjushri Chakrabarti drew the maps and Gauri Bandopadhyaya typed the manuscript: to both of them I remain grateful. I remember with special fondness the help and services I received from the entire staff of the Indian Institute Library in Oxford, especially from Mollie de Goris and Roberta Atherton. Jonathan Katz has been the most warm and helpful of friends. I much value the comradely eye he keeps on my English prose.

The book as it stands now is the product of many discussions I have had with Binay Chaudhuri, Partha Chatterjee, Tom Metcalf, Saugata Mukherjee, Peter Reeves and Sumit Sarkar. The errors that remain are despite their best efforts to make me see reason and knowledge. I am also grateful to the anonymous referee of the OUP who made many valuable suggestions. Mike Fisher helped in locating sources in the very early stages of research. Had it not been for the exertions of Tapan Raychaudhuri, my supervisor, and John Dunbabin, my college tutor, together with the suggestions of Simon Digby and Eric Stokes who examined the D. Phil. thesis, this book would have been far more vulnerable than it is. It is my eternal regret that Eric Stokes did not live to see this book in print. I had the good fortune to discuss my work with him and even where I disagree with him it is in the knowledge that without his pioneering efforts my work could hardly have begun.

Satyajit Ray, despite a very heavy schedule, designed the jacket. He has always been extremely generous with his time. The indulgence that I enjoy from him probably does not require a formal acknowledgement.

It is difficult for me to write about Barun De. Ever since I was an undergraduate his enthusiasm, guidance and range of historical learning has taught me more than he would care to admit. He suggested the theme and nursed the book to its present form. I don't have to thank him: he knows he is in this book wherever it rises above the puerile.

In spite of my anglicized education I find it impossible to formally thank the persons who will be the most proud to see this book. I know that for them, come what may, their honourable schoolboy will never change. It is only that certainty and confidence that gives me the courage to rush into print.

Calcutta Rudrangshu Mukherjee
September 1983

ABBREVIATIONS

BR	Board of Revenue
BROG	Board of Revenue Oudh General
Com./Commr.	Commissioner
Cons.	Consultations
CC	Chief Commissioner
C-in-C	Commander in Chief
For. Dept.	Foreign Department
Forrest, *Selections*	*Selections from Letters, Despatches and State Papers in the Military Department of the Government of India, 1857-58*, 4 vols. (Calcutta, 1893-1912).
F.S.U.P.	*Freedom Struggle in Uttar Pradesh*, ed. S.A. Rizvi and M.L. Bhargava (Lucknow, 1957).
GG	Governor-General
Kaye, *Sepoy War*	*History of the Sepoy War, 1857-58*, 3 vols. (London, vol. 1, 9th ed, 1880, Vol. 3, 4th ed., 1880).
O.G.	W.C. Benett (ed.), *A Gazetteer of the Province of Oudh* (Lucknow, 1877).
P.P.	Parliamentary Papers.
Proc.	Proceedings
Sec./Secy.	Secretary
Suppl.	Supplement

CONTENTS

	Introduction to the Paperback Edition	vii
	Preface	xviii
	Acknowledgements	xxiii
	Abbreviations	xxv
1	AGRARIAN RELATIONS IN PRE-ANNEXATION AWADH	1
	Land Revenue and the State	2
	Talukdars and Peasants	12
2	ANNEXATION AND THE SUMMARY SETTLEMENT OF 1856–7	32
	Annexation	32
	The Summary Settlement of 1856–7	38
3	THE REVOLT OF THE ARMY	64
	The Mutinies in Awadh	64
	The Fate of the Bengal Army	76
	The Awadh Countryside	79
4	THE REVOLT OF THE PEOPLE	82
	Rebels Gather in Lucknow: Chinhat to the First Relief	83
	The City and the Districts: First Relief to the Sack of Lucknow	88
	The Last Phase: Episodes in Retreat	107
5	ORGANIZATION AND IDEOLOGY	135
	A Rebel State?	135
	A War of Religion?	147
	A War of Restoration?	154
	Talukdars and Peasants: A Popular Resistance?	157

Epilogue	171
Appendices	175
to Ch. 2: List of Talukdars' Forts in Awadh	175
to Ch. 3: 1) Mutinies in North India	184
2) Disarmed Regiments	185
3) Other Corps That Mutinied	186
to Ch. 4: Begum's Plan for a Co-ordinated Attack	187
to Ch. 5: Talukdars in Southern Awadh and their Conduct During the Revolt	189
Glossary	205
Bibliography	208
Index	215

MAPS
   1) Villages Held by Talukdars Before Annexation
   2) Villages Held by Talukdars at the 1856–7 Settlement
   3) Mutinies in North India
   4) Winter Campaign of Lord Clyde

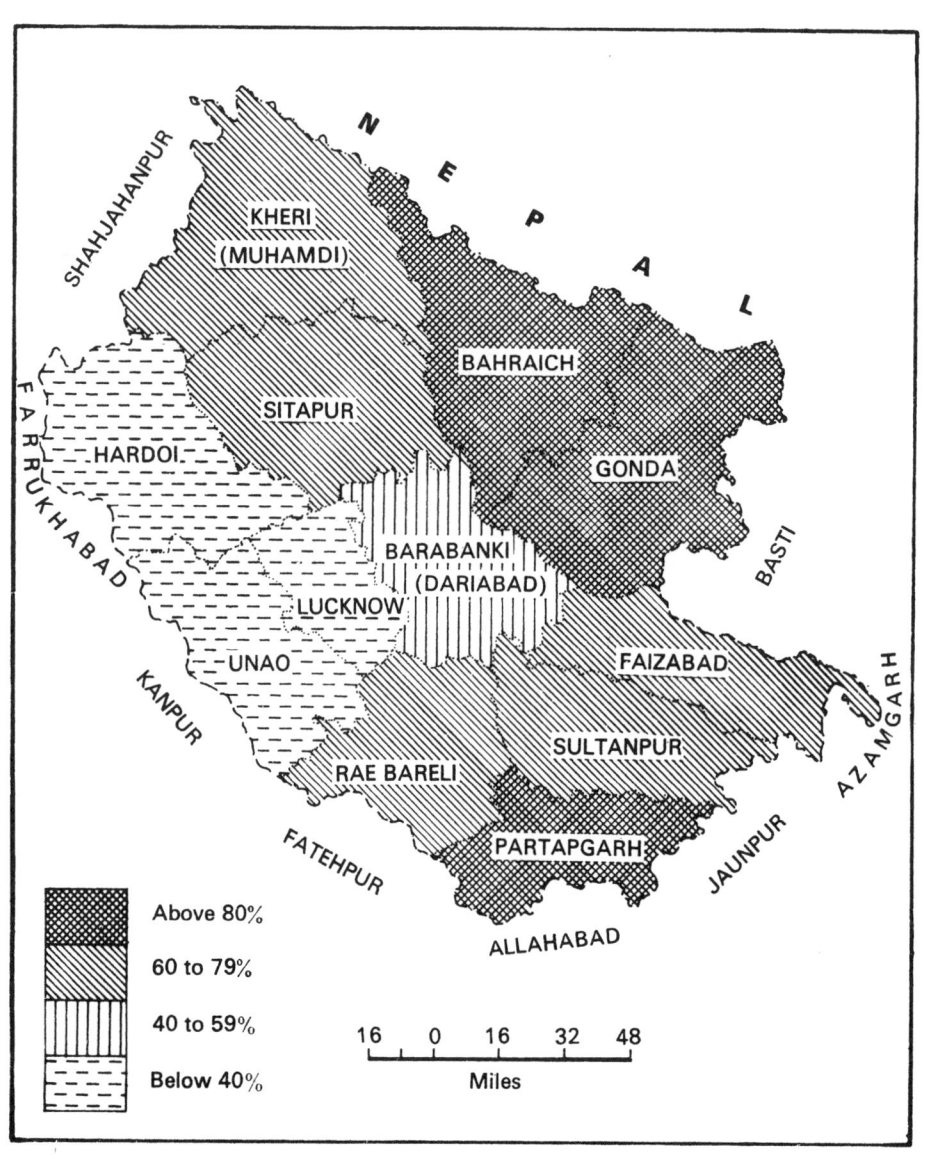

Map 1—Villages Held by Talukdars Before Annexation

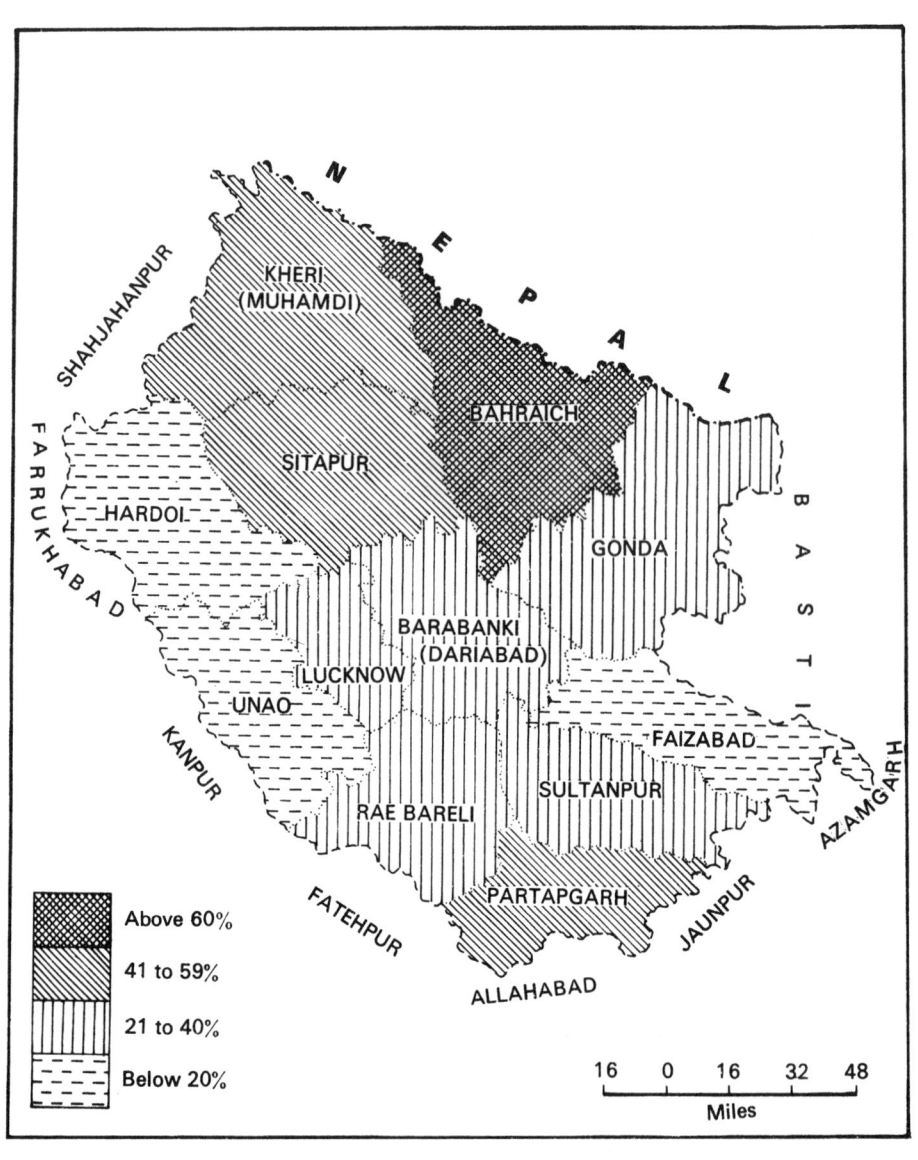

Map 2—Villages Held by Talukdars at the 1856–7 Settlement

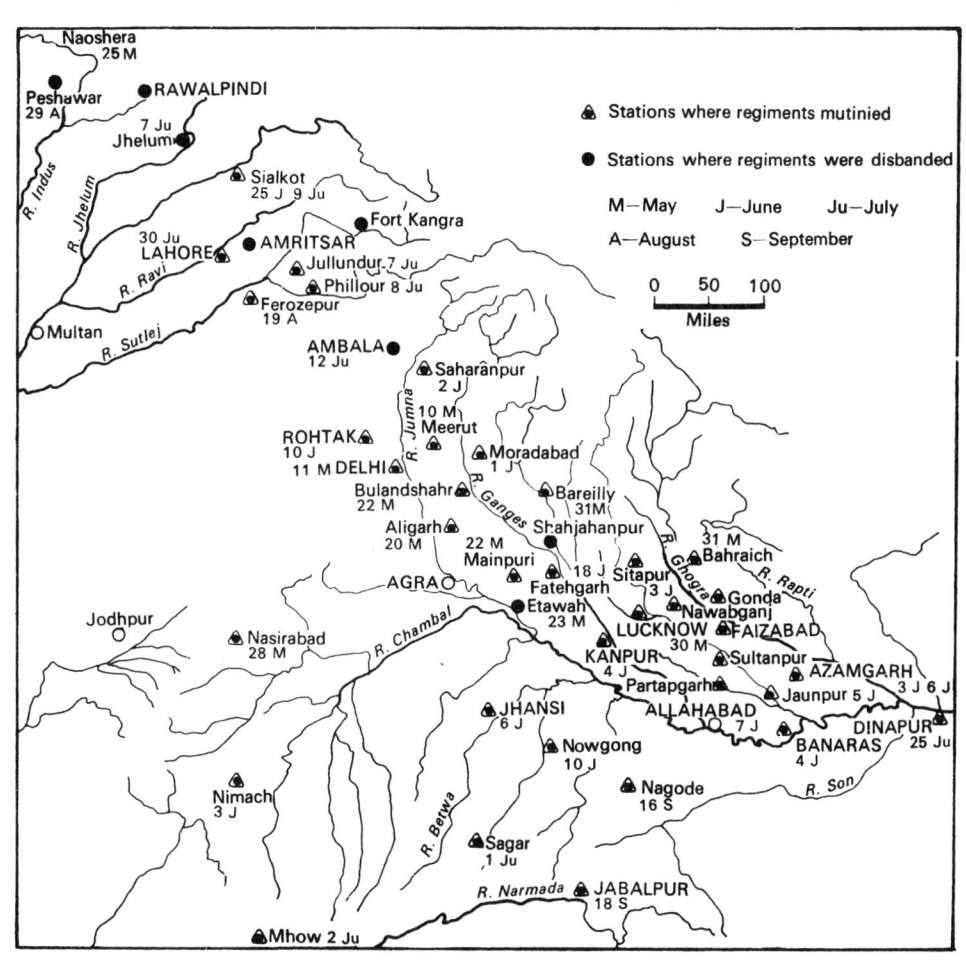

Map 3—Mutinies in North India

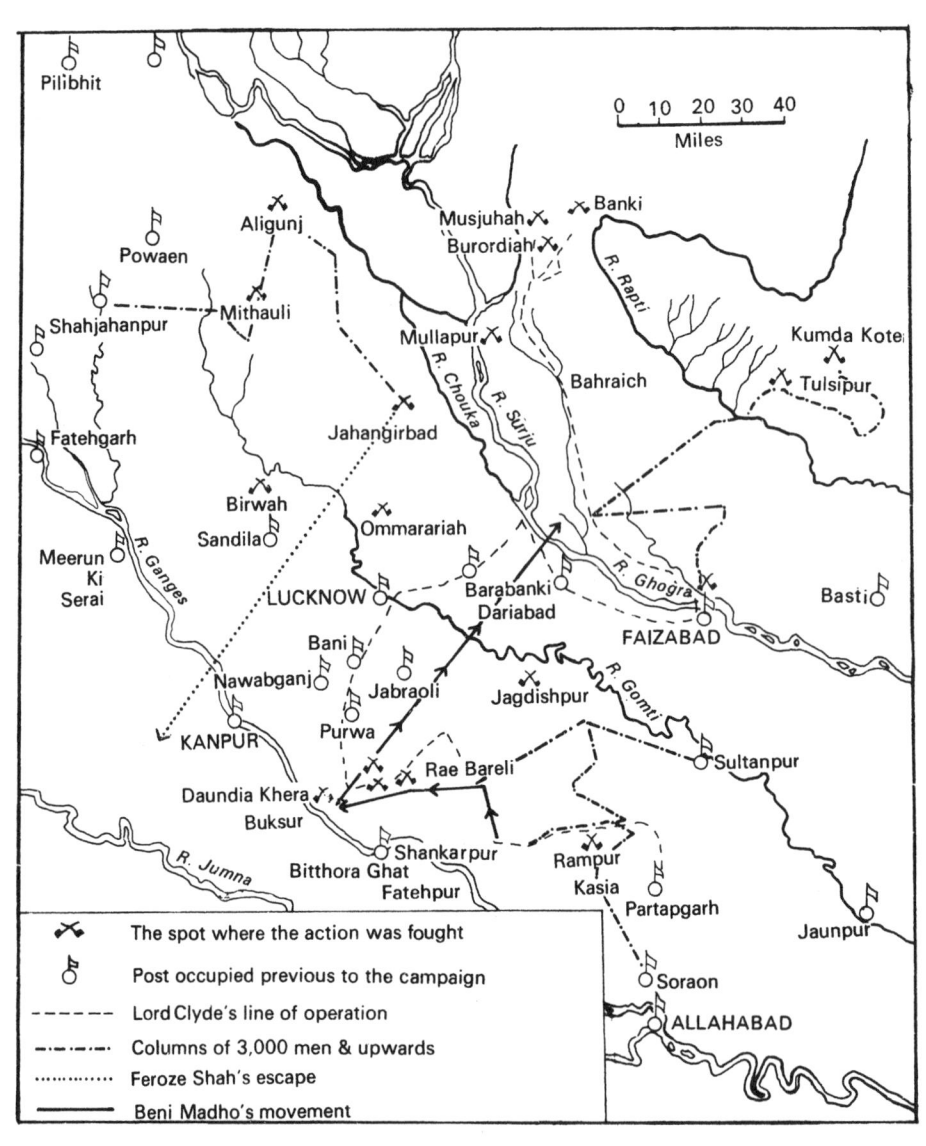

Map 4—Winter Campaign of Lord Clyde

CHAPTER 1
AGRARIAN RELATIONS IN PRE-ANNEXATION AWADH

In the eighteenth century, as the Mughal Empire declined as a centralizing force and the authority of the Emperor shrank, regional powers and regional focal points of loyalty emerged.[1] These successor states functioned at (what Bernard Cohn has delineated) the 'secondary' level.[2] Awadh was one of the biggest of these successor states. Founded in 1722 by an Iranian adventurer entitled Saadat Khan who refused the imperial order transferring him to Malwa,[3] it was among the first regional powers to become independent of Delhi.[4] Even after Wellesley had severely truncated Awadh in 1801, it still held an area of 23,923 square miles,[5] comprising the twelve districts of Lucknow, Sultanpur, Aldermau, Partapgarh, Panchamrat, Baiswara, Salon, Ahlad-

---

[1] Barun De, 'Some Implications of Political Tendencies and Social Factors in Eighteenth Century India' in O.P. Bhatnagar (ed.), *Studies in Social History (Modern India)* (Allahabad, 1964), pp. 219, 265 and *passim*. The process of the emergence of these successor states following the political breakdown of the Mughal Empire is best narrated and analysed in the *locus classicus* of eighteenth century political history of J.N. Sarkar, *Fall of the Mughal Empire*, 4 vols. (Calcutta reprint, 1972).

[2] See B.S. Cohn, 'Political Systems in Eighteenth Century India: The Banaras Region', *Journal of the American Oriental Society*, lxxxii; No. 3, July-Sept, 1962, p. 313. Cohn delineates four tiers in the political system: imperial, secondary, regional and local.

[3] Satish Chandra, *Parties and Politics in the Mughal Court 1707-1740* (Aligarh, 1959), pp. 185 and 136n; A.L. Srivastava, *First Two Nawabs of Oudh* (Lucknow, 1933), pp. 78-9 says that the independent state of Awadh might be dated from the time when Saadat Khan refused the imperial transfer to Malwa.

[4] Bengal under Murshid Quli had been administratively independent of Delhi though Murshid Quli continued to send the revenue regularly to Delhi till 1727. See Abdul Karim, *Murshid Quli and His Times* (Dacca, 1963), p. 84.

[5] D. Butter, *Outlines of Topography, and Statistics of the Southern Districts of Oudh* (Calcutta, 1839), p. 1.

ganj, Gonda-Bahraich, Sarkar-Khairabad, Sandi and Rasulabad.[6]

As in all pre-capitalist state formations the major source of revenue for the Awadh government was land. The surplus appropriated mainly from the land tilled by the labour of the peasant provided the sustenance and resources for the munificence and legendary luxuries of the Awadh Court: in fact Lucknow had become renowned as the only place where the grandeur associated with the Mughals still remained, where traditional forms of *adab* and culture held sway.[7]

Land Revenue and the State

The system by which the ruling power in Awadh appropriated the revenue from land was a carry-over of the Mughal land-revenue system in its essentials.[8] For land-revenue purposes the kingdom was administratively divided into *chaklas* (which numbered twelve) and then subdivided into parganas numbering seventy.[9] In theory each chakla was to be placed under a *chakladar*; but around 1838 six chakladars were appointed for the entire kingdom. One of the six held as many as seven chaklas and was virtually the supreme authority in southern Awadh.[10] When two or more chaklas were put under one officer he was called a *nazim*.[11] The nazim or chakladar who represented the state in the

[6]Ibid., p. 97; also see P. Reeves (ed.), *Sleeman in Oudh* (Cambridge, 1971), pp. 300-2. After the establishment of British power these districts were reorganized and renamed as follows: Lucknow, Sitapur, Hardoi, Kheri, Unao, Rae Bareli, Sultanpur, Bara Banki, Partapgarh, Faizabad, Gonda and Bahraich.

[7]For a description of the life of ease and culture prevalent in Lucknow see Abdul Halim Sharar, *Lucknow: The Last Phase of an Oriental Culture*, translated and edited by E.S. Harcourt and Fakhir Hussain (London, 1975).

[8]See C.A. Elliott, *The Chronicles of Oonao* (Allahabad, 1862), Chs. V and VI.

[9]Parganas were large tracts of land comprising a number of villages. Several parganas made up a chakla. Butter, pp. 97-8, gives a list of chaklas and parganas in Awadh.

[10]Butter, p. 97; also see H.C. Irwin, *The Garden of India, or Chapters in Oudh History and Affairs* (London, 1880), p. 123.

[11]Under the Mughal system a nazim was an officer in charge of law and police administration. See W.K. Firminger (ed.), *The Fifth Report from the Select Committee of the House of Commons on the Affairs of the East India Company* (Calcutta, 1917), Intro. p. xxxi. Under the Awadh administration a nazim had the duty of collecting the revenue.

countryside either collected direct from the proprietary right holder or coparcenary of every village or from landed magnates and chiefs who claimed through ancient prescription certain rights over clusters of villages.[12]

Viewed from the minarets of Chattar Manzil or the corridors of power in Qaiserbagh, land in Awadh was divided into four types: (a) *Khalsa* lands (b) *Huzur Tahsil* lands (c) *Ijara* lands and (d) *Amani* lands.[13] The Khalsa lands, as in Mughal times, were the crown estates. Revenue was paid direct to the Crown Treasury without the intervention of any middleman. This logically should have been the most lucrative source of revenue for the Awadh monarch. But due to the operation of corrupt chakladars and lack of supervision on the part of the Awadh monarch, the number of villages included in the khalsa declined drastically. For example in the district of Bahraich in 1807 the revenue from khalsa lands was worth Rs 7,25,000, but by 1849 it had declined to Rs 69,000.[14] The reason for this decline according to one British officer was that chakladars, in consideration of large bribes, had made over khalsa villages to talukdars. Thus khalsa villages in Bahraich, which had numbered more than 650, had declined to twenty or twenty-five villages by the 1850s. The talukdars of Ekona, Churdah and Bauchi had been the gainers.[15] All over Awadh, Outram noted, the same decline in khalsa lands could be observed.[16]

In the huzur tahsil system, the *malguzars* (the revenue payers) were permitted to pay their dues directly to the treasury through their own agents. Sleeman defined the system in very precise terms:

The term "Huzoor Tehseel" signifies the collecting of the revenue made by the governor himself whether of a district or of a kingdom. The estates of all landholders who pay their land-revenues direct to the governor, or to the deputy employed under him to receive such revenues and manage such estates are said to be in the "Huzoor Tehseel". The local authorities

---

[12]General Report on the Administration of the Province of Oudh, 1859 (henceforward cited as *General Report*, 1859), para 73.
[13]Outram to Sec., Govt. of India, 15 March 1855: *P.P.* XLV, 1856, para 25.
[14]W.H. Sleeman, *A Journey through the Kingdom of Oude*, 2 vols (London, 1858), i, p. 49.
[15]Outram's letter to Sec., Govt. of India, 15 March 1855, para 16.
[16]Ibid.

of the districts on which such estates are situated have nothing whatever to do with them.[17]

From all accounts this system was very popular with the people of Awadh since they enjoyed under it relative security and protection. When a landholder got his lands transferred to the huzur tahsil he paid a certain amount into the treasury and no more. The chakladar could not increase the *jama* nor could he seize the villagers for *begari* (forced labour) nor oppress the people in any other manner.[18]

Capt. Alexander Orr, who had toured nearly the whole of Awadh and who was one of those on whose local knowledge Outram based his letter to the Secretary, Government of India in March 1855, had this to say on the relative merits of the huzur tahsil system:

Under this system the ryot is invariably more contented, less tortured and generally exempt from furnishing forage. I speak not this from mere supposition, for an example of this is to be seen in the Baiswara district. All the great and powerful chiefs are under Huzoor Tehsil and it is a notorious [*sic*] fact that there is not in Oudh a better behaved set of men than these chiefs. I am not aware that they have ever shown bad faith towards their Government.[19]

Presumably, since the magnates were not harassed and oppressed by the demands of chakladars they left their raiyats in comparative peace and free from extortion.

Sleeman has described in detail the procedure adopted when a landholder paying into the huzur tahsil failed to pay his revenue. On such occasions a *jumogdar* was appointed and what followed is best left to Sleeman's own pen:

The landholder assembles his tenants, and they enter into pledges to pay direct to the Jumogdar the rents due by them to the landholder, under existing engagements, up to a certain time. This may be the whole, or

[17]Sleeman, *Journey*, i, p. 23 note.
[18]Outram to Sec., Govt. of India, 15 March 1855, para 26.
[19]Capt. A. Orr to Outram, 9 Jan 1855, para 19, Appendix B, to Inclosure 7 of No. 1 with Outram's letter to Sec., Govt. of India, 15 March, 1855. Irwin, *Garden of India*, p. 147, also mentions that the chiefs of Baiswara had their lands under huzur tahsil. Orr's point about the loyalty of the Baiswara chiefs needs to be underscored for my purposes. An example of the relative prosperity of the peasantry under the chiefs of Baiswara can be had from Sleeman's description of the lands under Beni Madho in Shankarpur; see Sleeman, *Journey*, i, pp. 252-3.

Agrarian Relations in Pre-Annexation Awadh

less than the whole, amount due to Government by the landholder. If any of them fail to pay what they promise to the Jumogdar the landholder is bound to make good the deficiency at the end of the year. He also binds himself to pay to Government whatever may be due over and above what the tenants pledge themselves to pay to the Jumogdar. This transfer of responsibility, from the landholder to his tenants, is called "*Jumog Lagana*", or transfer of the jumma. The assembly of the tenants, for the purpose of such adjustment, is called *zunjeer bundee*, or linking together. The adjustment thus made is called the *bilabundee*.[20]

In spite of the advantages of the huzur tahsil system and the king's awareness of these,[21] a very small portion of Awadh was under this sytem. In 1841 when the total collected revenue was Rs 1,15,72,491[22] the revenue from the huzur tahsil lands was only Rs 8,87,316, i.e. approximately eight per cent.[23] According to Sleeman in 1260 *fasli* (1852-3) the revenue from huzur tahsil lands had increased to Rs 22,76,711[24] but Col. Low, another Resident, was certain that this figure was baseless.[25] In fact, Col. Low's disagreement was well founded for by 1263 fasli (1855) the assessed revenue on huzur tahsil lands had fallen to a mere Rs 2,28,808 [26] Apart from the pressures from the chakladars to reduce lands included in the huzur tahsil so that they could have a field day, corruption had entered the *diwani* itself. The diwan arbitrarily began financial exactions and threatened to make over

---

[20] Sleeman, *Journey*, i, p. 203.
[21] Outram to Sec., Govt. of India, 15 March 1855, para 28.
[22] The figure for revenue collected is taken from Appendix of Inclosure 6 of No. 1 with Outram's letter, ibid.
[23] Outram to Sec., Govt. of India, 15 March 1855, para 28.
[24] Ibid.
[25] Col. Low wrote: 'Whence derived and how Colonel Sleeman relied on the correctness of this statement, I know not, and I have been unable myself to obtain any trustworthy information on the subject; but I cannot believe that Huzoor Tehseel estates can have increased to such an extent during the six years which intervened before the present king ascended the throne, during whose feeble reign they are more likely to have decreased. I am credibly informed, for instance, that in the Sultanpur Elaka, where formerly many villages were held under Huzoor Tehseel, none such exist, Agaie Alee Khan having stipulated with the Minister, when he became chukledar four years ago, that no land was to be therein held under that system, which agreement is said to have been strictly maintained'. Ibid.
[26] See 'Revenue Assessments of Oudh for 1263F (King's reign) according to statement of Jowahur Sing, Mohafiz Duftur Dewanee to HM of Oudh and who Before Mutiny was in Office of Financial Commr.', BROG File No. 1623.

the estate to a chakladar if the increase was not agreed to.[27]

The granting of ijaras, or the system of farming out the land-revenue to contractors, was fairly common among the later Mughals and its evils are well known.[28] As has often been pointed out, the ijara system had a built-in system of oppression and attracted bankers and speculators. This system was popular in Awadh, with disastrous consequences. It is possible to illustrate this with reference to a detailed fiscal history of pargana Mohan in zillah Purwa.[29]

This fiscal history stretches from 1240 fasli to 1262 fasli, i.e. 1833 to 1855. For the entire period the pargana was held in ijara. The first *ijaradar* from 1241 to 1246 fasli (1834-9) was Gangabishnu, a relative of Raja Balkishen, the diwan. These years were not characterized by any notable oppression and the condition of the people did not deteriorate significantly. Gangabishnu was followed by Beni Parshad, a nephew of a Lucknow-based *mahajan*. He increased the revenue demand by Rs 2,000, bringing it to Rs 72,000. In 1250 fasli (1843) the ijara went to a Lucknow kayasth called Laltaparshad at the increased sum of Rs 85,000. Laltaparshad fell into debt to his banker at Lucknow, and one Badri Nath took over the ijara in 1252 fasli (1845). According to local tradition it was under Badri Nath that the real oppression started. However, in 1259 fasli Badri Nath surrendered the ijara. Table 1 shows how much Badri Nath, his predecessors and his successor collected. It will be noticed that all the ijaradars collected an amount that was in excess of the government demand. Though tradition named Badri Nath as chief oppressor, in fact he was collecting approximately the same amount as his predecessors had. But his exactions following upon the exactions of the first three ijaradars meant that the people 'in Badri Nath's time could not pay without injury what they had paid before'. As Gubbins correctly noted, the marked feature of the fiscal account was that under the impact of the ijaradars'

---

[27]Outram to Sec., Govt. of India, 15 March 1855, para 27.

[28]Irfan Habib, *The Agrarian System of Mughal India* (London, 1963), pp. 234-5; and N.A. Siddiqi, *Land Revenue Administration Under the Mughals (1700-1750)* (Bombay, 1970), p. 98.

[29]The following account is taken from Martin Gubbins, 'Memo on the Assessment of Pergunnah Mohan, Zillah Poorwah, 17 Dec. 1856', BROG File No. 66, Part 1.

TABLE 1

Name of amil	Year	Govt ijara demand	amil's collection including nankar	Deduction or addition reqd. for comparison with the former status of pargana*	Amount	Amount of amil's collection including nankar now compounded
Ganga Bishnu	1241	70,000	85,128	*Add* for 9 villages held under huzur tahsil Rs 7000. *Deduct* for 5 villages granted in jagir Rs 4438 net addition per yr. Rs 2562	2562	87,690
	1242	70,000	85,083		2562	87,645
	1243	70,000	85,207		2562	87,769
	1244	70,000	83,158		2562	85,720
	1245	70,000	88,878		2562	91,440
	1246	70,000	92,610		2562	95,127
	1247	72,000	97,161		2562	99,723
Beni Parshad	1248	72,000	99,208		2562	1,01,570
	1249	72,000	97,119		2562	99,681
	1250	85,000	97,215		2562	99,777
Lalta- parshad	1251	85,000	91,823		2562	94,385
	1252	85,000	93,484		2562	96,046
Badri- nath	1253	92,000	98,469	Deduct only the jama of 5 villages	4438	94,031
	1254	92,000	1,01,678		4438	97,240
	1255	92,000	1,65,794		4438	1,01,256
	1256	92,000	65,251		4438	60,813
	1257	87,562	82,812	No additions or deductions		82,812
	1258	87,562	70,000			70,000
	1259	87,562	80,000			80,000
	1260	87,562	76,206			76,206
Habibur Rahaman	1261	87,562	70,958			70,958
	1262	87,562	65,421			65,421

*This adjustment is necessary because in 1241 fasli, 9 *mouzas* were put into *huzur tahsil* and were restored again in 1253 fasli. In 1257, 5 mouzas were taken off and granted in jagir. When the 9 mouzas were restored, ijara there was raised to **Rs 7,000**.

exactions the collections were deteriorating. Average collection between 1247 fasli and 1249 fasli had been 1,00,324, tapering off to 85,224 between 1252 and 1259 fasli, and falling to 70,895 between 1260 and 1262. This picture of deterioration is confirmed by Gubbins' description of the area when he toured it in late 1856:

> ... the present condition of the agriculturists of the Pergunnah ... [it] must be admitted is bad in the extreme.
> Mohan is peopled mainly by quiet and industrious classes. ... Poverty is everywhere written on the people and on their villages. Among the villages I visited I did not see half a dozen comfortable ones — several were without a house and in the great majority there were a great number of deserted houses.
> The inability of the people to lay out even small sums of money for the most necessary purposes, the repairs of wells and reconstruction of Kurcha ones is a marked indication of Poverty. Some villages which I visited, Tyzeellapoor and Chelwola, are now deserted and are represented to be without water. Throughout this pergunnah ... the wells are worked by manual labour instead of oxen. ... One of the village elders however declared that he could remember the day when their wells were worked by Bullocks. But that good stout cattle were needed to work a well and now they had none such. . .
> Again there is a great quantity of abandoned land of more or less recent abandonment. There is . . . no resisting the conclusion that the collections have not been fair. But have pressed unduly on the people.
> To throw as much light as possible on the subject I recorded the depositions of the Canoongoes and Mehtabray, Dewan to the ex-Chukladar, and enquired what share of the Nikasee they supposed that Budri Nath and Hubeeboo Rahman had left to the people whether 5, 10, 15, 20 or 30%. The only answer I could obtain was "They left nothing" and often made up their collections by cutting down and selling their ... household property and cattle.[30]

[30]Ibid. Sleeman, *Journey*, i, pp. 152-3 gives an account of the activities of Darshan Singh a typical ijaradar. A few telling lines may be quoted from Sleeman's description: 'He imposed upon the lands he coveted, rates which he knew they could never pay; took all the property of the proprietors for rent ... seized any neighbouring banker or capitalist whom he could lay hold of, and by confinement and harsh treatment, made him stand security for the suffering proprietors, for sums they never owed; and when these proprietors were made to appear to be irretrievably involved in debt to the State and to individuals, and had no hope of release from prison by any other means, they consented to sign the *bynamahs*, or sale deeds for lands, which their families had possessed for centuries... The proprietors ... plundered of all they had in the world, and without any hope of redress, left the country or took service under our Government, or that of Oude, or descended to the rank of day-labourers or cultivators in other estates'.

Agrarian Relations in Pre-Annexation Awadh 9

Under the final type of land-holding, the amani or trust management system, no amount was fixed and the collecting official was required to pay into the treasury all that he could collect. This system was obviously based on the integrity of the officials.[31] One of the conditions for its efficient operation was the confidence of the collector that he would retain a particular area for some length of time. But in Awadh in the middle of the nineteenth century this was not possible; court nepotism played such an important part that 'few Nazims reckon on holding their districts for more than one, or at the utmost two years. . .'[32] The British, who after their experiences with the 'public outcry' system in Bengal and Captain Hannay's activities in Gorakhpur[33] were suspicious of the ijara system, prompted the Awadh government to revert to the amani system based on a 'fair and moderate assessment'.[34] The result was a falling off in revenue collection and a persistence of the same rack-renting and corruption that prevailed in the ijara system.[35] The one major difference between the ijara and amani systems was that while in the former, despite the rack-renting, the state received its expected revenue, in the latter the same extortions prevailed but the state did not receive its due since the collector pocketed it.[36] Self-enrichment was the only motive of the collector and the amount he collected was far more than what went into the treasury. The additions made by the collector to the government assessment were styled *izafah*; and on the izafah was added the *nazrana* (additional presents and gifts). An instance of such methods can be seen from the following account of Agaie Ali Khan's[37] collection from the estate of Chandosi in Sultanpur on which the

[31]Outram's letter to Sec., Govt. of India, 15 March, 1855, para 30.
[32]Ibid.
[33]For the 'outcry' system see N.K. Sinha (ed.), *The History of Bengal 1757-1905* (University of Calcutta, 1967), pp. 89-90; and for Hannay see S.B. Chaudhuri, *Civil Disturbances During the British Rule in India (1765-1857)* (Calcutta, 1955), pp. 55ff.
[34]Outram to Sec., Govt. of India, 15 March 1855, paras 30-3.
[35]Ibid., paras 29 and 35.
[36]Ibid., para 39.
[37]From 1847 Agaie Ali Khan held the amani of the territory stretching from the river Gogra near Dariabad to the Jaunpur frontier about 90 miles and from East to West about 80 miles, i.e. nearly one-third of the Awadh territory, fetching a revenue of Rs 31,50,000, i.e. one-fourth of the entire revenue. Ibid.

government assessment was Rs 5,338. But Agaie Ali Khan's own assessment was Rs 7,200; and to this was added: Agaie Ali's nazrana Rs 1,500, Aga Hyder's (Agaie Ali's brother) nazrana Rs 1,200 as chakladar subordinate to Agaie Ali, Banda Hussein's nazrana Rs 1,100 as naib to Aga Hyder, and finally Ram Baksh's nazrana Rs 113 as diwan to Aga Hyder. All this adds up to a total payment of Rs 11,113, or more than double the government's assessment.[38] Further instances can be had from the Raja of Hussanpur Banduah in Sultanpur who was assessed (together with the izafah) in 1854 at 60,000. This was raised to 1,00,000 in 1855. Or the pargana of Kujrahat belonging to the *babu* of Bhiti which was so heavily taxed in 1261 fasli that some of the year's revenue was still outstanding even in the fifth month of 1262 fasli.[39]

The manner in which nazims and collectors performed their duty of collecting the revenue can be illustrated from the following details of Sultanpur *ilaqa*.[40] The *tashkhis*[41] of this ilaqa amounted to Rs 36 lakhs; from this was subtracted 9 lakhs on account of huzur tahsil lands and *nankar*; of the 27 lakhs that remained 17 were accounted for to the treasury and 10 were reserved for the nazim. To these 10 lakhs was often added one more, since the nazim practised other forms of extortion like seizure of the nankar lands or the appropriation of certain sums allowed by the government to each zamindar as subsistence money. The whole of the 17 lakhs that was accounted for to the government never reached the treasury since from it was deducted what was known as *samjhota* money, i.e. pay of the troops employed in reaching an 'understanding' about collection of the revenue, cost of repairs of the government forts, amounting in each fort from 200 to 500 rupees. expenses of grain, salt, etc. for artillery, cattle, food for nizamat elephants, construction of temporary cantonments, and expenditure on shot and powder in case of an attack against a fort. Over and above these deductions from the total *jama* were deductions made on account of revenue

[38]Ibid.
[39]These examples are taken from Capt. A. Orr to Outram, 9 Jan 1855, para 4.
[40]Ibid., paras 5-6.
[41]i.e. the net realizable revenue: Capt. A. Orr (ibid.) refers to it as *tuskerrie*. For the various forms of the word and its correct technical meaning see H.H. Wilson, *A Glossary of Judicial and Revenue Terms* (London, 1855), p. 513.

Agrarian Relations in Pre-Annexation Awadh 11

not collected from the zamindaris of certain notoriously 'bad characters', represented to the government as *ferari* landholders.[42] Many of the latter, Capt. Orr noted, had in fact paid their full revenue and 'also a "douceur" in order to carry on their lawless mode of existence'.

It is obvious that this corruption, rack-renting and extortion on the part of the collectors could mean, among other things, a declining amount of revenue being paid into the treasury and also an increasing gap between the amount of revenue assessed and the amount of revenue actually collected. Table 2[43] illustrates this trend for the years between 1838 and 1848.

TABLE 2 (amount in Rupees)

	Year	Jama	Collected	Balance
1245F	1838	1,39,95,792	1,31,83,833	8,11,958
1246F	1839	1,49,60,001	1,31,38,791	18,21,209
1247F	1840	1,38,62,012	1,26,87,730	11,74,282
1248F	1841	1,27,16,603	1,15,72,491	11,44,112
1249F	1842	1,28,32,724	1,09,58,195	18,74,529
1250F	1843	1,03,55,985	1,05,09,670	29,96,314
1251F	1844	1,35,87,143	89,70,464	46,16,678
1252F	1845	1,85,06,375	1,10,27,517	74,78,858
1253F	1846	2,09,96,702	1,16,65,050	93,31,651
1254F	1847	2,37,00,537	1,05,61,907	1,31,38,629
1255F	1848	2,70,21,035	1,06,32,072	1,63,88,962

This trend continued to the years before annexation: in 1853 the estimated revenue was Rs 1,21,66,214 out of which only 40 lakhs went into the treasury; and in 1854 the estimated revenue was Rs 1,22,30,082 and only 36 lakhs was paid into the treasury. It is possible that the increasing balance and uncollected jama could partly be a result of the peasants' inability to pay a high demand. Yet, after all that has been said about the activities of nazims, chakladars and ijaradars, it would not be far-fetched to conclude that a large portion of the uncollected revenue lined their pockets. This money in the hands of bureaucrats could only represent

---

[42]*Ferari* literally means 'absconding'. It refers in this case to landholders who took to the jungles as the chakladar approached to collect the land-revenue.

[43]See Appendix C to Inclosure 6 of No. 1 with Outram's letter to Sec., Govt. of India, 15 March 1855.

'an expanding margin of waste'[44] in the sense that these people, the nazims etc., were hardly likely to utilize such wealth for productive purposes.[45]

Talukdars and Peasants

Operating below this world of nazims and chakladars, partially subordinate and partially autonomous, were what Cohn has called the local structures.[46] These were the real mainstays, the permanent features of the Awadh countryside. Most of these local structures were controlled by Rajputs. How they had evolved is obscure. Our knowledge is solely based on local traditions.[47] These traditions usually stretch over a long period of history and describe how clan after clan of Rajputs fleeing eastwards in the face of Muslim aggression settled in particular regions. The process of a clan moving in to dominate previously settled peasants, and then in its turn being ousted or subordinated by another migrating clan continued till each major clan had, around Mughal times, established its own area of domination.[48] At

---

[44]This phrase is H. Trevor-Roper's. See H. Trevor-Roper, 'The General Crisis of the Seventeenth Century' in Trevor Aston (ed.), *Crisis in Europe 1560-1660* (London, paperback edn., 1974), p. 78. Trevor-Roper was referring to the 'waste which lay between the taxes imposed on the subject and the revenue collected by the Crown' in the Renaissance monarchies.

[45]It is interesting that in the eighteenth century the Mughal Empire was in a similar kind of crisis. There was a gap between the assessed revenue, the *hal-i-hasil* (collection) and the money paid into the treasury. (See Siddiqi, *Land Revenue Adm.*, p. 136). The surplus remained tied up with a bureaucratic class who could not effect a change in the agrarian relations and give the economy a new boost and direction. See S. Nurul Hasan, 'Zamindars Under the Mughals' in R.E. Frykenberg (ed.), *Land Control and Social Structure in Indian History* (Wisconsin, 1969), p. 29; Irfan Habib, 'Potentialities of Capitalistic Development in the Economy of Mughal India', in *Enquiry* (Winter 1971), *passim*; and Asok Sen, 'A Pre-British Economic Formation in India of the late Eighteenth century: Tipu Sultan's Mysore', in B. De (ed.), *Perspectives in Social Sciences I* (Calcutta, 1977), pp. 49-64.

[46]B.S. Cohn, 'Political Systems in Eighteenth Century India'.

[47]For Awadh the two classic accounts are C.A. Elliott, *Chronicles*, and W.C. Bennett, *A Report on the Family History of the Chief Clans of Roy Bareilly District* (Lucknow, 1870).

[48]An example of the extent of such domination can be seen from the name of the Mughal district of Baiswara which consisted of 'the many *mahals* that are the

some point in this process the domination of the victorious clans crystallized into certain superior rights for the clan, as well as over the people the clan had subjugated. Besides the Bais some of the others who settled in the same fashion were Dikhits, Janvars, Raikwars, Chouhans, Amethias and Kanhpurias.[49] Through the working of the law of inheritance and internal dissensions these clans were broken up into various houses and these houses became *talukas*.[50]

The establishment of superior rights by the Rajputs often took other forms.[51] These were:

(1) A tract of land lying waste would be made over by the imperial government to an enterprising officer or a court favourite either as a reward or to extend cultivation. In such situations the grantee — or the raja-to-be — would be absolutely independent. He himself would settle all the cultivators and the latter would all be in a state of villeinage without any rights of their own except those that the raja granted.[52] According to Benett, a good example of this type was the Charda ilaqa where a tract of waste was handed over in 1797 by the Nawab-Wazir of Awadh to a family which was to become the talukdars. A similar example was the estate of Nanpara.[53]

(2) A Rajput chief would be sent out to establish order in a lawless area. He would be authorized for this purpose to raise a number of men — mostly his kin and family followers. They would restore order in an area and if allowed to stay on there for any length of time, would normally bring their wives and children, thus transforming a 'temporary cantonment into a permanent village, which at the expiration of their term of

---

home of the seditious zamindars of the clan (*qaum*) of Bais'. See Habib, *Agrarian System*, p. 161.

[49] See Elliott, *Chronicles*, Ch. 3; and Benett, *passim*.

[50] See Elliott, *Chronicles*, p. 153; this process is best demonstrated by the Bais genealogy given on p. 70 of Elliott's book.

[51] Elliott, *Chronicles*, pp. 29-30, thinks that the settling in of the clans described in the previous paragraph was a feature of the first wave of colonists. The second wave which followed the establishment of Muslim power followed one or the other of the stereotypes I now discuss.

[52] W.C. Benett, *Gazetteer of the Province of Oudh*, 3 vols (Lucknow, 1877) i, p. 177. Henceforward cited as *O.G.*

[53] Ibid.

service, the Rajpoots would be loath to quit'.[54] This was the way in which the Sengurs and Gours settled near Kantha in the district of Unao.[55] Often after a Rajput chief had established order over an area, he would be granted the whole or a part of its revenue. Such grants would be for a lifetime, but in the more remote parts of Awadh they would become hereditary. Since the area had been reduced to subjection by the sword, the previous occupants would accept the overlordship and the lord on his part would be slow to recognize any right that was not of his own creation. The Ikauna estate in Bahraich was an example of this type. According to Benett the head of this house had been known as *risaldar* for seven generations. He never made any payments to the state yet the fiction was maintained that he was a servant of the government. When, in the course of events, the office was abolished and the revenue-free grant resumed, the grantee's position had become so powerful that he had to be recognized as the lord of the ilaqa.[56]

(3) Often superior rights developed independent of any grant from the ruling power. So long as a coparcenary community was small in number, equality of holdings could be maintained, but with expansion and growth a conflict of interests would inevitably develop, leading to partitions and ultimately to the superiority of the owners of one portion of the property over the others. In the process of attaining this superiority the division aspiring to it would inevitably choose a leader. This leader would, with the passage of time, aggrandize himself and his family at the expense of the rest of the community. His office would also become hereditary and thus a lord would emerge from a body of freemen.[57] Benett gave the following illustration of this type:

Of suzerainties of the class above described. I can name no notable instance . . . [than] the Sayyads of Jarwal. The number of shares into which the inhabited quarter of the village of Jarwal itself is divided, is clear proof of the equality of the interests of different divisions of the family in former days; but fifty years ago we find that there was only one man of mark in the whole family, who owned well nigh all the estate.

[54]Elliott, *Chronicles*, p. 30.
[55]Elliott, *Chronicles*, pp. 45-7, and *O.G.*, iii, p. 543.
[56]*O.G.*, i, p. 178.
[57]Ibid., p. 179.

The Balrampur estate is a modern instance of the gradual absorption by the chief of the family of all the rights belonging to the brotherhood.[58]

A fourth way through which superior rights could be established was the development of the 'auction taluka' as distinct from the 'hereditary taluka.'[59] I have so far described some of the ways in which the latter type could be formed. The former type was formed by sale, mortgage and fraud, or to use the local expression, by a talukdar who first 'approved' of a village and then 'digested' it.[60] How this occurred is best described by summarizing Elliott's account of the Morawan family. Chandan Lal who became a talukdar was (like his father and grandfather before him) originally a moneylender, merchant and treasurer to the nazim. Around 1814, when the operation of the contract system was resulting in the ruin of small landholders and the growth of large talukdari estates,[61] he began to think of buying land. The process of acquiring land came about, according to Elliott, in the following way: during the December settlement[62] the *patwari* and *tahsil-*

---

[58]Ibid.

[59]Elliott, *Chronicles*, pp. 154-5. See also Benett, *Chief Clans of Roy Bareilly*, p. 63: 'I may here remark that I consider that the division of the class into true talukdars and false talukdars, puts the matter in quite a wrong light. As a matter of fact all were exactly the same in as far as they were talukdars, middlemen put in by or forced on the Government, superintendents or arbitrary collections of villages, who as the central power grew weaker, were being gradually and surely transformed into landed proprietors. What has been called a true talukdar differs from what has been called a false talukdar only in the fact that while the former had been for centuries exercising an *imperium in imperio* on the spot, the latter was an outsider whose fortune, talents or wealth had secured him the position. Both were alike in being talukdars though they differed in every other particular'. While both Elliott and Benett disapproved of the distinction between 'true' and 'false' talukdar, it is not clear whether Benett accepted Elliott's differentiation between the 'hereditary' and 'auction' talukas. The 'hereditary' and 'auction' talukas might have differed in the process through which they were formed but in terms of the power and functioning of their holders they were the same.

[60]*O.G.*, i, pp. 179-80. The gobbling up of a small proprietors' lands by the talukdar, whether 'auction' or 'hereditary', was a common practice as Hanwant Singh told Sleeman, '. . all have been augmenting their own estates by absorbing those of smaller proprietors' . Sleeman, *Journey*, i, p. 245.

[61]Elliott, *Chronicles*, p. 134; Elliott noted how in Faizabad 'in 1814 no estate . . . paid a Revenue of Rs 10,000. In 1856 one Estate paid 2 Lacs, two paid Rs 70,000 and Rs 50,000 several Rs 30,000 and so on'.

[62]'The settlement, though annual, was done in two parts, the sums payable for each harvest being fixed separately. The Khureef settlement was done in

dar, probably in collusion with the moneylender, would recommend an increase on the previous year's revenue despite protests from the owner. To pay the increased demand the latter had then to borrow from the moneylender, and within three or four years had lost his villages to the moneylender. Alternatively, on hearing the protestations of the owner against the increase, the chakladar straightaway gave the village to the moneylender. The following year with the help of suitable gifts and bribes to the patwari, tahsildar and chakladar he got the assessment reduced or got himself awarded a nankar grant.[63] By such dubious operations Chandan Lal increased his holdings from three villages in 1810 to possessions yielding a revenue that fluctuated, between 1825 and 1850, from Rs 1.5 to 2.5 lakhs. Another example of an 'auction taluka' was the Mehdona estate in the Faizabad district. This sprawling estate, which stretched continuously without the interference of any other property, was formed after 1816 through purchases of land from revenue defaulters. Fraud and force were probably also freely used. Most of the land thus annexed belonged to the Chhatri clans who were not only warlike but also passionately attached to their lands. This latter characteristic leads to the conclusion that some amount of force must have been necessary to make them give up their property.[64]

September and was called the "Faisula". Land never changed hands at this time: the only point looked to was the amount of taxation, which was fixed in accordance with the assessment of last year. Thus if a village paid Rs 1,000 last year, as a general rule the "Faisula" for the Khureef was fixed at 500. But enquiries were made as to the nature of the crops sown: and if it were found that a large portion of the land was under rice or sugarcane cultivation, or other khureef crops, the Faisula would be 600 Rs or more, and if there were very few khureef crops, it would be 400 Rs. Whatever it was, it was divided into 5 portions, which had to be paid in five monthly instalments. But the actual settlement took place in December... By that time the Rubbie crops were well forward, and calculations could be formed as to the harvest which might be expected... But whatever the assessment is fixed at in this December settlement, the amount fixed for the khureef, and already paid in, was deducted, and the balance, divided into four instalments, had to be paid up in four months'. Elliott, *Chronicles*, pp. 138-9.

[63] This description is taken from ibid.
[64] *O.G.*, i, pp. 462-3. It is interesting that the then owner of the Mehdona estate, Bakhtawar Singh, secured the title of raja, granted in perpetuity by a *farman* given by Muhammad Ali Shah in 1837. See *O.G.*, iii, p. 38; see also P. Carnegy, *Historical Sketch of Tahsil Fyzabad, Zillah Fyzabad* (Lucknow, 1870), Pargana Pachhimrath, pp. 2-3.

Some confusion is often caused by the fact that in the context of Awadh the terms raja and talukdar are/were often used to denote the same set of people. This happened because in actual history the leaders of the various clans who had established themselves over areas and those who had established control over large tracts of territory became transformed into talukdars.[65] This was a direct consequence of the policy of Saadat Khan in the early eighteenth century. When Saadat Khan was establishing his authority in Awadh he was faced with the problem of reconciling his own authority with the power and control which the hereditary chieftains already enjoyed over large areas of the Awadh countryside. He solved it by acknowledging the control and power of the chieftains over their respective estates and appointing them to collect the government revenue.[66] This was a suitable arrangement since the chieftains retained their control, while at the same time Saadat Khan was provided with a body of hereditary revenue collectors who could also maintain law and order.

The control and power that the chieftains exercised was put to the test when an attempt was made, at the end of the eighteenth century, to set aside the chieftains and take engagements from the village proprietors. This was done to streamline the arrangements for revenue collection. This policy had the effect of reducing the chieftain to the same status as those who under him took land from existing talukdars, and it met with strong opposition. It became practically impossible to collect revenue. Chiefs were found repossessing villages and forming smaller estates which were to become the talukas that lasted through the nineteenth century.[67] Or often, as in the case of the raja of Gonda, attempts were made to supplant the raja by government officials. Such attempts also failed as the raja came back to his possession, even if

---

[65]Some writers distinguished between a raja and a talukdar in the following way: '... the distinction between the Raja ... and the Taluqdar presents itself as the difference between long prescriptive authority based on traditional reverence, and abrupt usurpation backed by violence and fraud', i.e. the raja was a person enjoying what Elliott called a 'hereditary taluka' while a talukdar enjoyed an 'auction taluka'. The quotation above is from Spencer Harcourt Butler, *Oudh Policy Considered Historically and With reference to the Present Political Situation* (Allahabad, 1896), p. 30.

[66]Benett, *Chief Clans of Roy Bareilly*, p. 59.

[67]See ibid., pp. 61-3.

to a smaller estate.[68] Benett summed up the whole process:

> Everywhere the rajas were stripped of their old position . . . everywhere they retained a footing, either by peaceful residence or by the maintenance through bands of desperate outlaws of a continual state of warfare; the officers of the king found it everywhere impossible to realize the revenue without the intervention of some powerful chief. . . . The result was that there grew up out of the old raj system a system of large estates, consisting each of a number of villages arbitrarily collected under a single revenue engagement. The old raj boundaries were rarely maintained. . . . But the new talukdars were almost always the old feudal lords.[69]

Whatever their genesis, it is unquestionable that the talukdars represented an *imperium in imperio* in rural Awadh. They enjoyed an independent right to a share of the produce and controlled law and order through their own militia. Much like the *seigneurie* holder of medieval Europe the raja-cum-talukdar also received numerous miscellaneous dues.[70] And, as in medieval Europe, what and how much these dues were to be was determined by custom. Custom, as engraved in the memory of the men of the estate, lay at the heart of the relationship between the lord of the estate and those below him.[71] Some idea of what such dues were in Awadh can be gleaned from a list of dues levied by the Raja of Utraula[72]:

---

[68]*O.G.*, i, p. xlvi.
[69]Ibid.
[70]See Marc Bloch, *French Rural History* (London, 1966), Ch. 3.
[71]Ibid., p. 70.
[72]This list is taken from W.C. Benett, *Final Settlement Report on the Gonda District* (Allahabad, 1878), pp. 41ff.: Benett notes that 'The list would vary slightly with every raj, but remain the same in its essential character'. (p. 41). It is interesting to compare the above list with the list submitted by H. Batson, collector of Moradabad: 'On every maund of produce of his estate where the rent is paid in kind, 1 seer; on every beegah of land cultivated in his estate where the rents are paid in cash, 1 anna; on every house, as house rent in every village of the estate per annum from 8 as to 1 Rupee; on every head of cattle grazing on the estate per annum 8 as; From every shepherd residing in the villages of the estate 2 sheep and 2 blankets; on every weaver's loom established in the villages of the estate per annum 1 Rupee; on every marriage celebrated in the Estate 1 Rupee; from every Fellmonger 2 hides per annum; on every hackery load of grass cut on the estate 4 annas; on each hackery load of bamboos 8 annas; on each hackery load of timber 8 annas; on each kiln of lime of Terrajaponica per annum 8 as to 1 Rs; . . . The raja also enjoyed a variety of other perquisites arising from the produce of jungles,

(i) *khatti*: a tax of two annas on each cart and one anna on each beast of burden bringing goods to the Raja's bazaar; a tax of 5% levied *ad valorem* on all goods sold in the raja's bazaar.
(ii) *mirbaha*: ferry dues levied on every ford of the area when crossing the Rapti, Kuana and Biswi. These varied in amount.
(iii) *pulahi*: a toll of a half-anna per cart, and a paisa per beast of burden, on each of the small faggot bridges. The collection of this toll was normally leased out by the rajas to contractors.
(iv) *tangarahi*: this was a charge levied from the inhabitants of neighbouring villages who came to cut wood from the forests. For villagers within the estate the cutting of wood for fuel was gratis, but they paid a nominal amount when taking timber for building.
(v) *subahi*: this was a lump sum collected on each bazaar payable by every tradesman. Each trade was organized in a guild under a special *chaudhuri* or headman, and the latter apportioned the total amount demanded by the raja among the members of the guild.
(vi) *sharakatana*: at times a very heavy contribution taken from the heads of villages towards any public expenditure especially towards war.
(vii) *khunt*: a toll on road where they entered the area even if this involved crossing a natural barrier viz stream or river.
(viii) (names unknown): a duty which was calculated as a proportion to the anticipated proceeds of the sale of spirits.
(ix) (names unknown): a duty of 8 annas per annum on each loom and on each cart.
(x) *bhent* or *nazarana*: miscellaneous dues which theoretically were supposed to be complimentary offerings but in practice were exacted regularly and on definite principles. Hide merchants, ferrymen, and owners of timber floating down the Rapti were expected to make yearly presents. Every year a *bhent* of Rs 2 and then a further Rs 3 had to be paid for first fruits taken from each village; there was also a fine levied on unsuccessful litigants.
(xi) *mendiawan*: a deposit of Rs 22 paid by each party when the raja arbitrated on a boundary dispute.
(xii) *gayari*: a right of escheat by which all property without legal heirs reverted to the raja.
(xiii) *bunda*: this was the name of the fines imposed by the raja on criminal cases.

Besides these the raja received further dues, namely clothes for a new-born son, money to celebrate the first shaving of his head, the

mangoe topes and fisheries, [he] also drew an income under the head of *rajahi* consisting of *jalkar, bankar, koont* and *abgeer* [jalkar was a tax on produce of ponds; bankar on the produce of forests and woods; koont on the transit of timber cut down and transported through an estate; and abgeer was a tax on the products grown in river beds]'. See A. Siddiqi, *Agrarian Change in a Northern Indian State, Uttar Pradesh 1819-1833* (Oxford, 1973), pp. 44-5 and note.

price of a horse or an elephant, and contributions for repairs to the fort; these were known as *kaprahi, mundan, ghurahi, hattiahi* and *kutahi* respectively. The raja in his turn had to contribute to the expenses for the rituals when a well-to-do subject lost a near relation or got married.

Waste lands were completely at the disposal of the raja. But once the land was granted the raja was bound by custom, though he had the right to resume the grant if the grantee failed to fulfil the conditions.[73] Similarly, wild produce and fish were the raja's property, though the cultivators had certain rights concerning grazing and fuel. A cultivator within the raja's estate could take from the raja's forests as much timber as he required for building, but he did not own the beams and had to leave them when he moved, the house becoming the property of the raja.[74] On the one hand these rights of the raja show the various economic and extra-economic instruments which he used to extract surplus over and above his 'legal' share of the produce; on the other they indicate the close ties determined and governed by custom that he had with the peasant.

The way the raja appropriated the surplus produce involved a process of 'pooling'[75] of resources which gave the *appearance* of sharing rather than of extraction. In fact the process was that of crop sharing and was well-known in Mughal times.[76] However, it is important to note that in the case described below the division took place within the raja's estate, irrespective of the Nawabi (in other words, the State) demand. Within the estate each person was entitled to a share in the produce when the grain heap was distributed. Benett systematized the operation thus:[77]

The assignments on the harvest in favour of the various members of the community are of three kinds: the first on the standing crop before it is cut; the second on the whole grain heap before the main division; the

[73]*Gonda Settlement Report*, p. 43.
[74]Ibid.
[75]I take this term from Marshall D. Sahlins, 'On the Sociology of Primitive Exchange' in *The Relevance of Models for Social Anthropology*, A.S.A. Monographs I (London, 1965), pp. 141ff.
[76]Habib, *Agrarian System*, pp. 197-8.
[77]*Gonda Settlement Report*, p. 47; see also M.L. Ferrar, *The Regular Settlement and Revised Assessment of the District of Sitapur* (Lucknow, 1875), p. 23 ff. I.F. Macandrew, *On Some Revenue Matters cheifly in the Province of Oudh* (Calcutta, 1876) pp. 63ff., gives the name of the various deductions.

third on the Raja's or cultivator's separate share, after the main division has been made. . . . At each harvest, while the crop is still on the ground, certain of the village servants select the twentieth part of a local bigha from the fields of each tenant, cut the produce before the rest of the field is touched, and take the whole of it for their own use. This right, known as biswa, is generally enjoyed by the watchman of the village site, the watchman of the outlying fields, the blacksmith, the carpenter, the herdsman, the priest, and, in many places, by the cultivator himself.

When the crop is cut it is brought into the threshing-floor, and the main deductions commence. The slave ploughman first takes his share, which varies from one-seventh of the gross produce in the better populated parts of the district to one-fifth close under the hills; and he receives in addition one panseri [78]. . . for every maund in his share. The cutters and threshers, for the whole village joins in the work, take a sixteenth part in rice, and select the fattest sheaf in thirty from other crops. As each man helps his neighbours, he recovers roughly from theirs, what he has paid on this account from his own crop, and the real weight of the deduction falls on the Raja's share of the produce. The carpenter, the blacksmith, the barber, the washerman, and the chaukidar take each twelve panseris from the beaten out grain of each cultivator for every four-bullock plough in his possession, and half as much for every two-bullock cart. The herdsman takes six panseris for every bullock left in his charge.

What is left is divided into two equal heaps, one for the Raja, the other for the cultivator. . . . One sir in every maund of the State share is then deducted and refunded to the cultivator, another sir in each maund is set aside for the village accountant; the priest takes a double handful (anjuri), and one-tenth of the heap falls to the mukaddam, who with respect to the crop from his own fields is treated like any other cultivator. Some small payments are also made from the tenant's heap, such as three panseris each to the blacksmith and carpenter, one panseri to the herdsman, a handful to the priest, and a sir or two for the patwari.

It is possible to get a more concrete computation of divisions between the raja and the peasant from other sources.[79] In Sitapur, for example, the peasant was allowed five seers out of the maund as *kur*;[80] the remainder was divided equally between raja and peasant, and then the latter had to contribute 2 or 2½ seers towards the patwari's account. In some areas over and above the 5 seers

[78]1 *panseri* was equal to 1 *seer* 12 *chitaks* 4 *tolas*: see *Gonda Settlement Report*, p. 73.

[79]*Sitapur Settlement Report*, p. 23. Macandrew, *Revenue Matters*, p. 67ff., gives a number of examples of such variations.

[80]This term is used in the *Sitapur Settlement Report* but it **is not defined; the** nearest equivalent I have been able to find is *koon* (meaning 'tillage') **in Wilson's** *Glossary*, p. 302.

granted as kur, certain tenants had a further let-off varying from 5 to 7½ seers. Thus, out of a maund the landlord got 12 to 15 seers and the tenant 25 to 27½ seers, subject to 2 seers deduction for the patwari.

It appears that in the estates of the rajas and talukdars there existed well-established customary relationships by which every member was seen to be linked in definite ways to the whole structure. His activities defined his position in the structure which in turn determined the share he was supposed to have from the entire produce. Each and every individual was assured of his proportion from the grain heap, and thus every villager was assured of a minimum income. Such a system of stability would of course be disturbed in a situation of falling prices or sudden drop in production. The pooling of resources and its distribution was the basis of the raja's authority. This whole mechanism bolstered chieftainship and subordination to the raja. At the same time such a system emphasizes the specially close relationship that existed between the raja/talukdar and his peasants. It highlights the elements of mutual co-operation that existed in the rural world of Awadh. In short, this system of pooling was double-edged; on the one hand it strengthened the dominance of the central authority and on the other fostered co-operation and interdependence: as Sahlins has noted 'pooling generates the spirit of unity and centricity. . . '[81]

This method of crop sharing, with its built in devices for providing everybody in the estate with subsistence, and the lord's willingness to bear the real weight of the many deductions[82] — leaving the peasant with 25 to 20 seers to the maund — satisfied the 'subsistence ethic' of the Awadh peasantry.[83] This established certain norms of mutual co-operation and common weal which created the interrelationships for establishing a moral economy in

[81]Sahlins, 'On the Sociology of Primitive Exchange', p. 143. Also see W. Neale 'Reciprocity and Redistribution in the Indian Village: Sequel to Some Notable Discussions' in K. Polanyi (ed.), *Trade and Market in the Early Empires* (Illinois 1957), pp. 218-36.

[82]This is clearly seen from the examples given by Macandrew, *Revenue Matters*.

[83]For the importance of the 'subsistence ethic' in Third World peasant life and its connections with the moral economy of the peasant see J.C. Scott, *The Moral Economy of the Peasant: Rebellion and Subsistence in Southeast Asia* (Yale, 1976), esp. Intro. and Ch. 1.

the countryside.[84] The Awadh peasant developed some notions of what was just and to be expected from the lord. He knew he would get his grain, protection and help when he got married or lost a close relative. He in turn tilled the soil, paid his dues and was expected to offer unflinching loyalty.

The peasant's loyalty was best revealed in his support to the talukdar in the face of extortionate revenue demands. It has already been noted in the context of the appointment of a jumogdar, how the peasants stood guarantors for payment of revenue when the raja had failed to pay. Similarly when a raja became *tut*, i.e. 'a broken man' because of the exactions of the chakladar, the raiyats would agree to advance the money so that the estate did not go out of the raja's hands to a merciless speculator or a nazim.[85] In fact to escape the extortions of the chakladars peasants would often bring their lands into a raja's estate to receive his protection.[86] That the loyalty of the peasant was taken as a matter of course is evident from the following account of Sleeman's conversation with Rana Beni Madho and Raja Hanwant Singh:

I asked Benee Madho . . . whether they [the tenants] would all have to follow his fortunes if he happened to take up arms against the Government "Assuredly", said he, "they would all be bound in honour to follow me, or to desert their lands at least".
"And if they did not, I suppose you would deem it a *point of honour* to plunder them?"
"That he assuredly would", said Rajah Hunwunt Singh; . . .
"And if any of them fell fighting on his side, would he think it a *point of honour* to provide for their families?"
"That we all do", said he, "they are always provided for, and taken the greatest possible care of".[87]

The well-knit relationship between lord and peasant and the care and protection the former provided is evident from the descriptions we have of well-cultivated lands under talukdars and of the relative prosperity of their peasantry. The tenants of Beni Madho looked 'happy' and the estate was 'admirably cultivated';[88]

---

[84]Ibid.; also see E.P. Thompson, 'The Moral Economy of the English Crowd in the 18th Century', *Past and Present*, No. 50 (1971).
[85]Butter, *Southern Oudh* p. 50.
[86]*O.G.*, i, p. 179; *General Report*, para 338.
[87]Sleeman, *Journey*, i, p. 254.
[88]Ibid., i, pp. 252-3.

the *kurmi* peasantry under Loni Singh in the Muhamdi district got 'all the aid they require from their new landlord';[89] according to Sleeman 'No lands could be better-cultivated' than those under Man Singh.[90] In the north, in the estate of Pyagpur, the peasants felt secure under their old raja.[91] Gonda-Bahraich, the major chunk of which was held by talukdars,[92] was rapidly progressing in cultivation and prosperity'.[93] In the context of the talukdars' relationship with their peasants and the protection they offered, the state of things in the Shahganj estate may be taken as typical. There, as Sleeman noted, the rajas kept their faith with the peasants, protected them from thieves, the violence of neighbouring rajas and the ravages of the king's troops.[94]

However, it is important not to romanticize the talukdar-peasant relationship. The situation was not idyllic, nor the relationship egalitarian. The very fact of surplus extraction, the grain heap notwithstanding, vitiated the possibilities of such an egalitarian idyll. Dominance of the talukdar was a singular fact of the rural world. Such dominance was, however, circumscribed by custom and mediated by various forms of paternalistic 'beneficence'.[95] In the rural world of Awadh there was a continuous interplay between the talukdars' rights and the peasants' obligation of allegiance, respect and duty; this entailed a certain complementarity in their relationship.[96] This was fortified by aspects of mutual co-operation already noted. Such co-operation,

[89] Ibid., ii, p. 88.
[90] Ibid., i, p. 171.
[91] Ibid., i, p. 82.
[92] See below, Table 3.
[93] Outram's letter to Sec., Govt. of India, March 15, 1855, para 42.
[94] Sleeman, *Journey*, i, p. 150; see also pp. 162-4 and vol. 2, pp. 116 and 223 for more descriptions of well-tilled lands and secure peasants under talukdars; and Butter, *Southern Oudh*, p. 110ff., for the peaceful and stable conditions in the lands under the Raja of Tiloi.
[95] For the notion of 'beneficence', see A.W. Gouldner, 'The Importance of Something for Nothing' in Gouldner, *For Sociology* (Pelican, 1975), pp. 266ff.
[96] For the concept of complementarity see A.W. Gouldner, 'The Norm of Reciprocity' in *For Sociology*, pp. 237ff. I should mention here that in my Oxford D. Phil thesis I described the talukdar-peasant relationship as being symbiotic. The characterization of such unequal but complementary relationships as symbiotic is not unknown. (See for example, F. Barth, *Political Leadership among the Swat Pathans*, London, 1959, p. 49). Subsequently, the criticism of friendly readers that the term symbiosis was misleading because it underplays

together with the prescriptions of custom, the proximate nature of the surplus appropriation through crop sharing and the norms of honour and loyalty which bound together the talukdar and peasant, provided the relationship with a human and agreeable dimension.[97] Contradictions and rapacity were also inherent, especially when talukdars refusing to pay the nazim retreated into their forts and gave battle, or when they disappeared into the jungle with the revenue. Such failures left the peasant at the mercy of the nazim; alternatively the peasants often had to organize themselves into fighting bands (*kammar bandhnewale*, i.e. those who tightened up their *dhoti* at the waist, an act symbolizing determination) to fight the nazim.[98] Again, internecine warfare within a family for control over the estate, like the kind going on at Nanpara and Tulsipur in the early 1850s, could leave the peasant without a protector, and open to ruin.[99] Nor must it be assumed that the talukdars looked after their peasants out of sheer altruism. They found it expedient to do so: the peasant tilled his land, paid his dues and provided fighting men. The peasants on their part received protection, security and occasional help in times of trouble; the distribution of the grain heap, governed by custom, guaranteed them subsistence. Elliott's summing up is well worth quoting:

The Talookdar could not afford to alienate his followers, . . . and the ryots and followers stuck by their masters, as they would be the sufferers if the zemindars were ruined and replaced by outsiders. They had no knowledge of an unchangeable law powerful enough to beat down all opposition; the right was not so very right, nor the wrong so extremely wrong; and all disputes were settled by mutual accommodation.[100]

Such a situation of mutual dependence included anger and

structures of dominance and appropriation led to second thoughts and reformulation.

[97] See K. Marx, 'His [the feudal lord] relation to them [those working on his estate] is therefore directly political, and even has an agreeable aspect'. *Economic and Philosophical Manuscripts* in Marx, *Early Writings*, ed. by L. Colletti (Harmondsworth, 1975), p. 318.

[98] Butter, *Southern Oudh*, pp. 50-1. It is important to note here that talukdars' forts (with surrounding jungles) dotted the Awadh countryside. I discuss the number of such forts and the extent of jungle in Chapter II (Appendix).

[99] Outram to Sec., Govt. of India, 6 Feb. 1855, *P.P.*, xlv, 1856.

[100] Elliott, *Chronicles*, p. 129; see also *General Report*, paras 336-7.

rapacity but perhaps precluded affirmative rebellion of the peasant against the raja.

It is necessary at this point to have an idea of the area under the control of talukdars. Table 3 attempts to show this. More than 60 per cent of the total villages were under talukdars; however it will be seen that talukdari control varied from district to district. It is possible to demarcate certain pockets where concentration of talukdari holding was heavy. The area around Lucknow and southwards towards Kanpur had the least number of villages under talukdars; talukdars held only around 30 per cent of the villages. The heavier concentration was around the east-south-east, in Rae Bareli, Sultanpur, Faizabad and Partapgarh, with nearly 70 per cent of the villages under talukdars; and this connected with the northern marches of Gonda-Bahraich merging into the Nepal Terai. Here the Nawab's authority had never effectively penetrated, and the talukdars held more than 85 per

TABLE 3

Villages under Talukdars before Annexation

District	Villages under Talukdars	Total No. of villages*		per cent	
Faizabad	3116	4215	(4215)	73.92	
Sultanpur	2113	3351	(3101)	63.05	(68.13)
Partapgarh	3032	3633	(3633)	83.45	
Lucknow	575	1570	(1569)	36.64	
Rae Bareli	1052	1551	(1602)	67.82	(65.66)
Unao	368	1236	(1236)	29.77	
Hardoi	464	1427	(1427)	32.51	
Dariabad	1087	2506	(2310)	43.37	(47.05)
Sitapur	2692	4422	(4539)	60.87	(59.30)
Gonda	3483	4129	(4240)	84.35	(82.14)
Bahraich	3761	3949	(3877)	95.23	(97.00)
Mohumdee	1759	3130	(3515)	56.19	(50.04)
Total	23,502	35119	(35264)	66.92	(66.64)

SOURCE: Summary Settlement in Oude. Collection to Political Despatches 33, Part 2, Collection No 37., I.O.L.R.

*The figures in brackets for total number of villages are taken from Statement showing what number of past settlements were upheld. The other figures, which are slightly different, of the total number of villages, are from comparative statements of charitable grants.

cent of the villages. Thus, roughly on an axis lying between Rae-Bareli and Bahraich would have been the control of the talukdars and the spread of peasant-talukdar interdependence and co-operation. The farflung north-west, Muhamdi and Sitapur, had more than 55 per cent of the villages under talukdars.

An indication of the importance of the talukdars in the Awadh agrarian scene can be had from the proportion of the total assessed revenue that they bore in the various districts. For example in Faizabad 90 per cent of the assessed revenue was set against the names of talukdars. In Salon (this district after 1858 was to be dismembered to form Rae Bareli and Partapgarh) the proportion was 89 per cent; in Bahraich over 97 per cent, in Gonda over 85 per cent and in Sitapur over 95 per cent. Even in districts where talukdars held less than 50 per cent of the total number of villages, as in Lucknow or Unao, 90 per cent of the assessed revenue was set against their names.[101] This lends itself to the conclusion that more often than not the talukdars controlled the best land in Awadh.

The talukdar's network of control and superiority was extended by the fact that he often brought his own kinsmen into his ilaqa and gave them land at favourable rates. This was given as a kind of 'blood money' in the sense that such men and their descendants were expected to fight for the talukdar and his family.[102] Men who were so settled did not see themselves as proprietors or as ex-proprietors. They maintained that:

Three or four generations ago, the then zemindars of the village, who were of the Bais caste invited us to leave our homes (naming some distant village) and to live with them; we gave them our daughters in marriage. They gave us land to cultivate at Rs 2 per Beegha; we have cultivated our lands, sometimes more and sometimes less for 60 years. . . Our honour was equal to that of the Talukdar; we sat in the same society as he did; we fought for him if anyone attacked him.[103]

These men formed a loyal base of support for the talukdar and formed the bulk of his fighting men. To keep them attached

---

[101] The proportion of assessed revenue borne by the talukdars is computed from 'Revenue Assessments of Oudh for 1263 F (King's Reign)': BROG File No. 1623.
[102] Bradford to Barrow, 13 April 1859, B.R. Faizabad File No. 11.
[103] Ouseley to Davies, 7 Dec. 1867: BROG File No. 1950, Pt. 1.

permanently to the village they were given a 'beegah or two in which to plant a grove of trees . . . they also received a beegah or two of land rent free on which to graze their plough cattle and their cows'.[104]

The talukdar's control often varied with the strength of the proprietary community below him and his relationship with them. Often, for example, a proprietary body under a talukdar not only paid a fixed sum for his villages but also enjoyed the entire produce of the estate. Again, the land directly under the plough of such a proprietary body would be rated low. Such arrangements were possible only where the underproprietors were on good terms with and subservient to the talukdar; or in situations where the talukdar was faced with a united and strong proprietary community and thus had to curtail his powers.[105] Or again, in cases where the talukdar was the chief of a large brotherhood and quite powerful, he frequently did not enjoy absolute control in matters affecting the community. The community acknowledged him as its head but did not permit any interference in village management. The proprietary community paid the talukdar a portion of the rent paid by the cultivators but 'they collect themselves, locate labourers, enjoy the spontaneous products of the jungle . . . and exercise all manorial rights'.[106] However, there were cases where the talukdar's control was absolute. He could often be found in perfect proprietary possession, those under him being in the position of simple cultivators. The talukdar collected direct from the cultivators and held all manorial rights.[107] What is important is that the existence of such kinsmen within the talukdar's domain reinforced and facilitated aspects of co-operation and dependence already noted.[108]

Despite the overall power and control of the talukdar, the simple cultivator under him had usufructuary rights. This seems obvious from evidence available from southern Awadh. For example in mouzah Kolapur a cultivator mortgaged a portion of his land in 1262 fasli for Rs 25. The annual rent of the land was

---

[104]Ibid.

[105]Bradford to Barrow, 13 Apr 1859, B.R. Faizabad File No. 11.

[106]Ibid.   [107]Ibid.

[108]For a general analysis of how kinship affects such aspects of sharing and co-operation see Sahlins, 'On the Sociology of Primitive Exchange', pp. 149ff.

Rs 16, but the talukdars received a rent of Rs. 10-8 as. The agreement between the mortgagor and mortgagee was that the mortgagee was to pay the rent and to keep Rs 5-8 as. as interest.[109] In another case in mouzah Kunjon, taluka Putti Syfabad, a cultivator, mortgaged his land for Rs 99 in 1264 fasli. The condition of the mortgage was that the mortgagor was to pay the rent of the land and that it was to be relinquished in 1273 fasli without the payment of any further sum: the mortgagee binding himself to consider his claim satisfied by the possession of the land for ten years.[110] These examples lead to the conclusion that some degree of permanency of occupancy was accepted in parts of Awadh.[111] It appears from the first settlement reports[112] that tenants were of two kinds, namely *chhapperband* (resident cultivators) and *pahikasht* (non-resident). Generally pahikasht cultivators were chhapperband cultivators in their own village. Their rights were the same, the only difference being that while the holdings of pahikasht peasants were constantly changing, those of the chhapperband cultivator changed with difficulty.

One particular element of the peasantry demands special mention, if only because it represented a group of such 'low social standing . . . that they could not call their lives their own much less the land which they tilled'.[113] Since the higher castes — the Brahmins, Chatris and most Kayasths—did not hold the plough, they often kept a bonded ploughman who also looked after the cattle. A person came to this status by a loan by which one of the lower castes, a *kori* or a *chamar*, bonded his own and his descendants' services in perpetuity, till such time as the loan was repaid. In return his subsistence was guaranteed because he had his fixed share from the grainheap. If needed he received further supplies from his master which were added to the loan. Such a ploughman was permitted to change masters, if he so wanted, by selling himself to a new master and clearing off his debt with the previous master with the proceeds of the sale. He was thus very different

---

[109]Ousley to Davies, 29 June 1867: BROG File No. 1950, pt 1.
[110]Ibid.   [111]Ibid.
[112]See especially *Gonda Settlement Report*, p. 88; and Macandrew, *Report of the Settlement of Eleven Pergunnas in the District of Roy Bareilly* (Lucknow, 1867), p. 23.
[113]Ouseley to Davies, 7 Dec. 1867: BROG File No. 1950, pt 1.

from an ordinary peasant and was the nearest approximation to a bonded labourer.[114] It is this type of labourer which Benett had called 'slave ploughman'.

Below the talukdar and above the cultivators there existed an entire complex of subordinate rights, with varying degrees of proprietary and usufructuary control. Such rights and tenures were very often the creation of the raja himself, either as grants/concessions to his kinsmen as 'blood money' (as noted earlier) or as rewards, or for maintenance; grants were also made to Brahmins. Such grants of land served to increase the talukdars' base of support and loyalty. It might perhaps be useful to describe a few such grants. It has been noted how peasants when unable to bear the oppression of the chakladar/nazim would often voluntarily bring their holdings into the protection of a talukdar. In such a case the talukdar would look after the land, take whatever accrued from it and give the former proprietor a piece of land which was rent-free for ever. Such a tenure was known as *didari*.[115] The commonest form of subordinate right was that of *seer* holdings. This was land, or portion thereof, which was held at privileged rates. According to Baden-Powell, the seer right originated when a former owner or co-sharer had lost all his other privileges but had managed to retain his own special holding. This holding he cultivated himself or with hired labour or with personal tenantry; he also held this land at a favourable rate of rent.[116] Another common underproprietary right was *birt*, a creation of the talukdar in return for money paid. Generally the rent paid on such land was low, and it was fixed.[117] A talukdar often created an underproprietary right for the family of a man slain while fight-

---

[114]The description of the 'slave ploughman' is from *Gonda Settlement Report*, p. 46.

[115]Macandrew, *Revenue Matters in Oudh*, p. 29.

[116]H. Baden-Powell, *Land Systems of British India*, 3 vols (Oxford, 1892), ii, p. 238.

[117]Macandrew, *Revenue Matters*, p. 35, cites the following as a typical *birt patta*: 'Birt patta dated Sawan Sudhi 8th 1238 fasli. Patta written by Rajah Shri Kishn Parshad Singh. I have given Tulsi Ram Misr a birt. He is to get (continuously) mauzah Garmeapur, tank, groves, dih, parjah, anjuri, biswa, bondha. He is to get (continuously) the zemindari hak, whether the village be pakka or Kacha. He is to take possession in confidence. Rupees 701 have been taken. Witness Banki Singh Sangam Misr. Written by Bhawani Baksh Mutsaddi'.

ing for the talukdar. Such a right was called *marwat* and paid a low rent and was never resumed.[118] Another subordinate proprietary tenure created by a talukdar was *purwa basna*, which was a grant to found a small hamlet or extend a village.[119] The point to notice and emphasize in the various forms of underproprietary rights discussed is the close interrelatedness the holders of such rights had with the raja or talukdar. It was from such interrelatedness that the talukdar came to occupy such a crucial and unassailable position in the rural world of Awadh.

Thus there existed in Awadh a base for united action at times when threats to the status quo were perceived. When the earliest policy prescriptions of the British raj assailed the position of the talukdar and thus challenged the existing rural structure, it did so react. The talukdars reverted to their previous types of autonomy and rights and in very many areas they, along with their subordinate peasantry, reacted with steadfastness, violence and internal solidarity.

---

[118] Macandrew, *Revenue Matters*, p. 37; Baden-Powell, p. 241.

[119] According to both Baden-Powell and Macandrew the following is a typical *sanad* for a *purwa*: 'Sanad granted by Thakar Ramdin to Jowahir to the following effect: Do you found a katra after the name of Bhagwan Bakhsh in Mauzah Deopur, and populate it, build your own house therein, and be assured that I have written off the zemindari of the same to you. Whoever comes and settles in it, do you remit his forced labour (begar). So long as you wish you may hold pakka (lease of the village), and when it is made kacha (direct collection from the cultivators) you may enjoy 10 bighas nankar and 15 bighas sir, assessed at one rupee eight annas and in addition take 10 bighas charri (grazing land). Dated Kuar Badi Panchmi Sambat 1901 (1252 fasli)'. This quotation is from Macandrew, *Revenue Matters*, pp. 33-4; Baden-Powell, p. 241, uses a slightly abbreviated version.

CHAPTER 2
ANNEXATION AND THE SUMMARY SETTLEMENT OF 1856-7

Annexation

Awadh was formally annexed to the British Empire in India on 7 February 1856 when the reigning monarch, Wajid Ali Shah, refused to sign a treaty handing over the administration to the East India Company. With this act Lord Dalhousie brought to a logical end the progressive subordination of Awadh to British economic and political control that had begun with the battle of Baksar.[1]

The rationale behind Lord Dalhousie's decision was his knowledge, based on the reports of Sleeman and subsequently of Outram, that misgovernment was rampant and that law and order (or for that matter any kind of efficient administration) had completely collapsed. Commenting on Outram's report Dalhousie wrote:

It seems impossible that the home authorities can any longer hesitate to overthrow this fortress of corruption and infamous misgovernment. I should not mind doing it as a parting *coup*.[2]

Earlier in 1851 he had described the kingdom of Awadh as 'a cherry which will drop into our mouths some day. It has long been ripening'.[3] It is true that a considerable degree of inefficiency

---

[1] For an analysis of the interrelatedness of British economic and political expansion into Awadh see R. Mukherjee, 'Trade and Empire in Awadh, 1765-1804', *Past and Present*, No. 94, Feb. 1982, pp. 85-102.

[2] Dalhousie to G.C. Bart, 2 May 1855: J.G.A. Baird (ed.), *Private Letters of the Marquess of Dalhousie* (London, 1910), p. 344.

[3] Dalhousie to G.C. Bart, 30 July 1851: ibid., p. 169. British Governors-General in India very often referred to Awadh as something to be eaten. Wellesley had promised London 'a supper of Oudh'. See C.H. Phillips, *The East India Company, 1784-1834* (Oxford, 1961), p. 104. This perhaps is an indication of how Awadh was viewed by British policy makers.

and corruption prevailed in the Awadh court.[4] What is not often emphasized is that the misgovernment was not merely a function of the king's inability to rule, as Dalhousie thought,[5] but was tied up with the nature of the British alliance with Awadh.

The subsidiary system had a ruinous effect on the Awadh administration. It made the administration increasingly dependent on British troops to enforce law and order and to put down recalcitrant talukdars. After 1830, when non-intervention in the internal affairs of native powers became the watchword, British troops were withdrawn. The Awadh rulers were thus left without any support. Time and again the British issued warnings to the Awadh king to improve the administration; but such warnings put him in a difficult position and so were self-defeating. As a recent writer has noted—

With the subsidiary alliance drawn tightly about him, he could not ignore the British and act as before. But he had neither the training nor the military force to act upon the injunction of his European advisers. So the Nawabs who succeeded Saadat Ali Khan, one after the other, increasingly abandoned the attempt to govern and retired into the *zanana*, where they amused themselves with wine, women and poetry. The sensuous life . . . did not reflect sheer perversity or weakness of character on the part of the Nawabs. Indolence was rather the only appropriate response to the situation in which the princes of Oudh were placed. . .[6]

This lucid statement highlights the political dimensions of misgovernment in Awadh. However, some vital aspects remain unnoticed. Misgovernment was not just a function of the British political presence in and around Awadh. Since 1765 the British presence had had an economic dimension, causing considerable drain and dislocation to the Awadh economy. Trade controlled by the Company or by European traders had channelled economic

---

[4]An example of the King's inability to enforce law and order is seen from the way Wajid Ali Shah vacillated when faced with the communal clashes concerning the Hanuman Ghari temple near Faizabad. The Muslims claimed that the temple was built on the site of a mosque. The consequent tension and fighting was brought to an end by the intervention of British troops who defeated and killed the fanatic Maulavi. See Foreign Dept. Pol. Proc., 28 Dec.1855, Nos. 339, 342, 351, 355, 360, 363, 365, 370, 378, 384, 388, 389, 394, 396, 398, 400, 409, 415, 417, 419 and 453.

[5]Dalhousie to G.C. Bart, 30 July 1851.

[6]Metcalf, *Land Landlords and the Raj*, pp. 39-40.

resources away from Awadh. This had eroded the very viability of the Awadh administration, leading to misgovernment, which in turn had become the rationale for annexing parts of Awadh, first Benares and then the whole of the Doab.[7] As a recent specialist on the history of Awadh has noted pithily, Awadh was important, after 1801, not for what it could do, but for what it had to offer.[8]

The attitude of taking from Awadh whatever it had to offer persisted till the middle of the nineteenth century. It is significant that in 1856 it was seen as a good area for investment in indigo. It was estimated that Awadh was capable of producing half the amount of indigo that was produced in Bengal and that the quality of the Awadh indigo would be as good as the indigo produced in the Doab. Fortunes would be easy to come by in indigo cultivations in Awadh as the capital outlay there 'would be small, mainly in sphere of building vats and "factories"'[9] Awadh was seen as an ideal region where private capital could be invested to develop raw material resources, especially cotton:

My firm belief is that it [the extension of cotton cultivation] can be effected by private capital and not by any Government interference or direct control. No country in the world affords a finer investment for capital than India and no part of India better than Oudh. With every variety of soil and with direct water communication with Calcutta . . . and a Railway at no great distance, nothing can be more favourable. Natives will not cultivate cotton or any other articles without some strong inducement, but I am quite sure that if a factory were established in Oudh, if seeds and advances are given the landowners would cultivate cotton to any extent required.[10]

Awadh was seen not only as a convenient field for the investment of private capital to extend the cultivation of cotton, but also, given proper transport facilities, as a market:

Were a good road made between Lucknow and Byram-Ghat, a place north-east by east about forty miles distant, where the Gogra and Gunduck unite, the former city would not only get up European articles of

[7] Mukherjee, 'Trade and Empire in Awadh', pp. 90ff.
[8] P. Reeves (ed.), *Sleeman in Oudh*, Intro., p. 6.
[9] Anon., 'The Physical Capabilities of Oude', *Calcutta Review*, vol. 26, June 1856, p. 437.
[10] S.A. Abbott, Commercial Suptd. Lucknow Divn. to G.R. Haywood, Sec. to Cotton Supply Association, 6 Dec. 1860: BROG File No. 2961.

consumption, so much in demand there . . . but it would also become the principal commercial mart in the Upper Provinces . . . its proximity also to Cawnpore, to which place a road is already in existence, would deprive Allahabad, Mirzapore and Benares of much of their commercial importance, and on the development of the numerous resources of Oude, this city might become . . . one of the most important commercial places in India.[11]

However, the annexation of Awadh in 1856 cannot be explained solely by economic considerations.[12] Yet two points need to be highlighted. Its misgovernment—the final rationale for annexation—was a function of the British political and economic presence in and around Awadh.[13] And immediately after the annexation Dalhousie's first thought was that 'our gracious Queen has 5,000,000 more subjects and £1,300,000 more revenue than she had yesterday'.[14] The emphasis on greater revenue acquires a special significance when we recall that

In the eight years of Dalhousie's administration £ 8,354,000 were added to the public debt; in the last three years there was a deficit of £ 2,044,000 in 1853-54 and of £ 1,850,000 in 1854-55.[15]

This apart, it should be remembered that by 1856 all the major areas of India had been conquered: the Maratha lands, the Doab, the Carnatic, Punjab and of course Bengal. A number of small princely states had fallen under Dalhousie's hammer. Awadh, though formally independent, would—with its sprawling boundaries and its own system of administration right in the heartland of north India—have presented administrative and political problems, especially in an age of expanding public works. It was expedient in such a context to bring Awadh into the British fold.

Whatever the amalgam of reasons that led to its annexation, there can hardly be any doubt that the people of Awadh were

---

[11]'The Physical Capabilities of Oude', p. 423; Sleeman had also written in the same vein to Sir J.W. Hogg, on 28 Oct. 1852: 'Oude would be covered with a network of fine macadamised roads, over which the produce of Oude and our own districts would pass freely to the benefit of the people of both; . . .', Sleeman, *Journey*, ii, p. 378.

[12]The economic dimensions are lucidly discussed in Reeves, pp. 20-1.

[13]Ibid., pp. 19ff., notes how the fact that Awadh was surrounded by British territories tended to undermine the effectiveness of the Awadh government.

[14]Dalhousie to Bart, 8 Feb. 1856: Baird, *Letters of Dalhousie*, p. 369.

[15]M.E. Bell, *Retrospects and Prospects of Indian Policy* (London, 1868), p. 221.

deeply moved by the fact that 'the honourable English came and took the country' (*Angrez Bahadur ain: mulk lai linho*).[16] They were especially moved by the plight of their king who had to leave his own homeland:

> Noble and peasant all wept together
> and all the world wept and wailed
> Alas! The chief has bidden adieu to
> his country and gone abroad.[17]

Distress and sorrow for the unfortunate king was widespread, and covered every age group.[18] People recited *nanha* (dirges) and followed their king all the way to Kanpur.[19] A contemporary observer wrote—

The condition of this town without any exaggeration was such that it appeared that on the departure of Jan-i Alam, the life was gone out of the body, and the body of this town had been left lifeless . . . there was no street or market and house which did not wail out the cry of agony in separation of Jan-i Alam.[20]

Immediately after the annexation there was an increase in the prices of essential commodities, which caused hardship.[21] The removal of the Lucknow Court affected the demand for indigenous goods; the cotton weavers in and around Awadh were particularly affected.[22]

Many self-styled religious leaders and messiahs flocked into Lucknow to denounce the annexation. The British were already unpopular with the Muslims for their action in quelling the tumult at Hanuman Ghari. Maulavi Ahmadullah—later famous for his activities in Faizabad during the events of 1857—arrived

---

[16]W. Crooke, 'Songs about the king of Oudh', *Indian Antiquary*, vol. XL., 1911, p. 62.

[17]Ibid.

[18]See *Bostan-i Avadh*, cited in G.D. Bhatnagar, 'The Annexation of Oudh', *Uttara Bharati*, vol. 3, (1956), p. 64.

[19]See Bhatnagar, p. 65, and references therein.

[20]*Qaisar-ut Tawarikh*, p. 180: cited in Bhatnagar, p. 65.

[21]*Tilism* (an Urdu daily published from Lucknow between 1856 and 1857), 8 Aug., 19 Dec., 26 Dec. 1856 and 16 Jan., 6 March 1857: cited in Iqbal Husain, 'Lucknow between Annexation and the Mutiny', (mimeographed paper from Aligarh Muslim University), p. 11.

[22]*Tilism*, 29 Aug. 1856: cited in Husain, p. 12.

in Lucknow in November 1856. People began to visit him in large numbers. He gave a call for jihad against the Company's rule.[23] A man called Qadir Ali Shah posed as a 'saint' and raised a force of 12,000 men. He fixed 11 Sept. 1856 (the tenth day of Muharram) for an uprising against the Company. This was foiled.[24] There were also a number of other incidents where 'saints' came to Lucknow ostensibly to restore the king.[25]

The people of Awadh did not accept the annexation as a *fait accompli*: in fact the chiefs proposed to collect men and oppose it.[26] Among the talukdars of Awadh there was a growing apprehension that the British would destroy their power and prestige once they took over. This was a deep rooted fear. Sleeman wrote:

In 1801 when the Oude territory was divided, and half taken by us and half left to Oude, the landed aristocracy of each were about equal. Now hardly a family of this class remains in our half, while in Oude it remains unimpaired. Everybody in Oude believes those families to have been systematically crushed.[27]

Apprehension was compounded into reality when the British, immediately after the take-over, ordered a wholesale disarming and demolition of the talukdars' forts. These forts, which dotted the Awadh countryside, were symbols of talukdar power and prestige.

An appendix to this chapter presents a list of talukdar forts in Awadh, with a special focus on southern Awadh where the talukdars were most entrenched and where the mutual dependence between talukdar and peasant was most marked. The forts were always strategically isolated by surrounding jungles or by deep trenches, or in the case of powerful talukdars (like Rana Beni Madho) by both; and the jungle could at times be as deep as eight miles. Most of the forts were *kutcha*, i.e. built of mud. Their

---

[23]*Tilism* 27 Nov., 12 Dec. 1856 and 30 Jan. and 6 March 1857: cited in ibid., p. 13.
[24]*Tilism*, 19 and 26 Sept. 1856: cited in ibid., pp. 12-13.
[25]See ibid., p. 14; also see M.C. Ommany., Judicial Commr. to G. Couper, 14 Nov. 1856, I.S. Banks, Com. of Lucknow to Judicial Com., 4 Nov., 1856, and Nawab Mahamudulah Bahadur to Dep. Com. Lucknow, 24 Sept. 1856: Foreign Dept. Secret, 26 Feb. 1858, Nos. 145-9.
[26]M.M. Khan, *Oude: Its Princes and its Government Vindicated* (London, 1857), p. 181; also see Bhatnagar, p. 64, Bhatnagar cites *Bostan-i Avadh* (p. 162) as his source.
[27]Sleeman to Colvin, 28 Dec. 1853: Sleeman, *Journey*, ii, p. 415.

strength varied: Man Singh's 'great fort' had as many as twenty-five guns, Beni Madho's had twelve, but the smaller ones had no guns at all. Often the more powerful talukdars owned many other small forts apart from the large ones in which they lived. Their military strength did not consist simply of guns, but also of cavalry and foot soldiers. The number of foot soldiers varied from 12,000 in some cases to one or two hundred among the smaller talukdars. These foot soldiers were directly in the pay of the talukdar and depended for their livelihood on the talukdars' patronage. It was perhaps inevitable that the talukdars, with such a remarkable diffusion of power and position of control in the Awadh countryside, were seen as political opponents by the British as soon as they assumed government.[28]

The annexation thus caused an emotional upheaval among the people by removing their king. The disruption of the court meant unemployment to retainers and the army, and also loss of work to people who supplied the court with its innumerable luxury items. To the lords of the countryside it meant a new government which appeared to have a bias against them. This feeling of discontent among sections of the population was to be exacerbated by the first British revenue measures.

The Summary Settlement of 1856-7

Once Awadh had been taken over by the Raj a major aim of the British government was to set up a system that would streamline the collection of revenue from the newly-acquired province. In this the British government faced certain obstacles almost immediately. In north India the revenue was collected in *kists* (instalments). In Awadh the payment of revenue was regulated by kists varying from nine to twelve in number, beginning with Kooar (Sept.-Oct.) and continuing monthly till Ashadh (June-July) or Bhadaun (Aug.-Sept.).[29] The time at which the annexation came

---

[28]Kaye, *Sepoy War*, iii, p. 422, notes how it was inevitable that the British would try to do away with the talukdars. Significantly, according to Kaye, this had nothing to do with the British officers considering talukdars to be interloping middlemen and originators of misrule. Kaye wrote, 'Practically, the same results would have followed annexation, if these men had been better landlords and better subjects'.

[29]Gubbins to Couper, 11 March 1856: For. Dept., Political Proceedings, 13 June

created problems but—

The matter was settled on a clear and unmistakable basis by adopting the native mode of accounts and by declaring that the first 4½ kists i.e. from Kooar to the 15th Maugh (Feb-March) belonged to the Oudh native government and that the remaining 7½ kists (or 5½ or 4½ where the kists are fewer than 12) appertained to the British Government.[30]

What created disaffection, however, was the actual collection of the revenue. The British decided to collect their own 7½ kists in two instalments (May and June) but at the same time they also summarily demanded the 4½ kists (i.e. the arrears). This 'became a source of great contention and embarrassment to Talooqdars and Zumeendars'.[31]

The revenue affairs thus began on the wrong foot: many of the big talukdars refusing to cough up their dues; and at the same time British revenue collectors appeared in an arbitrary garb. A military force had to be sent to arrest the raja of Tulsipur.[32] Man Singh refused to pay his dues, shut himself up in his fort and then fled at the approach of British forces. Similarly Hanwant Singh of Kalakankar, always a turbulent subject, refused to pay his revenue dues because he knew he was going to lose his villages.[33]

The instruction for the settlement proper, commencing on 1 May 1856, were very precise and specific. The settlement was to be made for three years, 'village by village, with the parties actually in possession'.[34] The assessments were to be based on detailed information and statements of (i) the past five years' jama (2) the nankar grants (3) rent-free villages, namely *mafi, jagir*, etc. (4) religious grants, and (5) patwaries and *chowkidaries* of the old system.[35] It was laid down as a leading principle that the settle-

1856, No. 317.
[30]Ibid.
[31]Barrow, 'Memo on former administration in Oudh': BROG File No. 305; also see Couper to Edmonstone, 4 July 1856: '. . . the steps taken by the Financial Commissioner for the realization of the 4½ kists of 1263 were calculated to excite the greatest distrust and suspicion among the people'. For. Dept., Political Consultations, 24 April, 1857, No. 164; see also *FSUP*, i, pp. 209ff.
[32]For. Dept., 27 June 1856, Cons. Nos. 186-8; 15 Aug. 1856, Cons. Nos. 56-7 and 63-4.
[33]Barrow, 'Memo on Hunwunt Singh, 25 Oct. 1858': BROG File No. 1037.
[34]Edmonstone to Outram, 4 Feb. 1856: *Papers Relating to Land Tenures and Revenue Settlement in Oude* (Calcutta, 1865), p. 3.
[35]Barrow, 'Memo on former administration', BROG File No. 305; also see

ment was to be made 'with the actual occupants of the soil', i.e. with village zamindars or with proprietary coparcenaries.[36]

The reasons behind such instructions are not far to seek. Awadh lay in the heart of north India with a long and contiguous boundary with the North-Western Provinces, large portions of which had before 1801 been a part of the old kingdom of Awadh. It was administratively convenient that Awadh be settled on the same pattern as the rest of north India. It was assumed that Awadh shared the same features as the rest of north India and hence could be settled in the same way:

> The tenures in land, the distinctive characteristics of proprietary village communities and the usages of the agricultural classes are believed to be identical with those in the North-Western Provinces...
>
> The tenures being identical, the existence of coparcenary communities of village proprietors being certain, and the nature of the country, as well as the agricultural usages of the people, being similar, the system of village settlements in the North-Western Provinces as fully and lucidly elaborated and explained in the *Directions for Settlement Officers*... should unquestionably be adopted.[37]

An anti-talukdar bias was inherent in the views of Bird and Thomason, the masterminds of the NWP settlement. For them a talukdar was not somebody connected with land for any length of time; he was an imposition from outside between the people and the government who had established his hold over land through force, influence and fraud.[38] For Bird and Thomason, following up on Holt Mackenzie, the village communities were the cornerstone of agrarian life in north India, and, where they did not exist,

'Chief Commissioner's observations regarding Summary Settlement': BROG File No. 2301.

[36]Edmonstone to Outram, 4 Feb. 1856: *Papers re to Land Tenure*, p. 4; also see 'CC's observations re Summary Settlement': BROG File No. 2301. In his 'Memo on former administration' Barrow explicated the instructions thus: 'The instructions for settlement made it nearly imperative on the District Officer to turn out the Talooqdar and reinstate the "Village Zamindar" the "Proprietor of the Soil"; no Talooqdar, middleman or farmer... was to be allowed and if long possession had given him a prescriptive right it was to be counterbalanced by a 10% Talooqdaree allowance, but this was ordered to be ignored as much as possible. If there was a village claimant he was to be put in'. See BROG File No. 305.

[37]Edmonstone to Outram, 4 Feb. 1856: *Papers re to Land Tenure*, pp. 6-8.

[38]See *Directions for Settlement Officers* (Calcutta, 1858), para 102; see also Elliott, *Chronicles*, pp. 146ff.

the key figure was the proprietor of every village.[39] Hence the emphasis on making the settlement with the 'actual proprietors' and on doing away with what was supposed to be an imposition between proprietor and government.

In practice the execution of the instructions did not turn out to be so simple. For one thing details of five years' jama of every village were scarcely available. In Awadh, villages grouped into talukas had been assessed for so long in the gross that 'there was no record whatever of what the villages paying jama was separately'.[40] As a last resort the settlement officers had to turn to *jamabandi* accounts kept by the talukdars' servants. And there they had to encounter the concealments and various other forms of corruption in which they indulged. The settlement and assessment was based on such dubious 'facts' and consequently contained 'many and grave errors'.[41]

There arose similar difficulties in dealing with seer lands, i.e. the lands held at a favourable assessment and cultivated by the landholder himself or by hired labour. It was difficult, first, to attain the quantity of seer land, and second, to find out at what rates they had previously been assessed. The settlement officers normally, after approximately ascertaining the quantity of seer land, added it to the total jamabandi at the highest rent paid per *bigha* for any land in the village.[42] There was thus a considerable gap in knowledge, and the settlement officers had often to depend on the rough and ready methods of trial and error — what in the context of eighteenth century British revenue practice in Bengal Warren Hastings had called the 'Rule of False'.[43]

Given the difficulties of getting information the officers, according to Major Barrow (a settlement officer in Salon who later supervised the 1859 settlement), had two courses open to

---

[39] E. Stokes, *English Utilitarians and India* (Oxford, 1959), p. 112; see also *Directions for Settlement Officers*, paras 76ff.

[40] Barrow 'Memo on former administration': BROG File no 305.

[41] Ibid. [42] Ibid.

[43] Hastings explained this in a letter to R.C. Barwell, 22 July 1772, reprinted in G.R. Gleig, *Memoirs of the Life of Warren Hastings*, 3 vols (London, 1841), i, pp. 314ff. According to Hastings this was a system whereby 'we must adopt a plan upon conjecture, try, execute, add and deduct from it, till it is brought into a perfect shape'. (Ibid. p. 316); see also R. Guha, *A Rule of Property for Bengal* (Paris, 1963), Introduction.

them.[44] One course was to take an approximate average of the last five years' jama, and then add to it the various nazranas and *sewais* which were extorted over and above the jama, to arrive at the total gross jama. From the latter figure could be deducted the money for the road fund, chowkidari and patwari, to arrive at the government jama. Another course was to find out the total village assessments as per the jamabandi returns, and an approximate figure for seer and mafi lands as well as for supposed concealments. Fifty per cent of the total thus arrived at would give the government jama. To the latter figure was added allocated amounts for the patwari, chowkidari and road fund to arrive at the total payment.

It was only after the settlement had commenced that it was realized that the chakladars and nazims had often taken whatever they could squeeze out from a village as jama so that the average of five years' jama was bound to be pitched too high; also that nazranas, sewais, etc. represented illegal extortions whose additions only inflated the already over-high jama. The second course too had an inbuilt propensity towards overassessment. The jamabandi rolls would also be inflated because of previous overassessment. Even in talukdari villages the patwaris (more often than not in the talukdars' pay) would give enhanced rates as the talukdar knew that according to the instructions he was going to lose the village anyway. And because of the short period available, detailed investigations were not possible and Barrow was certain that 'many mistakes must have accrued'.[45]

It is interesting that in Bengal in the late eighteenth century the British, lost amidst age-old customs and Persian hieroglyphics, had had to proceed on similar rules of thumb and had depended on Mir Kasim's inflated jama rolls, making overassessment rampant in their early revenue experiments.[46] Similarly in the revenue experiments in the North-Western Provinces when the first village settlements were being made, lack of time overruled the kind of detailed inquiry that Mackenzie's Minute and the Regulation of 1822 had prescribed; so the settlement officers often had to resort to 'guess and estimate' methods and overassessment

[44]Barrow, 'Memo on former administration': BROG File No. 305.
[45]Ibid.
[46]See N.K. Sinha (ed.), *The History of Bengal*, pp. 81ff.

Annexation and the Summary Settlement of 1856-7 43

was common.[47] This is not to say that experimentation and lack of knowledge were the only two factors behind overassessment. Maximization of land revenue was one of the driving forces of the British Raj.[48] In fact, underlying the decision to settle with 'actual proprietors' etc. was the fact that 'settlements with village occupants were often expected to yield a higher revenue'.[49] On the subject of overassessment it is well worth noting the following general but penetrating comment by an experienced India-hand in the nineteenth century:

> They [British civil administrators] had learnt, under Lord Dalhousie, that, on the annexation of a new province, it was expected that those, to whom its administration was intrusted, should demonstrate, by figured statements, that it would 'pay'. Perhaps the old 'mercantile bottom' of the East India Company was, in some measure, answerable for this. I do not underrate the importance of the consideration thus suggested. But the mistake always lay in the attempt made to bring out results by a forcing process of unwholesome rapidity. Officers trained in the essential business of 'settlement operations' had learnt that their efficiency as public servants was estimated in accordance with the success attending their efforts to screw up the revenue of their several districts to the highest possible pitch of productiveness. As long as the money was got, there was very little thought of the effect that might be produced on the minds of people by the manner of getting it. The black-and-white of demonstrable figures was greater in their minds than the animosities and resentments of an overtaxed people.[50]

Overassessment in Awadh varied from district to district; and though some districts were not overassessed on the whole, some parganas within the district were grossly overassessed. In pargana Pernagar of Sitapur district the total revenue demand for 1262 fasli under the Nawabi government had been Rs 24,392; the British demand in 1264 fasli had gone up to Rs 31,444, i.e. a 28 per cent rise.[51] In pargana Taddalpur there was a 63 per cent rise, from Rs 36,937 in 1262 fasli to Rs 60,216 in 1264 fasli.[52] In the same district

---

[47]Metcalf, *Land, Landlords and the Raj*, pp. 59-60.
[48]See I. Habib, 'Colonialization of the Indian Economy 1757-1900', *Social Scientist*, March 1975.
[49]A. Siddiqi, *Agrarian Change*, p. 91.
[50]Kaye, *Sepoy War*, iii, pp. 425-6.
[51]'Statement showing Revenue Assessment of zillah Seetapoor prior to Annexation in 1262F and after Annexation in 1264F at Summary Settlement': BROG File No. 1623.
[52]Ibid.

in pargana Hargaon the demand rose by 26 per cent from Rs 27,668 in 1262 fasli to Rs 34,886 in 1264 fasli.[53] However the overall demand in Sitapur had been reduced by 37 per cent from Rs 16,66,828 in 1262 fasli to Rs 10,43,315 in 1264 fasli.[54]

In Faizabad district where the Settlement Officer, Mr Forbes, had been the model of conscientiousness,[55] the settlement was based on the following data:

> First Mouzawar Nikasee collections of the past years furnished by the putwaries. These were again compared with returns of the Jumah assessed upon each Mouzah at the time when it was first incorporated in a Talooqa obtained from the Canoongoes . . . Secondly Mouzawar Returns of land cultivated during the last few years furnished by the Putwaries and thirdly Talooqdar Returns of Government Collections for the past five years.[56]

Detailed figures available for the district show that the total jama of the summary settlement, Rs 11,13,493, was 17 per cent higher than the average previous five years' collection which was Rs 9,50,963.[57] It is also important to underline that inspite of policy prescriptions to settle at half-assets and the Saharanpur Regulations of 1855,[58] the total jama represented 57 per cent of the estimated rental.[59] The estimated rental itself was 26 per cent more than the *nikasi* figures given by the patwaris.[60] It is worthwhile to go into some of the pargana figures of Faizabad district. In pargana Amsaw the total jama of Rs 33,747 was 27 per cent higher than the average of the previous five years' collection which was Rs 26,091. Even Gubbins admitted that 'The increase seems too great'.[61] In pargana Mangalsi the average of the previous five years' collection was Rs 56,628, and the total jama for 1856/7 was Rs 83,464, i.e. a 48 per cent increase.[62] In Pancham Rath the total

[53]Ibid.   [54]Ibid.
[55]M. Gubbins 'Minute on the Fyzabad Summary Settlement, dated 13 Feb. 1857': BROG File No. 66, pt. 1; referring to Mr Forbes' settlement volumes, Gubbins commented 'they are in fact just what ought everywhere to have been done. . .'
[56]Ibid. *Nikasi* here is probably used as a shorthand for *nikasi kham* which means the gross produce of an estate or village receivable from the cultivators by the zamindar, according to the accounts of the patwari. See Wilson's *Glossary*.
[57]Gubbins, 'Memo on Fyzabad Summary Settlement' BROG File No. 66, pt. 1.
[58]See R.C. Dutt, *The Economic History of India*, 2 vols (Delhi, repr. 1970), ii, p. 33.
[59]Gubbins, 'Memo on Fyzabad Summary Settlement', BROG File No. 66, pt. 1.
[60]Ibid.   [61]Ibid.   [62]Ibid.

Annexation and the Summary Settlement of 1856-7   45

jama (Rs 2,11,886) exceeded the average collections of the previous five years (Rs 1,61,520) by 31 per cent.[63] In Aldemau the previous five years' average collection was Rs 2,02,833 and the jama fixed at the summary settlement of Rs 2,39,805 showed an increase of 18 per cent.[64] In Akbarpur the increase was 16 per cent, the total jama being Rs 1,61,222 as compared to the average of the previous five years' collection, Rs 1,39,132.[65] In the pargana of Birhur the average previous five years' collection was Rs 94,272 and the total jama of 1856-7 was Rs 1,10,936 showing an increase of 18 per cent.[66] Since Faizabad is the only district for which such detailed figures are available, the data is set out in a tabular form (Table 4).

In pargana Mohan in the district of Purwa, an ilaqa that had no talukdars and had been ruined by the extortions of ijaradars,[67] the British revenue demand was 52 per cent of the estimated ren-

TABLE 4
Summary Settlement Assessment in Faizabad

Name of Pargana	Average of the previous five years' collection	Nikasi as given by Patwari	Estimate of Rental made by Settlement Officer	Total Jama	Total Jama as a percentage of Estimated Rental	Percentage increase of Total Jama compared to Past Collections
Havayli Oudh	75,669	1,26,886	1,41,121	80,006	56%	6%
Amsaw	26,091	52,753	59,729	33,747	55%	27%
Mangalsi	56,628	1,29,693	1,44,622	83,464	57%	48%
Pancham Rath	1,61,520	3,25,123	3,74,200	2,11,886	56%	31%
Tanda	41,780	48,530	81,904	45,065	55%	9%
Ittifatgunge	11,325	15,513	19,323	10,848	52%	—4%
Sultanpur	81,825	1,19,034	1,36,185	76,966	55%	—6%
Sirhurpur	27,790	35,017	49,910	28,505	57%	3%
Aldemau	2,02,833	2,83,070	4,61,738	2,39,805	51%	18%
Akbarpur	1,39,132	2,20,851	2,77,351	1,61,222	58%	16%
Birhur	94,272	1,40,162	1,82,136	1,10,936	60%	18%
Mujhoura	32,098	42,167	54,924	31,028	57%	—3%
	9,50,963	15,38,799	19,83,143	11,13,478	57%	17%

SOURCE: Gubbins, 'Memo on Summary Settlement in Fyzabad', Board of Revenue, Oudh, General File No. 66, Part I.

[63]Ibid. [64]Ibid. [65]Ibid. [66]Ibid.
[67]See Ch. 1.

tal.[68] Moreover, it was estimated that the amounts the zamindars had to pay in excess of the net jama as chowkidari and patwari allowances were in excess of what they had previously paid.[69]

In the district of Sultanpur, though the overall revenue demand was lower than the average of the previous five years' collection, the total jama represented approximately 60 per cent of the estimated rental and certain parganas and ilaqas were grossly overassessed.[70] For example in taluka Bhadiyan not only did the total jama (Rs 17,147) represent 60 per cent of the estimated rental (Rs 28,185) but it was also 13 per cent higher than the average of the previous five years' collection (Rs 15,127); the finance commissioner and the *quanungoes* of the area thought the assessment too high.[71] In taluka Kuumpur, the total jama of Rs 56,401 was 69 per cent of the estimated rental and was 40 per cent higher than the average of the previous five years' collection (Rs 40,607). According to the quanungoes, with such a demand the taluka would have only a surplus of three annas to the rupee.[72] In pargana Jagdishpur the average of the previous five years' collection had been computed at Rs 89,461 whereas the total jama of 1264 fasli was Rs 1,07,991, i.e. a 20 per cent rise. The total jama was 56 per cent of the estimated rental but there were at least eight villages in which the revenue swallowed up the entire assets, and in the rest left only six annas to four annas in the rupee.[73] In Amethi, the area under Raja Madho Singh, the total jama (Rs 2,02,305) was 36 per cent higher than Rs 1,48,659, which was the average of the previous five years' collection. The revenue demand was 56 per cent of the estimated rental but there were three mauzas in which there was no surplus left once the jama and the cesses had been

---

[68]Gubbins, 'Assessment of Pargana Mohan zillah Poorwah, 17 Dec. 1856': BROG File No. 66, pt. 1. Gubbins admitted that the past collections had been excessive and they were not a safe guide. It seems to be a safe assumption that the estimated rental was on the high side, especially as 'during the settlement of the neighbouring pergunnah, Suffeepoor, the assamees protested at the time of fixing the jumma that they would, abandon the land sooner than pay the excessive rents hitherto exacted'. (Ibid.) If the estimated rental itself was on the high side then the revenue demand probably represented more than 52 per cent of the *genuine* total assets of the area.

[69]Ibid.

[70]Gubbins, 'Minute on the Summary Settlement of Sultanpur, 17 Feb. 1857': BROG File No. 66, pt. 1.

[71]Ibid.   [72]Ibid.   [73]Ibid.

paid. And 'in no village is there a greater surplus after paying cesses than three to four annas' in the rupee.[74] In Chandab pargana the average of the previous five years' collection had been Rs 56,784, on which the revenue demand for 1264 fasli showed a 30 per cent hike. The estimated rental of the pargana is not available but the quanungoes noted that in the villages settled with the villagers themselves the assessment was generally moderate, leaving a surplus of eight annas in the rupee; but in the villages settled with the talukdars there was no more than a surplus of four annas in the rupee. There were four mauzas in which there was no surplus left over at all.[75] Even in parganas where the total jama was below the average past collections, there was often over-assessment in certain villages. In pargana Papurghat Kadam, where the revenue demand was 16 per cent below the past collections, the estimate of surplus left was generally four annas to the rupee. There was not a single village which had a surplus of eight annas, only three with a surplus of six annas and in a few there was absolutely nothing over.[76] In pargana Barsa Kadam, which had been badly broken up by severe past exactions, the British revenue demand was 75 per cent lower than the average of past collections but it was still 60 per cent of the estimated rental, and quanungoes and tahsildar thought the demand too heavy.[77] In Dyllappur where the revenue demand for the summary settlement was 11 per cent lower than the average of the previous five years' collection, there were eleven mauzas in which there was a surplus of only two annas in the rupee left over.[78]

In pargana Dariabad in the district of the same name, the figures of the past average collections were not always available, and the officer concerned 'assumed 70% or upwards of the Jummabundy as the Jummah'. At least thirty to forty villages objected. Gubbins thought the estimate of the total rental needed scaling down as well as the revenue demand. But even after reduction the total jama (Rs 1,68,221) represented 50 per cent of the total rental (Rs 2,92,238).[79]

In pargana Partabgunge of Lucknow district the average of the previous five years' collection was Rs 44,000 and the total jama

---

[74]Ibid. [75]Ibid. [76]Ibid. [77]Ibid. [78]Ibid.
[79]Gubbins, 'Minute on the Summary Settlement of the district of Durriabad, 5 Jan. 1857': BROG File No. 66, pt. 1.

(not including chowkidari, however) of the British was Rs 51,003, showing an increase of 16 per cent, and the total jama was 57 per cent of the estimated total rental. The Finance Commissioner did not think that the increase was justified, especially in the pattidari villages which were numerous. Gubbins had to suggest a considerable reduction but it was well into 1857 before the reduced settlement could be operative.[80]

In the pargana of Mugraer in ilaqa Daundiakhera in the heart of Baiswara the total jama of thirty out of thirty-five mauzas was slightly lower than the average of past collections (it is not certain from the document whether the average was of all the thirty-five mauzas or the thirty mauzas whose total jama is shown), but the total jama (Rs 21,194) represents 56 per cent of the estimated rental. Gubbins, the Commissioner of the Division and the Deputy Commissioner all agreed that there were some cases where the assessment was too high. A reduction of 7.5 per cent was suggested early in 1857. In fact the Deputy Commissioner of Purwa, Captain Evans, thought that a reduction of 7.5 per cent was applicable throughout the ilaqa of Daundia Khera.[81] Similarly, it was considered that parganas Harha, Unao, Purwa and Murawun had all been overassessed to some degree; the following rates of reduction were suggested in 1857: Harha: 15 per cent, Unao: 7.5 per cent (or 5 per cent), Purwa and Murawan 10 per cent each.[82]

The settlement of pargana Kakori in the district of Lucknow proceeded by the crudest possible trial and error method. The settlement officer 'did not make in any case a regular estimate of Rental. But fixed the jumah at what he considered just and assumed the Rental to be the double of it'.[83] The village of Rumermau refused to accept the jama thus fixed and in another village, Saifulpur, the resident villagers also declined to engage.[84] Gubbins suggested a radical revision. But even in the revised settlement the proposed jama (Rs 23,263 — not including chowki-

[80]Gubbins, 'Minute on the Summary Settlement of the Pergunnah of Pertabgunge, Zillah Lucknow, 1 Jan. 1857 BROG File No. 66, pt. 1.

[81]Gubbins, 'Minute on Pergunnah Mugraer Elaqua Daundia Khera, 7 Jan. 1857': BROG File No. 66, pt. 1

[82]Ibid.

[83]Gubbins, 'Minute on the Summary Settlement of Pergunnah Kakoree, zillah Lucknow, 29 Dec 1856': BROG File No. 66, pt. 1.

[84]Ibid.

dari) exceeded the average of past collections (Rs 20,145) by 15 per cent, and the proposed jama was 65 per cent of the estimated rental (Rs 35,085); and this demand was imposed despite Gubbins' awareness that the pargana had suffered considerably from the extortions of previous ijaradars.[85]

For the district of Salon the figures for the payable jama of 1262 fasli are all available; but unfortunately the figures for 1264 fasli (1856/7) are not available. This gap notwithstanding, a rough estimate to gauge the level of the revenue demand is possible by comparing the 1262 fasli figures with those of 1266 fasli (1859-60). This comparison seems fair especially as the overall assessment for 1266 fasli was lower than that of 1264 fasli.[86] Such a comparison shows that the 1266 jama was only 3 per cent lower than the payable jama of 1262 fasli. But in certain parganas the level of the demand in 1266 fasli showed an increase from 1262 fasli. In pargana Dalmhow the payable jama for 1262 fasli had been Rs 1,64,651 which was 28 per cent lower than the jama fixed for 1266 fasli — which was Rs 2,11,245.[87] In pargana Suraynee the total jama for 1266 fasli was Rs 79,675 which was 21 per cent higher than Rs 65,947, the payable jama for 1262 fasli.[88] In pargana Mohangunj the payable jama for 1262 fasli was Rs 54,727, and that of 1266 fasli was Rs 62,761, i.e. a 14 per cent increase.[89] There was an increase of 28 per cent in the pargana of Norkha where the payable jama rose from Rs 52,740 in 1262 fasli to Rs 67,381 in 1266 fasli.[90] Pargana Behar saw the massive increase of 35 per cent, the payable jama going up from Rs 1,17,477 in 1262 fasli to Rs 1,58,579 in 1266 fasli.[91] Similarly, pargana Rampirikythollah saw a hike of 28 per cent from Rs 75,318 in 1262 fasli to Rs 96,379 in 1266 fasli.[92] A further source of irritation, apart from the overassessment itself, was the fact that in Salon 113 villages which had been held mafi (i.e. rent-free) in 1262 fasli were assessed in 1264 fasli at a total jama of Rs 50,615.[93]

[85] Ibid.
[86] 'Summary Settlement in Oude: J.D. Forsythe, Sec. to CC Awadh to Sec. of Governor-General, 13 July 1859': Collection to Political Despatches, 33, pt. 2, Collection 37.
[87] 'Comparative Table of Jumma of Salone during 1262 and 1266': BR Oudh, Rae Bareli, File No. 62.
[88] Ibid. [89] Ibid. [90] Ibid.
[91] Ibid. [92] Ibid. [93] Ibid.

The settlement officer for pargana Partapgarh, Capt. A.P. Orr, admitted to overassessment in 1264 fasli.[94] *Asamis* (i.e. the actual cultivators) in many places demanded that their rents be reduced from their former level. According to Capt. A.P. Orr the British policy of taking half-assets of a village had 'so much reduced in favour of the zumeendar or Talooqdar, that they (the assamee) demanded corresponding reductions'.[95] But such reductions, according to Orr, were not possible because if granted they 'would have so depricated [sic] the value of land, that it would eventually interfere detrimentally with the regular settlement operations . . .'[96] Thus cultivators were often paying the exorbitant rents demanded of them in Nawabi times.

The 1264 fasli assessment has been presented in a tabular form (Table 5). A few words about the table and the figures in it are necessary. In most cases the figures for the payable jama of 1264 are not available. This is derived by adding to the net jama[97] (i.e. jama without cess) an approximate figure for the cesses. The rate of the cesses is the same as the one imposed by the British in 1859.[98] That the figures for the 1264 payable jama (arrived at

[94] Orr wrote to Barrow on 31 Dec. 1858: '. . . in 1264 I myself made the settlement of Pertaubgarh Purgunnah and on my recent return to the same district perfectly well remembered that my 1264 jumma of Untoo as well as that of some other estates was much too heavy'. See BR Rae Bareli File No. 62.

[95] Orr to Barrow, 8 Apr. 1859: BR Rae Bareli File No. 62.

[96] Ibid.

[97] The figure for the net jama is obtained from 'Statement of Present Summary Settlement compared with that of 1264' in Collection to Political Dispatches, 33, pt. 2, Collection 37.

[98] The figures for cesses will be found in 'Statement Showing what number of past settlements were upheld in 1859' in Collection to Political Dispatches, 33, pt. 2, Collection 36: I have computed the rates of the cesses as a percentage of the government jama as follows:

Lucknow	:	12%
Rae Bareli	:	14%
Unao	:	17%
Faizabad	:	13%
Sultanpur	:	15%
Partapgarh	:	15%
Gonda	:	9%
Bahraich	:	13%
Muhamdi	:	13%
Hardoi	:	12%
Dariabad	:	13%
Sitapur	:	13%

Annexation and the Summary Settlement of 1856-7   51

through such a computation) is not very off the mark is demonstrated by their nearness to the actual figures available for two or three districts. For the sake of consistency we have always taken the jama arrived at in this manner as the basis for comparison, even for the few cases where the actual figures were available. Given the lack of data about the 1264 settlement this set of approximate figures is a good enough tentative guide for comparison.

It is clear from Table 5 that taken at an aggregate the province of Awadh was assessed at a lower level than it was previous to the annexation. But at the same time there is evidence enough to show that overassessment often prevailed at a local level, and that the authorities were aware of it. An indirect proof that even the jama of 1264 fasli was not considered moderate is the fact that in the assessment of 1266 fasli, nine out of the twelve districts had their jama reduced, however slightly, and it was accepted that 'this diminution is . . . owing to the discovery of over-assessment in some estates'.[99] In making a comparison of the pre-British and British revenue assessments in Awadh it is always worthwhile to remember that the British revenue demands were following on the years of rack-renting that the chakladars, ijaradars and even some talukdars had indulged in. Thus while the British revenue demands could appear moderate or low in *relative* terms, i.e. compared to previous assessments, they could have been pitched too high in *absolute* terms, i.e. when compared to what remained of the revenue paying capacities of the area. Time and time again during the 1264 Summary Settlement, Gubbins recalled and emphasized that many areas had been ruined by exactions, and that it was important to bear this in mind when computing the assessment.[100]

It has to be underscored that the evidence I have presented of overassessment at the local level all comes (with the possible exception of certain cases from Lucknow and Sitapur) from the area of talukdar-peasant interdependence and complementarity. At the aggregate level, as the table shows, the two districts that mark an increase in 1264 fasli compared to 1262 fasli are Faizabad

---

[99]Forsyth to Sec. of Governor-General, 13 July 1859: Collection to Political Dispatches 33, pt. 2, Collection No. 37.

[100]See the various memos and minutes of Gubbins referred to above; see also Barrow 'Memo on Former Administration in Oudh': BROG File No. 305.

TABLE 5
Assessment at the Summary Settlement 1856-7

Districts	1264 Payable Jama	1262 Payable Jama	1266 Payable Jama	% increase or decrease in 1264 compared to 1262	% increase or decrease in 1266 compared to 1264
Lucknow	10,11,997 (10,26,738)*	11,41,149	10,04,379	—11.3%	— 0.7%
Rae Bareli	9,73,171	10,42,319	9,61,799	— 6.6%	— 1.2%
Unao	12,01,440	12,03,916	12,09,636	— 0.1%	0.6%
Faizabad	12,91,745 (11,13,493)**	11,85,889	15,17,691	8.9%	17.5%
Sultanpur	9,71,237 (13,89,754)+	13,17,600	9,57,782	—26.2%	— 1.4%
Partapgarh	10,00,787	11,20,574	9,77,284	—10.7%	— 2.2%
Gonda	10,01,571	12,74,777	10,09,426	—21.4%	0.7%
Bahraich	6,89,264	5,53,144	6,48,292	24.6%	— 5.9%
Mohmudee	5,04,983	6,71,080	4,52,583	—24.9%	—10.3%
Hardoi	11,84,264	13,84,339	11,61,132	—14.4%	— 1.9%
Dariabad	9,73,800	11,85,906	9,72,786	—17.8%	— 0.1%
Sitapur	10,95,745 (10,43,315)++	12,02,344	11,33,916	— 8.9%	3.4%

* Figure for 1264 fasli taken from BR Lucknow File No 68.
** Figure for 1264 fasli taken from Gubbins 'Memo on Summary Settlement in Fyzabad': BROG File No. 66, pt. 1.
+ Figure for 1264 fasli taken from Gubbins 'Memo on Summary Settlement in Sultanpur': BROG File No. 66, pt. 1
++ Figure for 1264 fasli taken from 'Statement showing Revenue Assessment of zillah Seetapoor prior to Annexation in 1262F and after Annexation 1264F at Summary Settlement': BROG File No. 1623.

Figures in brackets represent the actual (as distinct from our computed) figures for the jama where available. The method of computation is described in the text.

Source: 1. Comparative Statement showing Past and Present Assessments Nankar, Mafee Charitable Grants.
2. Statement of Present Summary Settlement Compared with that of 1264.
3. Statement showing what number of past settlements were upheld.

All three are in Collection to Political Dispatches, 33, pt. 2, Collection No. 37.

Annexation and the Summary Settlement of 1856-7 53

and Bahraich. The former lies squarely in that region of interdependence and the latter is very close to it. Such a configuration of overassessment, in and around the axis of talukdar-peasant interdependence, acquires an added significance once I have discussed how rights were disposed of in the Summary Settlement of 1856-7.

Ever since the uprising of 1857 the disposal of rights in the settlement operations of 1856 has been a much discussed subject. Armed with policy prescriptions to settle with the village proprietors, and with their conviction about the Thomasonian principles regarding the importance of village communities in rural society and the grasping and oppressive characteristics of talukdars, the revenue officers set about dispossessing talukdars as best as they could.[101] But this, like the fixing of the assessments, turned out not to be so easy in practice. For one thing the village zamindars did not initially come forward;[102] either they mistrusted the intentions of the British, or the talukdars had enough control to keep them back, or their interests were not at sufficient variance with the talukdars. Only gradually did the knowledge spread that the British were going to settle with the village zamindars whom they considered to be the 'actual proprietors of the soil'; and it was then that 'they came forward in thousands':[103]

> . . . and appeals were so numerous that District Officers were allowed and resorted to reverse their own settlements which had first been with the Talooqdar, in favour of the Zameendar, the contention was fierce, and the struggle ended in the dispossession of a large portion sometimes of all their estates to the Talooqdars. In many cases this result was hastened on by the Talooqdar's backwardness in paying his 7½ kists. For which there were two reasons, one that our demand was made for the crop when it was due, whereas according to Oude custom this was only properly due in the 7½ months following 15 February. Secondly the Talooqdar seeing his villages going away from him . . . held back from paying, besides which under the circumstances no muhajan would advance him money. Several Talooqdars resisted altogether and many lost their whole estates and became fugitives.[104]

The dispossession of talukdars was thus a consequence both of their reluctance to pay the rabi kists and of the British policy to stir 'up every ancient claim or title of a right that we could

---

[101]See Introduction to *O.G.*, i, p. lv.
[102]Barrow, 'Memo on Former Administration in Oudh'.
[103]Ibid.   [104]Ibid.

discover in every village in Oudh'.[105] As Barrow remarked later, 'No matter how remote the title it was allowed'.[106]

Once again lack of time and no fixed guideline regarding how many years possession/dispossession should be regarded as a just or unjust claim created confusion:

> ... in the hurry of proceedings it may be feared that many were too hurriedly dispossessed, more particularly the Talooqdars; in some divisions no period of dispossession debarred an applicants claim, in others 12 years was considered a sufficient plea to refer him to the Regular Settlement but there was no general rule as a guide.[107]

Barrow, the settlement officer in the district of Salon, could recall cases where people who had been dispossessed for over fifty years were settled with.[108] There were also instances 'where parties were resident but had not held the Puttah for perhaps 80 or 100 years ...[and were] restored to what was called their Rights'.[109] Conversely there were also cases, such as ilaqa Karimullahpur in the district of Salon, where the Bais talukdar of Ganghur 'was dispossessed after 80 or 90 years possession'.[110] Barrow considered this to be a good illustration of the 1264 fasli settlement.[111]

Data on how much individual talukdars lost is extremely scanty. Some prominent examples can, however, be given. Lal Madho Singh of pargana Amethi originally held 807 villages, but under the 1264 settlement had only 302 villages settled with him.[112] Man Singh of the Mehdona estate, in revenue paying terms by far the biggest talukdar in Faizabad (paying a revenue of Rs 1,37,347),[113] lost all but three of his villages.[114] Hanwant Singh and Beni Madho, two names that have become practically synonymous with the archetypal talukdar, lost 55 per cent and 44 per cent of their villages respectively (Hanwant Singh lost 161 of his 292 villages and Beni Madho 119 out of 269).[115] Fortunately the

[105]Ibid. [106]Ibid. [107]Ibid. [108]Ibid. [109]Ibid.
[110]Barrow's Memo dated 16 Dec. 1858: BR Rae Bareli File No. 62.
[111]Ibid.
[112]Gubbins,'Minute on Summary Settlement in Sultanpur': BROG File No. 66 pt. 1.
[113]Man Singh's revenue figures are from 'List of Talukdars': BROG File No. 396.
[114]Irwin, Garden of India, p. 180; Metcalf, Land, Landlords and the Raj, p. 169, gives six villages.
[115]For Hanwant Singh see Barrow, 'Memo on Hunwant Singh', 25 Oct. 1858:

detailed breakdown of how each talukdar was dealt with in Sitapur is available, and forms the basis of Table 6. Table 7 shows how Loni Singh, one of the most important talukdars in Awadh,[116] was treated in the 1264 settlement. It will be seen from Table 6 that barring only seventeen talukdars, each one lost some villages; quite a few lost all the villages they held. Admittedly, at an overall calculation the talukdars, in Sitapur at least, held most of their villages. However it is important to remember their losses because given their position of control in the rural scene, even the loss of one village at an individual level could be interpreted as a blow to power and prestige.

It is the historians' hindsight that tends to see and analyse things in aggregates or in macro terms. Yet it is more than possible that in 1857 each talukdar remembered only his individual losses, and the loss of 90 villages (e.g. Mahmudabad) or all 49 villages (e.g. Seo Singh) left wounds that festered; Loni Singh is a similar case in point. Though he retained most of his villages he lost, as Table 7 shows, villages which he had held for a decade, and in one case lost four *mahals* which he had held for thirty-five years. It would be surprising indeed if such losses did not rankle.

The layout of Table 8 calls for some explanation. All previous writers who have focused on the losses suffered by the talukdars in the 1856/7 Summary Settlement have made the mistake of assuming that the villages held by talukdars prior to annexation were the same as the total number of villages in Awadh. Thus Jagdish Raj writes:

Out of the total of 23,522 villages, 13,640 were settled with the taluqdars and only 9,903 villages with persons other than taluqdars. The taluqdars retained more than half the province in their possession.[117]

And more recently Majid Siddiqi follows suit with similar figures.[118] T.R. Metcalf, who has a small section on the Summary

---

BROG File No. 1037; and for Beni Madho, Metcalf, *Land, Landlords and the Raj*, p. 178.

[116]Sleeman, *Journey*, ii, pp. 89-94.

[117]J. Raj, *The Mutiny and British Land Policy in North India* (London, 1965), pp. 18-19.

[118]M. Siddiqi, *Agrarian Unrest in North India, The United Provinces 1918-22* (New Delhi, 1978), pp. 6-7.

TABLE 6
Settlement with Talukdars and others in Sitapur in 1264F

Talukdar	Name of Taluka	No. of villages in Taluka	No. of villages settled with Talukdars	Jama	No. of villages settled with others	Jama
Seo Singh	Jurgaon	49	—	—	49	7,902
Md. Hosein Khan	Kalli	28	28	7,559	—	—
Mirza Ahmed Beg	K. Nagar	37	37	10,000	—	—
Shankar Bahadur	S. Nagar	19	17	3,800	2	170
Reza Cooly Khan	W. Nagar	16	—	—	16	3,200
Basti Singh	Kachusi	20	20	2,900	—	—
Sew Buksh Singh	Bhutpurowa	35	30	6,100	5	375
Bakhtawar Singh	Neeri	42	42	8,870	—	—
Balwant Singh	Shrarn	53	53	2,240	—	—
Ali Bahadur	Aurangabad	59	59	15,000	—	—
Loni Singh	Mithowli	208	176	27,266	32	5,240
Kalka Baksh	Hempur	12	12	2,844	—	—
Gyadin Singh } Amber Singh	Sherepur	22½	22½	7,722	—	—
Rughbir Singh	Burgawa	18	18	2,050	—	—
Kalka Baksh	Seraiah	16	13	2,628	3	348
Ram Narain	Umowrah	35	26	4,942	9	2,142
Bijoy Singh } Jotin Singh	Behut	49	48	6,180	1	236
Seobur Singh	Shikree Sipowlee	29	—	—	29	8,233
Bhawunidin	Nilgaon	19	18	9,220	1	325
Balbahadhur Singh	Bujehra	41	30	8,000	11	2,390
Raja Ibadulla Khan	Pantypur	74	74	34,000	—	—
Rao Monessur Buksh	Mullapur	220	220	33,196	—	—
Ranjit Singh	Deolalea	38	38	16,367	—	—
Darreeao Singh	Rampurkula	33	33	9,200	—	—
Hoosein Buksh	Surwa Jala	30	30	9,000	—	—
Bhowaniparsad	Mudurpur	10	10	3,200	—	—
Gooman Singh	Rempur Muthra	86	86	25,419	—	—
Rughbur Singh } Jaskar Singh Bhowanidin Salig Singh	Tumbore	22	21	4,676	1	61
Thakurain Bhugwani Coour	Rebur	33	32	4,333	1	500
Rughunath Singh	Bhimman	16	16	5,420	—	—
Balkhadur Singh	Chelasi	96	—	—	96	22,837

Annexation and the Summary Settlement of 1856-7

Talukdar	Name of Taluka	No. of villages in Taluka	No. of villages settled with Talukdars	Jama	No. of villages settled with others	Jama
Murlay Monohar	Mouzadeepur	68	51	16,572	17	5,789
Amirhusein Khan	Mahumudabad	551	461	1,30,852	90	23,323
Newar Singh	Burgawa	88	66	8,176	22	1,900
Jomahir Singh	Bittowli	79	68	15,068	11	2,780
Bani Singh	Kunmowdosi	47	38	1,121	9	2,300
Munooro Dowlah	Kunowa	151	93	21,371	58	11,531
Amrot Singh	Shahudut	23	18	5,327	5	453
Bahadur Singh	Kesopur	19	11	3,848	8	4,699
Fuzul Ali	Keotee	73	73	17,398	—	—
Seo Buksh Singh	Kutehsar	88	70	38,444	18	4,485
Kalka Buksh	Rumkote	38	38	7,500	—	—

SOURCE: Comparative Statement of Settlements with the Talukdars of Zillah Sitapur (14 June 1859), BR Sitapur File No. 36.

Settlement, notes very pertinently the mistake that Jagdish Raj is making. But he himself fails to highlight the extent of the upheaval by only providing figures for the number of villages settled with talukdars and for those settled with others; these figures are then set beside the number of villages held by talukdars prior to annexation.[119] Perhaps a better way to underline the degree to which talukdars were dispossessed in Awadh is to compare the *proportion* of the total number of villages they held under the Nawab's government to the *proportion* of the total number of villages settled with them in 1264 fasli. Such a comparison shows that their holdings were very nearly halved in the first British revenue settlement: whereas in Nawabi times they held approximately 67 per cent of the total number of villages, by the 1264 fasli settlement this had been reduced to a mere 38 per cent. The regional breakdown is even more significant. In Faizabad the talukdars held 74 per cent of the villages in Nawabi times. In the 1264 fasli settlement this had been drastically reduced to only 17 per cent. In Sultanpur the proportion had fallen from 63 per cent to 37 per cent; in Partapgarh from 83 per cent to 45 per cent; in Rae Bareli from 67 per cent to 35 per cent. This is to say that in

[119]Metcalf, *Land, Landlords and the Raj*, Table 17 on p. 171 and p. 172n.

TABLE 7
Estates held by Loni Singh in the Muhamdi District in 1263F and their Settlement in 1264F

Pargana	No. of villages held by him	No. of villages settled with him in 1264F	Jama	No. of villages settled with others in 1264	Jama	Year when they came into Loni Singh's possession
Kustah	whole pargana	96 villages	17,580	4 mahals	3,664	1229F
Ulgaon	whole pargana	whole pargana	6,208	—	—	—
Pala	whole pargana	115 villages	14,408	19 villages in 10 mahals	1,962	1248F
Aurangabad	20 villages	13 villages	1,886	2 villages in 1 mahal	—	—
				5 villages in 1 mahal		
Burwar	1 village	1 village	195	—	—	—
Mugdapur	4 villages	4 villages	2,700	—	—	—
Hyderabad	48 villages	39 villages	5,211	7 villages in 1 mahal	1,267	1255F
				2 villages in 1 mahal	196	1257F
Aligunge	32 villages	20 villages	1,560	1 village in 1 mahal	250	1257F
				3 villages in 1 mahal	400	1257F
				5 villages in 1 mahal	700	1257F
				3 villages in 1 mahal	600	1257F
Kurumpur	10 villages	10 villages	700	—	—	—

SOURCE: BR Sitapur File No. 190

Annexation and the Summary Settlement of 1856-7 59

southern Awadh the area under the control of the big Bais chiefs, the traditional chieftains, had suffered enormously in the new settlement made by the British. Up in the northern reaches in Gonda and Bahraich, where the talukdars had held more than 80 per cent of the total number of villages, they had lost out considerably. By the 1856-7 settlement they held only 33 per cent of the total number in Gonda (as compared to 84 per cent previously) and 70 per cent in Bahraich (as compared to 95 per cent previously). In terms of my analysis, precisely the area I have delineated as the area of talukdar-peasant interdependence and complementarity, the area where 'well-cultivated lands and happy peasants'[120] had been observed, was the hardest hit in terms of losses suffered by the talukdars. It is unfortunate that the available records do not permit us to reconstruct how each individual talukdar of this area was affected. But it is a reasonable surmise that the effect must have been tremendous, both in terms of material losses and in terms of loss of power and prestige. In fact it was a veritable rupture from the traditional order of things. The effect was exacerbated of course by the fact that the incidence of overassessment seems to have been the highest in the same areas where the mutual dependence of talukdar and peasant was disrupted. The talukdar lost not only his land but also all the other rights that he enjoyed. Moreover, the pattern of settlement with village proprietors disturbed the internal structure of the estates described in the previous chapter. The complementarity of talukdar and peasant was disrupted. The moral economy of the rural world received a sudden shock. The peasant, exposed directly to the overassessment of the Raj and the strict methods of British revenue collection, now no longer had the talukdar as his lord and protector to turn to. There was no more the guarantee that in times of hardship or crop failure the effects of the calamity would be shared equally in the village, nor was there the chance of being helped out in special circumstances such as marriage of death. Instead there was a large and fixed revenue demand to be paid with regularity.

It is obvious how adversely the shift from grain-sharing to a fixed revenue demand commuted in money terms affected the peasant. When the peasant paid a fixed proportion of the grain

[120] See Chapter 1.

TABLE 8

Comparative Statement showing Villages held by Talukdars and others in Nawabi times and subsequently at the Summary Settlement of 1856-7

District	Total No. of villages	Villages held by Talukdars in Nawabi times	% of total villages held by Talukdars under Nawabi	Villages held by others in Nawabi times	% of total villages held by others	Villages held by talukdars at 1264F settlement	% of Total Villages held by Talukdars at 1264F settlement	Villages held by others at 1264F settlement	% of total villages held by others at 1264 settlement
	1	2	3	4	5	6	7	8	9
Faizabad	4,215	3,116	73.92	1,099	26.07	687	16.29	3,479	82.53
Sultanpur	3,351	2,113	63.05	1,238	36.94	1,240	37.00	2,129	63.53
	(3,101)		(68.13)	(988)	(31.86)		(39.98)	(1,879)	(60.59)
Partapgarh	3,633	3,032	83.45	601	16.54	1,648	45.36	1,985	54.63
Lucknow	1,570	575	36.64	995	63.37	407	25.92	1,163	74.07
	(1,569)			(994)				(1,162)	
Rae Bareli	1,551	1,052	67.82	499	32.17	553	35.65	1,001	64.53
	(1,602)		(65.66)	(550)	(34.33)		(34.51)	(1,052)	(65.66)
Unao	1,236	368	29.77	868	70.22	1,640	13.26	1,101	89.07
Hardoi	1,427	464	32.51	963	67.48	271	18.99	1,158	81.14
Dariabad	2,506	1,087	43.37	1,419	56.62	760	30.32	1,746	69.67
	(2,310)		(47.05)	(1,223)	(52.94)		(32.90)	(1,550)	(67.09)
Sitapur	4,422	2,692	60.87	1,730	39.12	2,296	51.92	2,224	50.29
	(4,539)		(59.30)	(1,847)	(40.69)		(50.58)	(2,341)	(51.57)

Annexation and the Summary Settlement of 1856-7   61

Gonda	4,129	3,483	84.35	646	15.64	1,377	33.34	2,750	66.60
	(4,240)		(82.14)	(757)	(17.85)		(32.47)	(2,861)	(67.47)
Bahraich	3,949	3,761	95.23	188	4.76	2,769	70.11	1,164	29.47
	(3,877)		(97.00)	(116)	(3.00)		(71.42)	(1,092)	(28.16)
Mohumdee	3,130	1,759	56.19	1,371	43.80	1,468	46.90	1,620	51.75
	(3,515)		(50.04)	(1,756)	(49.95)		(41.76)	(2,005)	(57.04)
Total	35,119	23,502	66.92	11,617	33.07	13,640	38.83	21,520	61.27
	(35,264)		(66.64)	(11,762)	(33.35)		(38.67)	(21,665)	(61.43)

Figures in columns 6 and 8 do not add up to those of column 1 because there was some reorganization of villages at the 1264 fasli settlement; but more than that there are some obvious discrepancies in the sources. I have, however, kept to the figures as given in the original.

Figures in column 4 are arrived at by subtracting figures in col. 2 from those of 1. Figures in col. 8 are arrived at by adding figures from 4 to figures of no. of village previously in talukas but settled with others in 1264 from Final Report of Settlement in Collection to Political Dispatches 33 pt. 2 Collection No. 37.

Figures for column 6 are also from Final Report of Settlement (ibid.)

For columns 1 and 2 and for those in brackets see Table 3 in Chapter 1.

heap he shared with the raja-cum-talukdar the benefit or loss resulting from price or harvest variations. But when, as under the revenue settlement of the Raj, the revenue demand was fixed the burden of the overassessment or of bad harvest or low prices fell directly on him.[121] This disturbed the 'subsistence ethic' of the Awadh peasantry, and the violation of such an ethic is known to have created resentment and tension elsewhere.[122] For the Awadh peasantry this meant that it had shifted from a realm of dependency which provided a certain amount of security by guaranteeing subsistence to a more forthright unprotected relationship with a colonial state whose operation was alien to its world. The alienness was best expressed in the words of a folk song of the period: 'The British began to measure the land in iron chains'.[123]

It is perhaps necessary at this point to recapitulate the highlights of the preceding analysis:

1. The Summary Settlement of 1856-7 in Awadh witnessed gross overassessment in certain pockets, although the overall assessment was reduced.

2. The Settlement was aimed at destroying the power of the talukdars; the latter's holdings were halved.

3. The regions of overassessment and talukdars' losses fell within the axis of what has been called areas of talukdar-peasant complementarity.

Like the Awadh nawabs the British Raj was faced with the problem of collecting maximum revenue, though through a collecting agency that would not only be dependable but also subordinate. The British sought to solve the problem by removing the existing intermediary collecting agencies who, in their eyes, were all interlopers without any long-standing connection with the people, and by bringing the bureaucratic structure of the Raj into direct contact with the 'actual proprietors'. An attempt has been made to show that the talukdars were not always interlopers and that in fact they had a certain stake in the continuity of cultivation and

[121]Cf. Siddiqi, *Agrarian Change*, p. 77.
[122]See Scott, *The Moral Economy of the Peasant*, p. 6 and *passim*.
[123]W. Crooke, 'Songs about the King of Oudh', No. 5, verse 15: *The Indian Antiquary*, vol. XL., 1911, pp. 61-7.

property. The wealth that accrued to the talukdars was never invested in any kind of productive enterprise. But it did serve to maintain a certain type of lifestyle where networks of patronage, protection and loyalty held sway. The attempt to remove the talukdar meant the destruction of that entire world; it also meant that that part of the surplus which previously remained with the talukdar, portions of which circulated in the rural economy as salaries to retainers and other forms of patronage, were now totally extracted by the bureaucratic machinery of the Raj. From the network of co-operation and patronage the rural world was thrown directly into the world of colonial revenue policy and its efficient bureaucratic implementation.[124]

This perceived change tied up the assault on the talukdar into a broad consensus of grievances against the *firangi* Raj. Everything became a grievance.[125] In fact the annexation of Awadh and the policy prescriptions that followed had a snowballing effect. The act of annexation itself alienated the people of Awadh by removing their king. What followed was seen as various orders that rendered topsy-turvy the traditional world of Awadh. What at the time of the annexation was a mere emotional grievance against a foreign power became linked with real bread and butter grievances as the talukdars and peasants were hit by the Summary Settlement. This amalgam lay at the heart of many of the events that began in Awadh with the emeute on the night of 30 May 1857.

---

[124] This change frightened peasants, as they told Sleeman about British administration, '. . . we cannot understand the *'aen* and *kanoon'* (rules and regulations) . . .' and the peasants contrasted British courts and administration with the strength of custom in the villages. The peasants were emphatic in their preference for 'native' rule over the British Raj. Sleeman, *Journey*, ii, pp. 66-7.

[125] G. Hutchinson, *Narrative of the Mutinies in Oude* (London, 1859), p. 56.

CHAPTER 3
THE REVOLT OF THE ARMY

The last chapter attempted to analyse some of the factors which created disaffection among the populace of Awadh. The rebellion of 1857, however, was not started within the ranks of the civil population. It began within the sepoys of the British army. It was their actions which precipitated the rebellion. There seems hardly any scope for disagreement on this score. The grievances particular to the sepoys of the Bengal Army have also been written of *ad infinitum* in every book on 1857, scholarly and potboiler. What is not often, if ever, enquired into is whether the mutinies followed any kind of pattern in types of action and in their spread from station to station. Also none of the extant studies asks what the springboards of sepoy action were really and whether such actions can be seen to have some distinctive character other than that of sheer mob violence. Moreover, what were the links of the mutinous sepoys with the countryside, especially that of Awadh, and how did the lords of the land respond? This chapter tries to answer some of these questions.

The Mutinies in Awadh

The existing literature on the uprisings of 1857, by viewing the mutinies of the native regiments from a geographical standpoint, fails to discover any kind of pattern in the way the mutinies spread. For the convenience of narration it writes about the mutinies in terms of administrative divisions or regions. This has become accepted practice since Kaye's pioneer work on the subject.[1] Approached differently, however, the events do suggest a pattern, one that is connected with the 'movement' or diffusion of the mutinies. Such a pattern is in fact quite clearly discernible if

---

[1] J.W. Kaye, *Sepoy War*. A glance at the title of the various 'books' in Kaye's account will make this obvious: 'vol. 2, Book IV: The Rising in the North-West,

one studies the mutinies in north India in a more or less chronological order. There seems to have been a contagion of movement in the way the uprisings spread.

The mutinies started in Meerut on 10 May 1857. The circumstances of the mutiny outbreak in Meerut have been analysed in detail.[2] It is well known that the mutineers of Meerut made for Delhi. It is more than a chronological coincidence that despite growing tension between 10 May and 14 May none of the major stations in north India witnessed a mutiny. Indeed regiments in other parts of north India mutinied only after Delhi had fallen (11-12 May) — the garrison there had revolted, massacring the British population, and Bahadur Shah had accepted the nominal leadership of the revolt.[3] The spread of the word that the British had been expelled from Delhi — interpreted as the breakdown of British authority[4] — acted as a catalyst for mutiny as well as revolt. In fact the uprisings that followed the fall of Delhi saw a greater degree of activity on the part of the civil population.[5]

The dates of the mutinies after the massacre at Delhi seem to indicate a pattern: 20 May Aligarh, 23 May Etawah and Mainpuri and 27 May Etah. It was as if the mutinies were travelling down the Ganges valley from Meerut and Delhi, with a time-gap

---

Book V: Progress of Rebellion in Upper India, Book VI: The Punjab and Delhi; vol. 3, Book VII: Bengal, Behar and the North-West Provinces, Book VIII: Mutiny and Rebellion in the North-West Provinces, Book IX: Lucknow and Delhi.' Similarly the more recent accounts follow the same division. S.N. Sen, *Eighteen Fifty Seven* (Delhi, 1957), divides his description of the events into Delhi, Kanpur, Oudh, Bihar, Jhansi, Rajputana and Central India and the Punjab. R.C. Majumdar, *The Sepoy Mutiny and the Revolt of 1857* (Calcutta, 1957), divides Book II, which contains the description of the mutinies, into Meerut, Delhi, Bihar and Bengal, the Deccan, the Punjab, Central India and Rajasthan. Chaudhuri, *Civil Rebellion*, follows a straightforward regional division, e.g. Upper India, Eastern India, Western India, etc.

[2] J.A.B. Palmer, *The Mutiny Outbreak at Meerut in 1857* (Cambridge, 1966).

[3] The mutiny in Delhi is summarized in C. Hibbert, *The Great Mutiny, India 1857* (Pelican edn., 1980), Ch. 5; also see, especially for Bahadur Shah, T.G.P. Spear, *Twilight of the Mughals* (Cambridge, 1951), pp. 203ff.

[4] Kaye, *Sepoy War*, iii, pp. 247-8. Henry Lawrence perceived the importance of the fall of Delhi; he wrote to Edmonstone, 29 May 1857: 'Tranquility cannot be much longer maintained unless Delhi be speedily captured'. Inclosure 135 in No. 19, Appendix Papers Relative to the Mutinies in the East Indies, p. 341, *Papers Relating to Indian Mutinies*, 3 vols (London, 1857).

[5] Kaye, *Sepoy War*, iii, pp. 246ff.

between the various stations required for the news to travel from one place to another.[6] The mutiny reached Lucknow on 30 May; that night the garrison there rose. Rumours had been rampant that 30 May 1857 was the day fixed for a total destruction of white men all over north India.[7]

In Lucknow people had been tense and apprehensive since early May when the 7th Regiment of the Awadh Irregular Infantry refused to accept the new cartridges that were furnished to them.[8] In the days immediately after the fall of Delhi there were signs of smouldering discontent, especially among the populace at Lucknow. Proclamations in Hindi, Urdu and Persian were put up all over the city calling upon the populace, both Hindus and Muslims, to unite, rise and exterminate the firangis.[9] People began indulging in the acts of symbolic violence known to accompany moments of popular unrest as symptoms of popular hatred and anger.[10] For example, figures were dressed up as Europeans and their heads were cut off in public places to the appreciation and amusement of the people around.[11]

It was generally felt in the city that things were going to happen suddenly. Grain merchants and shopkeepers who had given credit to the British refused to supply them with food and provisions without getting ready money.[12] As one observer noted, 'The city people . . . await the signal for them to rise en masse on the mutiny of the native troops'.[13]

Among the sepoys of the regiments stationed in Lucknow there seems to have been some communication about the mutiny. The 7th Awadh Irregular Infantry who had refused to take the cartridges early in May, wrote to the 48th Native Infantry saying that

[6]This is indicated by the following comment of Kaye (ibid., p. 432): 'At this time [i.e. after the fall of Delhi] news was travelling through the country. . .'
[7]Ibid., p. 270.
[8]Henry Lawrence to Canning, 3 May 1857: For. Dept. Secret Cons., 18 Dec. 1857, No. 565; see also Forrest, *Selections*, ii, p. 8.
[9]*F.S.U.P.*, ii, pp. 5 and 7-8.
[10]Ibid., p. 8.
[11]G. Rude, *Paris and London in the 18th Century* (1974, repr. Fontana), p. 19, mentions that burning of the effigy of the villain of the hour was a typical action of the pre-industrial crowd in popular movements.
[12]*F.S.U.P.*, ii, p. 8.
[13]Ibid., p. 5.

'they had acted for the faith and awaited the 48th orders'.[14] Men had also been sent to Lucknow from Benares and other places to 'corrupt the troops'.[15] A former *havildar* of the 63rd Native Infantry, Ranjit Singh Bissein, who had served for twenty-seven years before being pensioned off, came into Lucknow in May 1857 at the request of his former officer Captain Hawes. His experiences *en route* to Lucknow highlight the temper and attitude of the soldiery and police during that fateful month. On the morning of 24 May he was on his way to Machi Bhavan via Makaliganj and he had to pass a police station:

... the police (who were new servants, recently entertained) were lounging on their charpoys. They called him to come and sit down and talk. They said they were new levies stationed there. He asked what duty was assigned them? They said that they were to oppose any of the Sepoys ... and fight them. But they added 'We shall not fight them. Kala Kala admee Sab eyk hyn. Deen Kee bat hyn. Hum log Kahi ko bey dhurm ho'. [All black men are one. It is a matter of religion. Why should we lose our religion.][16]

This striking statement indicates the bonds of fraternal unity that extended not only within the armed forces but through all who were of one colour, as against the white man.

The expected uprising did not occur till the night of 30 May. It was as if, to use the words of Kaye, the troops in the cantonment had been in an 'uncertain state of semi-mutiny' waiting for events to develop 'sufficiently ... elsewhere to encourage a general rising of the troops at Lucknow'.[17] It was only after all the major stations between Delhi and Lucknow had risen and the word was around that the rule of the Company *Bahadur* had collapsed[18] that the regiments in Lucknow mutinied. It was not just that they waited for events to develop elsewhere — even on the night of 30

---

[14] Henry Lawrence to Canning 3 May 1857: For Dept. Secret Cons., 18 Dec. 1857, No. 565; also see Forrest, *Selections*, ii, p. 8.

[15] *F.S.U.P.*, ii, p. 14.

[16] Gubbins to Couper, 27 May 1857, enclosing statement made by Runjeet Sing Bissein: For. Dept. Secret Consultations, 26 June 1857, Nos. 52-4.

[17] Kaye, *Sepoy War*, iii, p. 440.

[18] A district officer in Awadh wrote on 29 May: 'I wish we could hear of the fall of Delhi, for deserters are coming in fast and spreading wonderful reports of the utter cowardice and alarm of the sahibs in the North-West'. Kaye, *Sepoy War*, iii, p. 458. This statement is an indication of how fast word was spreading.

May the actual mutiny itself waited for a prearranged signal: the firing of the nine o'clock gun.[19]

In Lucknow, as in Meerut and elsewhere, the outbreak commenced with the burning of bungalows, general firing and attacks on the lines of British officers.[20] The preparations of Henry Lawrence and his officers enabled them to control the activity of the mutineers who sped off towards Sitapur. The party that went towards Sitapur consisted of half of the 48th Native Infantry, about half of the 71st, some few of the 13th and two troops of the 7th cavalry.[21] After the departure of the mutineers, the people of Lucknow, 6,000 strong, attempted a general uprising in the city. Their original intention had been to join up with the mutineers.[22] The British were convinced 'of an extensive conspiracy in the city and in the cantonments'.[23] Numerous arrests were made. It is significant that among the arrested were fairly important personages of Nawabi Lucknow like Sharrafuddowla. the prime minister of Mohammed Ali Shah, Amjad Ali Shah[24] and Rukunuddowla (the son of Saadat Ali, who Lawrence had tried to befriend).[25] Others arrested included the raja of Tulsipur, Mustapha Ali Khan, the elder brother of Wajid Ali, and two brothers connected with the royal family in Delhi.[26] Henry Lawrence with his wonted perspicacity had noted that 'These people however can only *by possibility* be dangerous, with our own troops'.[27]

While events in Lucknow were being brought under control by

---

[19]It was generally believed at the time that the firing of the gun was to be the arranged signal for mutiny. (Kaye, *Sepoy War*, iii, p. 442). It is significant that in Bareilly on 31 May, the sound of the artillery firing ' . . . was a signal for general action'. (Ibid., p. 270).

[20]Descriptions of the Lucknow mutiny through contemporary eyes are available in M.R. Gubbins, *An Account of the Mutinies in Oudh* (London, 1858), Ch. 7; Hutchinson, *Narrative*, pp. 59ff.

[21]Lawrence to GG in Council, 31 May 1857: For Dept. Secret Consultations, 18 Dec. 1857, No. 575.

[22]Gubbins, *Mutinies*, pp. 112-13; Hutchinson, *Narrative*, p. 71.

[23]Hutchinson, *Narrative*, p. 72.

[24]Ibid., p. 73.

[25]Lawrence to Canning, 2 May 1857, For. Dept., Secret Cons. 18 Dec. 1857, No. 564.

[26]Hutchinson, *Narrative*, p. 74.

[27]Lawrence to Canning, 2 May 1857.

Lawrence and his officers, events in the surrounding districts of Awadh were moving swiftly towards a crisis. In fact Lawrence had predicted this. Soon after the emeute in Lucknow, in his cable to Canning, he had voiced his anxieties about the districts.[28] The districts had been flooded with rumours and were on the verge of rebellion. In fact just as Lucknow and the other towns of north India had waited for Delhi to rise and the news to travel, similarly the district stations of Awadh waited for Lucknow. As Hutchinson wrote, they were 'only waiting for Lucknow to do so, that they might follow their example'.[29] Once the Lucknow garrison had mutinied the out stations followed in quick succession: Sitapur, Faizabad, Gonda-Bahraich, Sultanpur and Salon.

The fall of one station contributed to the rising in another garrison. Each successful mutiny was seen as the growing weakness — or the fall — of British power. In Sitapur the mutinous troops from Lucknow arrived around the beginning of June, the mutiny followed immediately after on 3 June. In Gonda-Bahraich, it seems evident from Wingfield's narrative, the fast departing confidence in the permanence of British power was leading to disaffection among sepoys.[30] In Sultanpur, it was evident from the thin attendance in the *Kachari* (office for public business) and slow collection of revenue, that the people had lost confidence in the authority of the British.[31] Even in Salon, a district which in contrast to the others had remained relatively calm with the collection of rabi kists proceeding peacefully, things started being disorderly with the news of the mutinies, especially those of Faizabad and Sultanpur.[32]

In most of these stations people from outside were communicating with and provoking the troops. The Faizabad sepoy lines were full of mutineers from Azamgarh, Jaunpur and Benares who were urging the Faizabad sepoys to rise. In fact the Faizabad mutineers were possibly in direct communication with the 17th

---

[28] Lawrence to GG, 31 May 1857: For. Dept. Secret Cons., 18 Dec. 1857, No. 575.
[29] Hutchinson, *Narrative*, p. 56; also see Sitaram, *From Sepoy to Subedar*, tr. by Lt. Col. Norgate, ed. James Lunt (London, 1970), pp. 163-4.
[30] Wingfield's narrative quoted *in extenso* by Hutchinson, *Narrative*, pp. 130-6.
[31] J.A. Grant to Edmonstone, 21 June 1857: For. Dept., Secret Cons., 31 July 1857, Cons. No. 92.
[32] Barrow's narrative in Hutchinson, *Narrative*, pp. 127ff.

Native Infantry which had mutinied in Azamgarh.[33] The Faizabad troops had also 'received a perwana from the King of Delhi setting forth that he had possession of the whole country, and summoning them to join his standard'.[34] Similarly, Sultanpur and its neighbourhood was swarming with mutineers from Benares and Jaunpur; these sepoys boasted of having taken over Benares and Allahabad and claimed that it was now the 'Telinga Raj'.[35] Salon was an example where the troops mutinied only after mutineers from Allahabad, Sultanpur and Partapgarh had come in and 'goaded' their brothers to rise.[36]

These mutinies were not always chaotic and disorderly in their occurrence. Some of them showed remarkable co-ordination in the way they happened or the way events developed. In Faizabad, for example, the mutiny took off with the pre-appointed signal—the sounding of the bugle at 10 p.m.[37] The troops quickly organized themselves. In a co-ordinated manner they stopped the *golandazes* (the gunners) from touching their guns. Under the direction of a *risaldar* (infantry officer) the officers of the 22nd and the 6th were placed with the Quarter-Guard. The *sawars* patrolled all roads and approaches to the cantonment.[38] In Sikrora the mutineers remained in contact with the regiments in Gonda.[39] In Gonda the British had planned to move the treasure to Lucknow but the sepoys expressed their determination that they would not let that happen.[40] In this context of co-ordination

---

[33]E.O. Bradford to Edmonstone, 2 July 1857: For. Dept. Secret Cons., 25 Sept., 1857, Cons. No. 398. (hereafter Bradford).

[34]Reid's Memo of events immediately preceding the mutiny of the Native Troops at Faizabad: For. Dept. Secret Cons. 28 May 1858, Cons. No. 419 (hereafter Reid).

[35]Deposition of Sheikh Emambux, late gaoler in the Sultanpur district of Oude, taken on 3 Sept. 1858: Hutchinson, *Narrative*, pp. 147ff. The phrase 'Telinga Raj' originates from sepoys being known as 'Telingas' from the first Telegu speaking sepoys brought by Clive in 1756-7 from Madras. This name persisted even when the Company's sepoy army was recruited largely from north India. The name was greatly feared in the eighteenth century. See A.M. Khan, *The Transition in Bengal, 1756-1775* (Cambridge, 1969), p. 123, note 3.

[36]Barrow's narrative.
[37]Bradford.
[38]Ibid.
[39]Wingfield's narrative: Hutchinson, *Narrative*, p. 133.
[40]Ibid.

The Revolt of the Army

the experience of Captain Hearsey is worth noting. Captain Hearsey had been given protection by the Military Police. But the 41st Native Infantry insisted that as they had murdered all their officers, it was imperatively necessary that the military police must either follow their example, or deliver me up a prisoner to them'.[41] On the Military Police's refusal to comply, it was mutually decided to settle the matter by *panchayat*, i.e. by arbitration of a certain number of native officers from each regiment.[42]

The common pattern running through the mutinies was destruction. In each and every station there were scenes of extensive firing, burning of bungalows and property owned by the British, looting of the treasury and breaking open of jails. This was not just a symptom of mindless pathological disorder on the part of a mob. The destruction of property — or direct action — is a common phenomenon in 'popular movements' involving crowds or 'mobs'.[43] Property owned, used or lived in by the firangi were the objects of the wrath of the mutinous sepoys. The sepoys saw in the Raj an entity and structure that was intervening in their way of life and they frontally assaulted and destroyed the proximate symbols of that structure. There was also sheer greed for money, evident from the plunder of the treasury and the sepoys' concern about the movement of the treasure. This may be explained as a natural act on the part of a body of men who were proverbially ill-paid. Henry Lawrence highlighted the underpayment in the native army:

Also we should expect the Soobedar and Jemadar to be content with 67 and 24 rupees a month respectively while in the Civil Department their fellows, ten and twenty years younger enjoy 500,600 and even 1000 Rupees and while they themselves if under a native ruler would be Generals if not Rajahs or Nawabs.[44]

There were also cold-blooded murders by assemblies of mutinous sepoys. Their blood lust has been written about in vivid

---

[41]Capt. Hearsey's narrative: Hutchinson, *Narrative*, p. 97.
[42]Ibid.
[43]Rude, *Paris and London*, pp. 19, 296 and *passim*., and *The Crowd in the French Revolution* (Oxford, 1959), Ch. 13.
[44]Henry Lawrence to Canning, 2 May 1857: For Dept. Secret Cons., 18 Dec. 1857: Cons. No. 564.

detail by all contemporary narrators whose accounts abound in adjectives like *badmashes*, murderers, wretches, and such like — and these have been repeated even by most twentieth century writers. There should of course be no attempt to condone the killings that the sepoys perpetrated. By any yardstick their butcheries — such as the massacre of the Faizabad refugees on the river, the murder of Mr Christian and his family in Sitapur, the cold-blooded behind-the-back shooting of Fisher in Sultanpur (to give just a few examples) — are repellant. However, the blood lust of the sepoys has other important implications which should not be overlooked. Throughout the previous century of colonial rule the sepoys had seen how harshly their masters dealt with the sepoys' own crimes and disobedience. Their movement, like other movements of the 'lower orders' of society, could hardly fail to learn from the example set by social superiors.[45] Sepoys had had to tolerate abuse and kickings, disgrace in front of comrades, and floggings; they had seen their comrades blown from guns. They had also seen the ruthlessness with which the British had fought and won wars in India. So when they began what they thought was their own war against the firangi, they replicated the mercilessness and violence they had seen in the sahib. It is perhaps worth noting that in all the internecine wars of the eighteenth century or the encounters between the Company and Indian powers, there were no parallels for the sadistic cruelty one associates with the 'Mutiny'.

One aspect of the mutinies which is not very often noted or emphasized is the way rumours and panic often acted as the springboard for sepoy action. Here perhaps is a remarkable parallel with France during the Revolution.[46] Like the fear of the *complot aristocratique* in France, there spread in north India the

---

[45]Rude, *Paris and London*, p. 26: 'The eighteenth century crowd, in particular, could hardly fail to be corrupted by the example set them by their social betters. It was an age of brutal floggings, torture of prisoners and public executions'; also see R. Cobb, *The Police and the People: French Popular Protest, 1789-1820* (Oxford, paperback edn., 1972), pp. 88-9 for a counterposing of the violence of the *sans cullotes* and that of the *ancien regime* — a line of argument which I found very suggestive.

[46]See G. Lefebvre, *The Great Fear of 1789: Rural Panic in Revolutionary France* (London, 1973).

alarm of a deliberate British plot to despoil the religion of the Hindus and Muslims:

> Government it was said, had sent up cartloads and boatloads of bone-dust, which was to be mixed with the flour and sweetmeats sold in the bazaar, whereby the whole population would lose their caste. The public mind became greatly excited. On one day, at Sultanpoor, it was spread over the station that a boat had reached a certain ghaut on the river Goomtee, laden with bone-dust, and the sepoys were hardly restrained from outbreak. A few days later, at the station of Salone, two camels, laden with ammunition, arrived at the house of Captain Thompson, the commandant. It was rumoured that the packages contained bone-dust and a panic spread through the station. Not only the sepoys in their lines, but the domestic servants about the officers' bungalows, and the villagers and zemindars attending court, hastily flung away, untasted, the food which they had cooked and fasted for the day. At Lucknow, the rumours which were whispered about were perpetual, and the public mind was never allowed to rest. Now it was at one shop, the next day in another bazaar, that despatches of bone-dust had, it was asserted, been received. It was in vain that facts were opposed to this prevailing panic.[47]

In Sitapur, a day before the mutiny, the sepoys refused to touch the *atta* (ground wheat) procured for them because they

> ... imagined it was adulterated, and declared it would destroy their caste if they made use of it. This idea seemed to pervade the whole Regiment, who declined to use the flour, notwithstanding the remonstrance of the commanding officer, whose efforts to convince them of the purity of the atta were entirely unavailing, and the men insisted on the whole being thrown into the river.[48]

Henry Lawrence 'was startled by the dogged persistence' of a *jamadar* of the Awadh artillery (a man of "excellent character") 'in the belief that for ten years past Government had been engaged in measures for the forcible or rather fraudulent, conversion of all natives'.[49] The belief and the fear of conversion were so strong that in Sitapur the very name of the Commissioner — Mr Christian — became identified with the religion, increasing the wrath and fury of rebels.[50]

Throughout the summer of 1857, when the mutinies were tak-

---

[47]Gubbins, *Mutinies*, p. 86.

[48]Narrative of the emeute at Sitapur, 3 June 1857: For. Dept. Political Cons., 18 March 1859: Cons. No. 129.

[49]Lawrence to Canning, 9 May 1857: quoted in H.B. Edwardes and M. Merivale, *Life of Sir Henry Lawrence*, 2 vols. (London, 1872), ii, p. 322.

[50]Kaye, *Sepoy War*, iii, p. 456.

ing place, rumours about British atrocities and rebel activity spread panic and the desire for vengeance in which much of the violent action was rooted. Reid, while escaping from Faizabad, heard a sepoy of the 37th Native Infantry telling the village pundit who had provided shelter to the Faizabad refugees:

> that the native troops at Benares had been disarmed, and then massacred by artillery and a regiment of European infantry; that, afterwards, the Rajah of Benares, who was in league with the native troops, had come with a great force and killed every European in the place . . . The disarming and massacring story, which was industriously promulgated all over the country, was almost universally believed, and may have had most injurious effect. A native, in whom I placed considerable reliance, assured me that it was the immediate cause of the mutiny and cruel murders at Allahabad. The news of the capture by the mutineers of the fort of Allahabad was also circulated through Oude and even we believed it for a time.[51]

In Sikrora (Bahraich district) the mutiny was precipitated by the widespread belief among the sepoys that the British officers 'had tried to murder them in their sleep'.[52]

What was important in all this was not the objective truth, but what the people believed the Company was going to do or doing. And it was the *belief* about what was being done and the consequent panic that stirred men into feverish activity. Fear bred fear, and rumour spread from one sepoy line to another, generating activity and more panic. Rumour, fear and panic, for all their irrationality, brought men together, stoked their hatred and spurred them to violent action. The transmission of rumours and panic was facilitated by the fact that the sepoys shared a common life style; very often (as will be seen in the next section of this chapter) they came from the same background. Communication of fears and passions comes easy in such a context. Events such as the seizure of Awadh or the way the first summary settlement in Awadh was disrupting the familiar world, when discussed in the sepoy lines, could reinforce feelings of shared misfortune and generate mass violence.[53] Rumours of attempts to undermine

---

[51]Reid.

[52]Wingfield's narrative in Hutchinson, *Narrative*, p. 131; this fear was caused by the sergeants who when woken by a false alarm had, as a precaution, turned the guns on the infantry lines.

[53]Sitaram, *Sepoy to Subedar*, pp. 161-2 mentions how the annexation of Awadh

caste purity must have created widespread panic, stirring up the 'wind of madness'. Fantasy, which revealed a deep-rooted distrust, combined with facts to produce an image of the firangi Raj as the monolith that was out to destroy all that was cherished and sacred. The episode of the 'greased cartridge' must have provided the crucial element of psychological over-stimulation, transforming perception into action. The mutinies thus expressed a collective mentality of opposition that embodied in it a whole matrix of panic, anxiety and hope.[54]

Added to the force of rumours was the circulation of mysterious objects like chapatis and lotus flowers — the most commonly referred to incident of the mutiny — conveying unknown messages. Here is a parallel with the 'Swing Riots' of early nineteenth century England when there were stories about mysterious 'strangers' riding around in gigs.[55] In this context it is worthwhile recalling, especially as religion had an obvious hold over the nineteenth century Indian mind, that there was current in India during this time the prophecy that the end of British rule was not far off:

> ... the ancient works, both of the Hindoos and the Mahommedans, the writings of the miracle workers, and the calculations of the astrologers, pundits and rammals, all agree in asserting that the English will no longer have any footing in India or elsewhere.[56]

The prophesied end of British rule in India was expected to concide with the centenary of the battle of Plassey.[57] During the mutinies it was a strongly held belief that the expulsion of the British was final.[58] And often, perhaps strengthened by the oracles' prophecy, the troops even made no pretence of a grievance.

---

was discussed and how regiments communicated with each other about the 'greased cartridge'.

[54]This paragraph owes a lot to my reading of G. Lefebvre, 'Revolutionary Crowds' in J. Kaplow (ed.), *New Perspectives on the French Revolution*. (New York, 1965), pp. 173-90.

[55]G. Rude and E. Hobsbawm, *Captain Swing*, (Penguin Univ. Books,1973), p. 182.

[56]Proclamation of Bahadur Shah: 25 Aug. 1857: *F.S.U.P.*, i, pp. 453ff.

[57]'Our learned men... told us that the Company's rule would come to an end in 1857, since this was one hundred years after the Company's first great battle...', Sitaram, p. 173.

[58]Bradford.

They openly declared that 'they were strong enough to turn us out of the country and intended to do it'.[59] It is conceivable that for many sepoys who took to arms in 1857 the fight represented the pursuit of the centennium.

In the way the mutinies diffused themselves along the Ganges valley, there is evidence of events being generated by 'contagion' or chain reaction. Rumours, panic and 'other irrational elements' acted as motors of collective action and thus provided the links. The sepoys used remarkably similar methods everywhere to destroy the firangi and all that belonged to him. There is evidence of a certain element of co-ordination and communication among the mutinous regiments and in their action, though the co-ordinators themselves remain anonymous. In all this there was a method in the so called 'criminal madness' of the sepoys.

The Fate of the Bengal Army

Before one explores the links between the mutinies and the discontent in the Awadh countryside, it is necessary to digress a little and shift the focus away from Awadh. In terms of the overall argument of this book it is necessary to indicate the areas in north India (the term north India is used loosely to denote that area north of the Vindhyas, excluding Kashmir and Assam) that witnessed the rising of the native regiments. An appendix to this chapter provides a more or less complete list of all the mutinies in north India, the dates on which they occurred, and a map which shows their locations.

It will be seen that the mutinies were concentrated around an area bounded by Delhi in the west and Ghazipur in the east with roughly the Jamuna acting as the southern boundary. This was, as it were, the core of the mutiny area. It is also noticeable that even in the chronology of the mutinies there is 'a unity of time' in this area; they all took place between May and June. The other areas where the native regiments mutinied are clusters around this core, in the Punjab, in central India (i.e. south-west of the Jamuna) and scattered stations in the east. With few exceptions, the mutinies around the core took place after the mutinies within it as a kind of spread-effect. This pattern of physical distribution

[59]Reid.

had causal links with the concentration of the revolt in Awadh. These can be explained with reference to the pattern of recruitment in the Bengal Army.

The areas from which the sepoys of the Bengal Army were recruited are always referred to in very general terms. Amiya Barat in her detailed study of the Bengal Native Infantry devotes only seven to eight pages to the subject.[60] It is very difficult to find more specific quantitative statements than 'the Bengal sepoys were largely drawn from Oude',[61] or that the sepoys of the Bengal Army came 'chiefly from Oude'.[62] Butter called Awadh the 'great nursery for the armies of British India'.[63] Some officials did attempt rough estimates of the number of men who came from Awadh. In his testimony before the Commission for the Reorganization of the Indian Army, 1859, Colonel Keith Young remarked that 'Oude and the adjacent districts that were formerly under the Oude Government furnish about three-fourths of the recruits for the Bengal infantry'.[64] According to Sleeman the area of Baiswara and its neighbourhood alone provided about 30,000 men to the army around 1825.[65] William Howard Russell noted in his diary that 'the Byswara district. . . furnished in the old days about 40,000 of the finest of our sepoys to the Bengal army. . .'[66]

It would have been very enlightening were it possible to identify the precise areas from which the sepoys of the particular regiments which mutinied were recruited. But a search for that kind of data did not prove fruitful. It is possible that such detailed recruitment data was normally never kept or recorded, since recruitment of sepoys was often done in a haphazard manner, at least till the middle of the nineteenth century.[67] There was no

[60]A. Barat, *The Bengal Native Infantry: Its Organisation and Discipline* (Calcutta, 1962), pp. 118-20, 126-9.

[61]R.M. Martin, *The Indian Empire* (London, n.d.), p. 111.

[62]Organization of Army (Indian): replies of Sir Patrick Grant, *P.P.*, vol. v (1859), p. 481. In fact most officials who gave evidence before the commission said that Awadh was the chief recruiting ground.

[63]Butter, *Southern Oude*, p. 156.

[64]Reorganization of Indian Army: Papers received from Col. Keith Young, *P.P.*, vol. viii (1859-session 2), p. 789.

[65]Sleeman, *Journey*, i, p. 170.

[66]W.H. Russell, *My Indian Mutiny Diary*, ed. M. Edwardes (London, 1957), p. 227.

[67]Barat, *Native Infantry*, p. 128.

special agency for recruitment and new recruits were mostly brought back from the villages by sepoys who had gone home on leave — the case of Sitaram who was brought back by his uncle is a typical example.[68] After 1852 orders were given that in future detailed and verified lists of new recruits were to be prepared.[69] Unfortunately such lists have probably not survived. Barat does not refer to them and I have been unable to find any.

In spite of the non-availability of such complete lists there is one document which offers a fairly detailed account of the extent of recruitment from Awadh. This is a descriptive roll of deserting non-commissioned officers and sepoys of the 22nd Native Infantry. This list provides the names, castes, villages and parganas of 280 men.[70] Of these only fourteen men (i.e. 5 per cent) came from districts that were not in Awadh. Of the remaining 266 men who came from Awadh, 140 (i.e. 53 per cent) were clearly from southern Awadh, i.e. the districts of Sultanpur, Partapgarh and Rae Bareli, the area corresponding roughly to Baiswara and its neighbourhood. This breakdown, even though it refers only to one regiment, reinforces my general argument regarding the importance of the area of talukdar-peasant complementarity as a source of recruitment. And given the mass of statements about Awadh, and especially Baiswara, being the main recruiting area, there is no reason to surmise that the sample available from the 22nd N.I. is necessarily atypical.

This concentration of recruits from one particular area gave the Bengal Native Army the character of 'one great fraternity'.[71] It also helps to explain how rumour and panic spread so rapidly among the sepoys. Hedayat Ali Khan, a subahdar in the native army, who wrote an account in Urdu of why the mutinies took place, noted how quickly the story that the British were going to despoil caste and religion and the resultant fears spread among the sepoys.[72] Such swift movement of rumour and panic is very

[68] Sitaram, *Sepoy to Subedar*, pp. 6ff.
[69] Barat, p. 128.
[70] Proceedings of A Special Commission of Enquiry, Berhampore, 13 Dec. 1824: Bengal Military Consultations, 6 Jan. 1825, Range 31, vol. 10, Cons. No. 33.
[71] See John Lawrence's answers to questions by the Commission for the Reorganization of the Indian Army: *P.P.*, vol. viii (1859-session 2), p. 673.
[72] 'A few words relative to the Mutiny of the Bengal Army and the Rebellion in the Bengal Presidency, by Sheikh Hedayut Ali, Subedar and Sirdar Bahadur,

easy within a body of men whose bonds of understanding are strong. The ties of the village world, which were automatically carried over into the army by the sepoys' common origins, facilitated the workings of the grapevine.

There was one other consequence, after the mutinies had begun, of the fact that recruits came principally from one particular area. As regiment after regiment mutinied or was disbanded, sepoys often made tracks for their own villages. Sitaram notes how, after the mutinies of the regiments in the various stations of Awadh, 'the country was overrun with sepoys from these regiments'.[73] Once they returned to their villages their grievances and fears coalesced with those of their village brethren whose traditional rural world had been totally disrupted. The return was especially easy as most of the mutinies took place in north or central India, within what was walking distance for an Indian peasant. It is true that not all the sepoys returned home — large numbers moved towards Delhi, or followed local leaders like Nana Sahib in Kanpur or Kunwar Singh in Bihar. But the homeward journeys continued as Delhi and other stations were recovered by the British. The sepoys returned home to fight in Awadh, either immediately after mutiny or after fighting and losing somewhere else; elements of some twenty-nine native regiments were recorded as fighting against the British in Awadh in 1857-58.[74] This was one reason why operations there were more intense and prolonged than elsewhere.

The Awadh Countryside

While the regiments were rising in mutiny in the various towns and military stations of north India, the Awadh countryside and its leaders, the talukdars, were quiet. In retrospect it looks as if

Bengal, Seikh Police Battalion, commanded by Captain T. Rattray, who has translated this paper from the original Oordoo', reproduced in K.K. Datta, 'A Contemporary Account of the Indian Movement of 1857-59', *The Journal of the Bihar Research Society*, vol. xxxvi, pts. 3-4 (Sept.-Dec. 1950), pp. 96-133.

[73]Sitaram, *Sepoy to Subedar*, p. 164 also Wingfield to (illegible) 4 July 1857: 'All accounts that I receive write in describing the roads as (full) with sepoys returning to their homes. . . , For. Dept., Secret Cons. 25 Sept. 1857, No. 519.

[74]This point can be strengthened by enumerating which regiments or parts thereof were observed fighting in Awadh between 1857 and 1859: 1st N.I., 6th N.I.,

they were waiting to see which way events would turn. No doubt there was disaffection in the countryside, but there was no attempt at this point to activate it. Only when the mutinies in each and every station had succeeded and British administration in Awadh had collapsed (as Gubbins noted, 'like a house made of cards')[75] did the talukdars and their men decide to act. Before this almost every talukdar looked on while the sepoys raised the banner of mutiny. Some of them even rendered valuable service to the British by providing shelter to fleeing British officers and their families. In this context the name of Man Singh of Shahganj is most often remembered. He warned the British that the sepoys would rise, gave shelter to officers and their families and even provided boats for their safe passage to Dinapur. When all trace of British administration and authority had disappeared from Awadh Man Singh was seen as the last loyal ally in Awadh, and rewards were offered to him for continuing support.[76] Apart from Man Singh, among the talukdars who helped British officers were Dirg Bijay Singh of Balrampur, Lal Madho Singh of Amethi, Rustam Sah of Dera and Hanwant Singh of Kalakankar. Theirs were not acts of loyalty *per se*; most of the talukdars had no reason to remain loyal to an administration which had taken away their land, power and prestige, as well as their king. They preferred to lend a helping hand to the British out of gentlemanly pity or out of a romantic and feudal sense of honour and chivalry. Their action was in no way an act of collaboration and alliance. Barring the raja of Balrampur and Rustom Sah, every talukdar who provided shelter to the British at the beginning of the mutiny later joined the cause of the rebels. The attitude of the talukdars at this

---

7th N.I., 9th N.I., 10th N.I., 12th N.I., 15th N.I., 17th N.I., 18th N.I., 22nd N.I., 28th N.I., 37th N.I., 41st N.I., 48th N.I., 53rd N.I., 54th N.I., 56th N.I., 71st N.I., 74th N.I., 2nd Light Cavalry, 3rd Light Cavalry, 4th Light Cavalry, 7th Light Cavalry, 11th Irregular Cavalry, 12th Irregular Cavalry, 13th Irregular Cavalry, 15th Irregular Cavalry, the Awadh Irregular Force fought against the British in Awadh, Regiment of Ludhiana, 4th Troop of 1st Brigade Horse Artillery, 5th Co. 7th Battalion Foot Artillery. These facts are gleaned from G.H.D. Gimlett, *A Postscript to the Records of the Indian Mutiny: an attempt to trace the subsequent careers and fate of the rebel Bengal regiments, 1857-58* (London, 1927).

[75]Gubbins, *Mutinies*, p. 118.

[76]Ibid. pp. 133ff ; also see 'Copies of Reports and Despatches relative to the Protection afforded by Mann Singh and others to Fugitive Europeans at the Outbreak of the Sepoy Mutiny': *P.P.*, vol. xliv, part 1 (1857-58), pp. 29ff.

The Revolt of the Army

point of time is best summed up by the words of Hanwant Singh to Barrow:

Sahib, your countrymen came into this country and drove out our King. You sent your officers round the districts to examine the titles to the estates. At one blow you took from me lands which from time immemorial had been in my family. I submitted. Suddenly misfortune fell upon you. The people of the land rose against you. You came to me whom you had despoiled. I have saved you. But now, — now I march at the head of my retainers to Lakhnao to try and drive you from the country.[77]

Every sentence of this remarkable statement deserves close scrutiny. There is mention of injustice to the king and of dispossession as the major sources of disaffection. The mutinous sepoys are identified as the people of the country — corroboration of the point made earlier that the sepoys were basically peasants in uniform. There is also a recognition of the time gap between the sepoy uprisings and the talukdars joining the revolt.

As the uprisings took place in the various Awadh stations and British administration collapsed, the talukdars recovered the land they had lost. Very often in a remarkable act of loyalty the village proprietors returned the land voluntarily to the talukdar. Capt. Barrow, who had sought shelter with Hanwant Singh, watched this act of allegiance.[78] The return of the sepoys from the mutinous regiments provided the talukdars with fighting men, and the allegiance of the village proprietors gave them a popular base. It was only then that conditions were fulfilled for the revolt of the army to be transformed into a revolt of the people.

---

[77]G.B. Malleson, *History of the Indian Mutiny, 1857-58*, 3 vols. (London, 2nd ed., 1878), i., pp. 407-8n.

[78]Barrow to Edmonstone, 24 June 1857: For. Dept., Secret Cons., 31 July 1857 Cons. No. 98; also Barrow's 'Memo on Hunwant Sing', 25 Oct. 1858: BROG File No. 1037; T.R. Metcalf, 'From Raja to Landlord' in R.E. Frykenberg (ed.), *Land Control and Social Structure in Indian History* (Wisconsin, 1969), p. 126, refers to the incident without mentioning the source.

CHAPTER 4
THE REVOLT OF THE PEOPLE

There were three distinct phases in the transformation of the army revolt into a general uprising of the people of Awadh and in the subsequent progress of the rebellion. The first phase was a direct sequel to the mutinies in the districts. With the collapse of British administration in the districts the only area where British authority survived was Lucknow, in the neighbourhood of the Residency. Naturally the rebel forces were then concentrated around Lucknow. The concentration increased once the British suffered their first major setback in the battle of Chinhat (30 June 1857). From the battle of Chinhat to the first relief of Lucknow in September 1857 by Havelock and Outram, the city was under siege and was the centre of the revolt in Awadh. The second phase, perhaps in one sense the most crucial, lasted from the first relief to the final fall of Lucknow in March 1858. During this phase too the city was the focus and the fighting was for its control. The British were still in a precarious condition and under siege. The city had to be evacuated by them in November 1857, and from then until March the British and the rebels maintained the struggle for Lucknow because both sides realized the importance of holding it. But the fight was slowly spreading to the countryside. The third phase was after March 1858 when the rebels, having lost the capital, dispersed into the countryside. This is the phase both of desperate struggle to continue the revolt and of conciliation and surrender to the columns of Lord Clyde which were then sweeping through Awadh. All three stages of the rebellion had, in a way, the capital city for their focal point. First, events sparked off at Lucknow swiftly affected the districts. Then there was a movement back into the city, and finally in the third stage back again into the districts.

This chapter attempts to present the events of the revolt within this chronological framework. But its emphasis is different from that of most standard works on the subject — these have been written from a predominantly British viewpoint, whatever the nationality of their authors. The unconscious adoption of a British viewpoint by Indian writers on 1857 is best exemplified by S.N. Sen's chapter on 'Oudh'.[1] This recounts in detail the moves made by British generals, efforts to defend the Residency, day-to-day life within the walls of the Residency (including what the officers had for dinner), how much the belongings of Lawrence fetched and how such-and-such officer missed his cigar. Lost in such delightful trivia the reader looks in vain for some glimpse of what the rebels were doing. Among Indian writers R.C. Majumdar does try to concentrate on the rebels, but his account is marred by his bias against popular participation in the uprisings.[2] S.B. Chaudhuri also concentrates on the rebels but his otherwise remarkable account of the civil rebellion — he treats the action in different centres and districts separately — misses out on the all-important linkages.[3] My attempt in this chapter is to emphasize the movements of the rebels (as distinct from those of the British troops) to assess their strength and organization and explore in particular the precise role played by the talukdars and their men at the various stages.

Rebels Gather in Lucknow: Chinhat to the First Relief

By the end of June 1857 rebels from the districts had started moving towards Lucknow. They were all gathering at Nawabganj, about twenty miles from Lucknow. They were apparently in communication with the Nana Saheb in Kanpur and as soon as they heard that the entrenchment there had fallen they moved at once upon Lucknow.[4] They were about 7,000 strong.[5] Gubbins, who had a fairly accurate idea of their composition, reports:

The force of the mutineers ... consisted altogether of regiments stationed in the province...

---

[1] Sen, *1857* pp. 172-244.
[2] This point is made by S.B. Chaudhuri, *English Historical Writings on the Indian Mutiny 1857-59* (Calcutta, 1979), pp. 188ff.
[3] Chaudhuri, *Civil Rebellion*, pp. 118-143.
[4] Gubbins, *Mutinies*, p. 181.
[5] Telegram from H. Tucker to Canning, 11 July 1857: Forrest, *Selections*, ii, p. 32.

They had the two 9-pounder batteries from Secrora and Fyzabad, each of six guns, making twelve pieces of artillery. They possessed besides, three or four small native guns, which could have been of no service in the field, and which they had obtained in the districts.

There were about 700 or 800 cavalry, made up of parties from the 15th Irregulars at Sultanpoor, and the three Oudh local regiments, Daly's, Gall's and Hardinge's, with some of Weston's police troopers. Of infantry, there were the following corps:

NATIVE INFANTRY
the 22nd Regt. from Fyzabad only
OUDH IRREGULAR INFANTRY
A few men of the 1st from Salone.
The 2nd from Secrora.
The 3rd from Gondah.
The 5th from Duriabad.
The 6th from Fyzabad.
The 8th from Sultanpoor.
The 9th from Seetapoor.
MILITARY POLICE
The 1st Regt. from Sultanpoor.
The 2nd Regt. from Seetapoor.[6]

What Gubbins did not note (or perhaps did not know) at that point of time was that some of the talukdars and members of the nawabi bureaucracy had already joined the rebellion and were providing the leadership. The raja of Mahmudabad was the first to join, providing leadership to the Sitapur rebels who fought under his naib (deputy) Khan Ali Khan (an ex-chakladar of Salon) at Chinhat. Raja Jailal Singh, the nazim of Azamgarh, was elected the mouthpiece of the soldiery and as their chief.[7] In fact the talukdars, especially in southern Awadh, had begun to collect men, recruit sepoys and prepare ammunition as soon as they were sure that British authority had collapsed in the districts.[8]

The news of the British defeat at Chinhat spread quickly. It became an accepted fact that the Company's rule had 'past [sic] away for ever and the "Nawabee" is restored as a matter of course'. The British could come back only with the help of a 'reliable armed

---

[6]Gubbins, *Mutinies*, pp. 189-90.

[7]Trial Proceedings, Govt. vs. Raja Jai Lal Singh, Govt. Decision: Lucknow Collectorate Mutiny *Basta: F.S.U.P.*, ii, p. 51.

[8]Letter form Lalu Harshay, Extra Asstt. Comm. of Sultanpur, to Outram, 16 Sept. 1857: Mutiny Papers of Outram, Havelock and Campbell, Eur. Mss. C124, I.O.L.R.

force'.⁹ The news of the defeat also augmented the efforts of talukdars and their peasants to join the fight:

> ... several people of the neighbourhood of Cusbah Jyee (in Salon) together with the revolters of that place, have collected a number of men. ... Hunoomanpershad with his friends and relations has employed 2.000 persons and has an intention of creating a disturbance... The Government Treasury has been plundered by the people of the above Mouza, as well as by the neighbouring zemindars. No servants of the Government are in this place... In Cusbah Jyee nothing but the firing of guns and muskets can be heard. Some men... have been... instigating the people to create disturbances. Any one who refuses to follow them is subjected to great disgrace.¹⁰

In the countryside the rebellion was already becoming general and acquiring a popular character.

In Lucknow the British were pushed back into the Residency and surrounded by rebel forces:

> I heard they were in the Residency and the insurgents surrounding them, fighting going on daily but the number of the insurgents are overpowering. People say not less than 35,000 of which 10,000 are mutineers of different Regiments and the rest the followers of Talooqdars for instance Goorbux Sing of Ramnuggur, Nawab Ally Khan, the Puthuns of 'Mulleabad' and Murdham Sing a Talooqdar and many others ... it is reported that the insurgents have ruined it [the Residency] ... orders have been sent to all the Talooqdars to repair with all their retainers to Lucknow. Everyday their numbers increase. They are repairing all the guns of the late Native Government which the English disabled at annexation...¹¹

The situation was so desperate that Henry Lawrence thought they could hold out only for fifteen or twenty days.¹²

To the south of Lucknow, in Unao, the rebels, now indistinguishable from the rural populace, were busy putting off Havelock's advance from Kanpur into Lucknow. The British general was forced to fall back again and again because of the strength of the popular opposition. As an officer noted:

⁹Wingfield to Edmonstone, 1 July 1857: For. Secret Cons., 25 Sept. 1857, No. 520.

¹⁰Abstract translation of a letter from Sahikh Enaeth Ashroff to Ashroff Hossein Khan, 3 July 1857: For Dept. Secret Cons., 28 Aug. 1857, No. 310.

¹¹Extract from a letter of Man Singh to Wingfield, 10 July 1857, For. Secret Cons., 25 Sept. 1857: No. 516.

¹²Neill to Canning, 10 July 1857, quoting message from Lawrence dated 30 June: Forrest, *Selections*, ii, p. 31.

> It became painfully evident to all that we could never reach Lucknow; we had three strong positions to force, defended by fifty guns and 30,000 men ... the men are cowed by the numbers opposed to them, and the endless fighting. Every village is held against us, the zemindars have risen to oppose us; ... We know them to be all around us in bodies of 500 or 600 independent of the regular levies.[13]

The villages had the character of 'almost impregnable fortifications', and the villagers had converted themselves into "excellent garrison troops'.[14] Charles Ball, basing himself on despatches from Havelock's camp, describes the fighting qualities of the rebels; the description shows that though the rebels could be outclassed in the open, they made 'excellent garrison troops':

> A hundred Oude men would flee from the attack of ten English soldiers on an open plain; but if ten Oudians are placed behind a loopholed mud wall, they will hold their position without shrinking... Such was the case in the petty village of Oonao. The enemy were completely hidden behind walls: the British troops were in the place and all round it, and yet they could comparatively do nothing...[15]

There was a plan on the part of the British to approach Lucknow via the river Gogra but it had to be abandoned because the opposition of 'the warlike population of Oude ... swarmed by mutinous troops' was apprehended to be 'too strong'.[16] In Lucknow itself the rebels were so strong that, according to Havelock, to encounter them too quickly 'would be to court annihilation'.[17]

The spirit and tenacity of the rebels is highlighted by incidents such as the following:

> The pertinacity of one of the villagers ... was remarkable. He had stationed himself in a little mud fort at the entrance of the place [Bashirhatganj in Unao] ... and had contrived to hide himself, thus escaping the fate of his comrades in the general bayoneting. As soon as the main body of the English had passed on, this man emerged from his shelter, and plied his solitary matchlock with effect at the guns, the baggage, the elephants ... the poor wretch was shot through the head as he was

---

[13]Telegram from Lt. Col., Tytler to the C.-in-C., 6 Aug. 1857: Forrest, *Selections*, ii, p. 173.

[14]C. Ball, *The History of the Indian Mutiny*, 2 vols. (London, n.d.), ii, p. 17.

[15]Ibid.

[16]Officer Commanding at Allahabad to C.-in-C., 18 Aug. 1857: Inclosure 97 in No. 2 *Further Papers* (No 4), p. 101, *Papers Relating to Indian Mutinies*.

[17]Havelock to C.-in-C., 6 Aug. 1857: Inclosure 56 in ibid., p. 83.

crossing over the parapet for a last hit at his enemies.[18]

Such desperate courage, by no means uncommon among the rebels, was an indication of their commitment to a cause which evidently had a very powerful appeal.

In Lucknow the rebels went around in groups crying 'Bom Mahadeo' (a peculiarly Hindu evocation of the god Shiva), called Birjis Qadr from the palace, embraced him and said 'You are Kanhaiya [Krishna]'.[19] But their activities were not limited to such celebrations. Outram realized how precarious they had made the position of the Lucknow garrison:

> Since we have obtained access to the exterior of this entrenchment we find that they had completed six mines in the most artistic manner (one of them from a distance of 200 feet) under our principal defensive works, which were ready for loading, and the firing of which must have placed the garrison entirely at their mercy. The delay of another day therefore might have sealed their fate.[20]

Time and again the ingenuity of the rebel gunners around the Residency baffled the British:

> They soon had from twenty to twenty-five guns in position, some of them of very large calibre. These were planted all round our post at small distances, some being actually within fifty yards of our defences, but in places where our own heavy guns could not reply to them; while the perseverance and ingenuity of the enemy in erecting barricades in front of, and around their guns in a very short time, rendered all attempts to silence them by musketry entirely unavailing. Neither could they be effectually silenced by shells, by reason of their extreme proximity to our position, and because moreover, the enemy had recourse to digging very narrow trenches, about eight feet in depth, in rear of each gun; in which the men lay while our shells were flying, and which so effectually concealed them, even while working the gun, that our baffled sharpshooters could only see their hands while in the act of loading.[21]

Most of the besiegers of the Residency were thought to be talukdars' men, and it was believed that 'nearly every Talooqdar except

[18]Ball, *The Mutiny*, ii, p. 18.

[19]Saiyid Kamaluddin Haidar Husaini, *Qaisar-ut-Tawarikh*, 2 vols. (Lucknow, 1897), ii, p. 230: cited in *F.S.U.P.*, ii, p. 166.

[20]Outram to Campbell, 31 Sept. 1857: Mutiny Papers of Outram, Havelock and Campbell; details of the mining are given in McLeod Innes, *Lucknow and Oude in the Mutiny* (London, 1895), pp. 136ff., 160-1 and 165ff.

[21]Inglis to Sec. to Govt. Military Dept., 26 Sept. 1857, quoted by Ball, *The Mutiny*, ii, p. 50.

the Raja of Balrampoor and Man Sing have [sic] sent his contingent to assist in the siege'.[22]

Even after the British force under Havelock and Outram had entered the Residency on 25 September 1857, the condition of the British in Lucknow remained vulnerable in the extreme. Outram and Havelock had succeeded in getting to the Residency, but once in there they were completely isolated. All around them the rebels swarmed: so strong and numerous were they that the British generals could not establish contact with their stores at Alambagh, nor could they evacuate the Residency. As Outram noted:

To force our way through the city would have proved a very desperate operation, if indeed it could have been accomplished.[23]

In a telegram to the Commander-in-Chief he admitted that 'the insurgents are too strong to admit of withdrawing from this garrison'.[24]

In fact what is called the first relief of Lucknow was for practical purposes no relief at all. The British were still under siege. Rebel enthusiasm was in no way dampened by the arrival of the force under Outram and Havelock. On the contrary they intensified their efforts to throw out the British from Awadh. At best 'round one' was a draw, but it had shown that the sepoys, talukdars and their men were fighting together and valiantly, that a unified objective had emerged and that the revolt was no longer confined to mutinous soldiers.

The City and the Districts: First Relief to the Sack of Lucknow

Finding themselves in a vulnerable position inside the Residency, with their supply line cut off, the British attempted to negotiate with the rebels. But every overture made by Outram to the influential citizens of Lucknow was spurned.[25] Even after November, when Sir Colin Campbell's army had moved into Lucknow, the native population refused to co-operate in any way

[22]Letter to Outram (signature illegible), 30 Aug. 1857: Mutiny Papers of Outram, Havelock and Campbell.
[23]Outram to Campbell, 31 Sept. 1857: ibid.
[24]Outram to C.-in-C., 2 Oct. 1857: Forrest, *Selections*, ii, p. 293.
[25]Ball, *The Mutiny*, ii, p. 44.

with the British. Like Outram before him Campbell—

did his utmost to open communications with the Chiefs and Nobles and other influential inhabitants who might be well-disposed towards us. With this object he issued proclamations declaring that all people who had taken no part in the disturbances would be treated with every consideration by the British Government. Such persons were invited to come and have an interview with the CC and shopkeepers and artisans were also assured that they would be treated with kindness and receive their own prices for their goods. . . . These proclamations however were unattended with the slightest effect. Not a seer of provisions could be obtained nor did a man attempt to open communication with us. . .[26]

This was an indication of how wide the base of the rebellion had become, also perhaps of the strength of anti-British feeling. Evidently, neither blandishments nor implied threats had any impact on the people or their commitment to the destruction of firangi Raj. True there was an element of fear, but that itself can be seen as a recognition of who the Awadh people thought were on the winning side between September 1857 and March 1858.

The rebels themselves were busy improving their organization. Shortage of ammunition was being overcome. Percussion caps and all kinds of ammunition were being produced in Lucknow. Artisans were brought in from Delhi especially for this purpose.[27] The services of a Christian who had been taken prisoner were commandeered.[28] Supplies of ammunition from the districts were also maintained. A huge quantity of lead was found in the Dilkhusa and then converted into bullets.[29] Similarly, 3,000 nine pound and 2,000 eighteen pound shot were recovered from wells where the British had left them when they evacuated the Residency.[30] A workshop was set up in Faizabad for the purpose of repairing heavy guns.[31]

[26]Couper to Edmonstone, 21 Nov. 1857: For. Secret Cons., 29 Jan. 1858, Cons. No. 341.
[27]R. Strachey to Edmonstone, 25 Jan. 1858 forwarding Mr Carnegy's Intelligence, For. Dept., Secret Branch, 26 Feb. 1858, Cons., No. 228 (News of mid-Nov 1857).
[28]Ibid., Cons. No. 227 (News of 7 Jan. 1858).
[29]Extracts of Intelligence from Carnegy, 13 Oct. 1857, Inclosure 30 in No. 7; *Further Papers* (No. 7), p. 75, *Papers Relating to Indian Mutinies* (News of 13 Oct. 1857).
[30]Couper to Edmonstone, 15 Dec. 1857, For. Dept. Secret Cons., 26 March 1858, No. 63.
[31]Extracts of Intelligence from Carnegy, 13 Oct. 1857.

Lucknow became the chief focus of fighting. Both the rebels and the English realized the importance of having control over the city. It became the symbol of power and authority. As Outram noted:

> I regard the re-establishment of our Government as an impossibility, so long as the capital, which is looked upon by every native as the seat of government is in the hands of the rebels.[32]

Colin Campbell shared his feelings:

> It is moreover the deliberate opinion of the CC that the subjugation of the province will follow the fall of Lucknow as surely the conquest of France would follow the capture of Paris.[33]

Khan Bahadur Khan, the leader of the rebellion in Rohilkhand, noted how the complete re-establishment of British power in Rohilkhand was impossible so long as Lucknow remained beyond their grasp:

> ... there are still two places, Barreilly and Lucknow (which is an imperial city) against which the efforts of the British have been unsuccessful... If God be with us, it [British rule] shall never be again known in these two cities. If the English are kept in check at Barreilly and if Lucknow is not threatened, assistance will certainly reach Barreilly from the last mentioned city if Lucknow is taken by the English Barreilly *must* fall but if on the contrary Barreilly is first taken by the British it can easily be reconquered by the assistance of the Oudh troops.[34]

The importance of Lucknow to the rebels is evident from the concentration of their forces in and near the city. Around October 1857 twelve infantry and three cavalry regiments had been reported to be fighting in Lucknow. They were reinforced by

---

[32]Outram to Canning, 29 Nov. 1857: For. Dept., Secret Cons., 16 March 1858, No. 62. Outram emphasized the symbolic importance of Lucknow in a telegram to Canning, 17 Sept. 1857: 'The moral effect of abandoning Lucknow will be very serious against us; the many well-disposed chiefs in Oude and Rohilcund, who are now watching the turn of affairs, would regard the loss of Lucknow as the forerunner of the end of our rule'. Inclosure 83 in No. 4, *Further Papers* (No. 4), p. 245, *Papers Relating to Indian Mutinies*.

[33]Couper to Edmonstone, 18 Jan. 1858: For. Dept. Secret Cons., 29 Jan. 1858, Cons. No. 361.

[34]Translation of a letter arrived from Lucknow dated 15 Feb. 1858: For. Dept. Political, 30 Dec. 1859, Supplement No. 952; also available in For. Dept. Secret Cons., 26 March 1858, No. 79.

talukdars and their men — 'almost all the Oude Talookdars sent men and agents'.[35] Man Singh, Hanwant Singh, Bishwanath Baksh, the son of Sangram Singh of Allahabad, the raja of Amethi and Davi Buksh were the chief talukdars who were personally fighting in Lucknow.[36] Rana Beni Madho with 2,000 men, Raghunath Singh of Khajurgaon with 2,000 men, Bishon Singh of Simerpaha with 1,000 men, Bhagwan Baksh of Nain with 1,000 and Sahajram of Pakhramow with 1,000 men were also entrenched in the city and received *khilats* (dresses of honour) binding them to attack the English in Alambagh.[37] The intensity can be assessed from the fact that early in October 5,000 rebels were either killed or wounded in an encounter outside the palace gates when 200 Europeans were trying to reach the Residency.[38]

By the end of September 1857 the revolt in Delhi and its neighbourhood had been suppressed and British authority reestablished. As the imperial city was recaptured, the rebels who had fought there turned to the other seat of power in north India — Lucknow — as their haven. The Awadh capital still remained outside British control; it was seen as the place where the cause could still be defended, where money, food and shelter were still available. Right through October and November mutineers and rebels were flocking into Lucknow. On 6 November two regiments and 200 men of the Sappers and Miners, 300 sowars and eight guns arrived from Delhi. On 19 November, five Delhi regiments and six guns arrived; the Begum called upon them in the name *khuda* (God) to help her, and they joined in the fight immediately, infusing new enthusiasm into the rebel camp.[39]

Other rebel objectives throughout October and November were to cut off the British contact with Kanpur and to destroy the British entrenchment at Alambagh. Thus when a company of British troops from Kanpur arrived at Bani Banthara, (about thirty-six miles from Lucknow), Raja Hicha Ram proceeded with four regiments to oppose them.[40] Lal Madho Singh also went off to fight at Bani Banthara with 2,000 men and four guns. He lost 200 of his men and two guns in the fight. Madho Singh warned

---

[35]Carnegy's Intelligence, For. Dept., Secret Branch, 26 Feb. 1858, Cons. No. 228 (News of 4 Oct 1857).
[36]Ibid. [37]Ibid. (news of 23 Oct. 1857).
[38]Ibid. (news of 15 Oct. 1857). [39]Ibid. [40]Ibid. (news of 2 Nov. 1857).

the Begum that unless the British advance was stopped they would be at Alambagh.[41] Some Badshahi regiments were sent off to fight the British and simultaneously the attack on Alambagh was strengthened:

The Moorchabundee of the forces surrounding the Alumbagh is as follows:— 1st at the Talab Futeh Allee, Rajah Madho Sing with 1,600 men and 4 guns also Rajah Rambuksh Pokrawallah with 700 men and 1 gun and 500 sowars of 15th Risala. 2nd — at the Jurnel Bagh, talab Dwarakadas Rao Dorrgabuksh commander with 2 Regiments the 'Jurrar' and 'Burk' and 1 gun, also Raja Suhujram with 1,000 men and 3 guns. 3rd—at Husnapoor 1 Regiment of 500 men, 4th—at the Fort of Jullalabad 1 Regiment (the 71st) also 500 Nujeebs and 1,200 sowars of the 12th and 15th Irregular and 2 guns. 6th — at Julalpoor Mullo Sing zemindar of Nara with 500 men. 7th at Tipra Khairah the Regiment of Toorum Baz Khan 700 men. 8th at Gurh Kuniarpoor, the Regiment of Wazeer Khan 500 men and 1 gun (kalanag). 9th at Jhangeers Regiment Nasir Beg 400 men and 1 Goorda gun. 15th 200 Nujeebs and 1 gun (the numbers omitted are not mentioned in the letter)[42].

As soon as news of the arrival of British reinforcements at Alambagh reached Lucknow these forces were reinforced, with Raja Jailal Singh leading three regiments, 500 sowars and four guns, and also by Raja Man Singh who had with him 2,000 of his 7,000 men.[43] As the reinforcements advanced towards Lucknow the rebel army geared up its efforts to block their progress:

The disposition of the troops now is on the west and east sides of the English; in the centre surrounding the Palace, the King's army; in the Satara Peshwa's house, the Moulvie; in Hazratgunge the mutineers and the Talooqdars' men. Access by the Goomtee is closed except by the Stone Bridge. The rebels now reinforced by the Delhie Regiments have sworn to die in Lucknow; and further reinforcement are pouring in from the districts and all are now of one mind.[44]

The Bailee Guard was surrounded by guns on all sides: four on the east, three on the north, five on the west and four on the south; 'besides these 6 or 7 guns are in position in different lanes and streets about the place'.[45] Fighting was particularly heavy around 16, 17, and 18 November, when Colin Campbell's relief force

---

[41]Ibid. (news of 4 Nov. 1857). [42]Ibid. (news of 2 Nov. 1857).
[43]Ibid. (news of 6 Nov. 1857). [44]Ibid. (news of 16 Nov. 1857).
[45]Ibid. (news of mid-Nov.).

The Revolt of the People

finally entered Lucknow. Streets were blocked up with dead bodies.[46]

Table 9 gives the breakdown of rebel fighting men who were at Lucknow during Campbell's relief.

TABLE 9[47]

Regiment	Strength
Regt. of Captains Soobah Singh and Akipal Singh	700
Regt. No 8 Rightwing Capt. Gajadhar Singh	700
The Nadir Shahie Regt., Seetul Singh Adjt	400
The Right Wing of Akhtari Regt., Capt. Bhowani Singh	950
Barlow's Regiment (6th Oude Locals), Capt. Umrao Singh	700
The Akhtari Regt., Capt. Fida Hussain	600
The Volunteers (37th N.I.), Capt. Gauri Shanker	750
The 'Bole' Regt. (22nd N.I.) Capt. Rajman Tiwari	700
Left Wing of Burbury's Regiment (8th Oude locals) Capt. Mukhodom Baksh	700
Left Wing of Robert's Regiment	600
Right Wing of Robert's Regiment	550
Regt. No. 9, Capt. Gajen Singh	600
King's Regiments	
Regt. of Agha Hussain Salar (general)	400
Regt. of Jafir Ali, Salar	350
Regt. of Sheik Ali Bagar, Salar	400
Regt. of Bahadur Ali Salar	250
Regt. of Mir Nagi, Ali Khan, Salar	762
Regt. of Mirza Shehar Yar, Salar	882
Remains of other Regiments, approximately	2,556
Cavalry	
Regt. No. 12 Capt. Hari Singh	700
Regt. No. 15	800
Regt. No. 11	600
King's Cavalry	
Tahwar Khan Rissaladar's Regt.	500
The Tircha Regt.	700
The Maiman-i Shahi Regt.	700
The Mesurrah Regt.	900

[46]Ibid. (news of 17 Nov. 1857).

[47]Ibid. (News of 15 Dec. 1857); Chaudhuri, *Civil Rebellion*, p. 130, gives the aggregate figures but not the details of the breakdown. He also makes the mistake of dating the list as pertaining to forces in mid-December 1857. It is true that the newsletter which contained the list was dated 15 Dec. 1857, but it also made clear that it was at least a fortnight old. I think it is safe to assume that the list is of men in Lucknow around the time of Campbell's relief since that was the period when the fighting was at its heaviest.

Ali Buksh Khan's Regt.	800
Mahomed Akbar's Regt.	900
The Regiment No. 9	1,000
The New Regt.	120
Talukdars' Troops	
Raja Hardat Singh Bahadur Bahraich	200
Raghunath Singh of Raipur	200
The Ikauna Men	240
The Changapur Men	150
Hardat Singh of Churda	300
The Tepurdha Men	100
The Balrajkumars	200
The Shahpur Men	100
Kishandatt Pandey's Men	1,200
Sadun Salgunge	1,000
Bhinga Men	300
Tulsipur Men	500
Nanpara Men	400
Raghunath Singh of Baiswara	1,000
Raja of Tiloi (Shanker Singh)	80
Sheo Shankar Singh Jorapur	500
Lal Bahadur Sipah Salar of Kalakunkur	1,000
Rampur Katowalah (Men)	400
Beni Madho Singh	1,000
Raja Man Singh	7,000
Raja of Amethi	2,500
Raja Sahaj Ram of Banthra	2,000
Raja Gurbux Singh of Ramnagar	2,500
Raja Nawab Ali Khan, Mahmudabad	2,200
Raja Baljandur Singh of Palpur	1,500
Surujpur Burhilah	2,000
Baley Dube of Amooah	100
Umrao Singh of Mowhah	1,000
Umrao Singh of Ajuldhukwa	500
Jai Narain Singh of Dhorahrah	300
Balapur Rao Khairabad	800
Isanagar, Jai Prakash	500
Miscellaneous	300
This detail gives:	
Sepoys	7,950
Oude Regts.	5,600
Cavalry	7,720
Talukdars' Men	32,080
	53,350

This breakdown clearly shows that the rebellion in Awadh had transcended a purely sepoy base. For one thing the fighting force was quite large and for another more than sixty per cent of the fighting force was drawn from the general rural populace. It is more than probable, given the ties of loyalty that existed in the rural world of Awadh, that the thousands of men supplied by the talukdars were not all just their retainers but also drawn from tenants, peasants and clansmen who lived on their land. Also, it should be emphasized that the data cited is a snippet from the reports of a spy, and refers to events during only a few days in November. Hence it is conceivable that more talukdars and their men were fighting in and around Lucknow before or even during November. In fact, this report of the number of fighting men ends with the words 'which numbers are being daily reinforced.'

Of the thirty-two talukdars (or their men) in the list, the places of origin of twenty-one talukdars are readily identifiable: nine come from districts in southern Awadh, nine from Gonda and Bahraich and two and one from Dariabad and Sitapur respectively. The evidence of this list thus suggests strongly that the districts in which the talukdars' control was the strongest and where they had lost heavily in the Summary Settlement supplied the bulk of the rebel forces. In other words the areas delineated as those of talukdar-peasant complementarity had joined in the revolt most readily and with most men:

The number of fighting men in Lucknow and its neighbourhood increased after the evacuation of the British from the city on November 1857. In fact Campbell's decision to evacuate the city gave a fillip to the rebellion.

It was then proclaimed in the city that the Europeans had abandoned the place, and addresses to the same purport were sent to the district authorities and to the king of Delhie. The Chief Begum has given Shurruffooddowlah written instructions to occupy Benares and Allahabad, and the Nuwab is making the necessary military preparations to carry out these orders. Councils of war are constantly being held... It is known that the Bala Sahib, and the Nana Sahib with the Gwalior troops have surrounded Cawnpoor. The War is now fully believed throughout Lucknow to be a religious crusade, and crowds of people are flocking into the capital from the districts to take part in the struggle.[48]

---

[48]Carnegy's Intelligence (News of 25 Nov. 1857).

By January, Lucknow was 'swarming with fighting men'.[49] The talukdars were still fighting in Lucknow, led by Man Singh with four to five thousand men and by the raja of Amethi with four guns and 3,000 men.[50] It was estimated that 'the army now at Lucknow is a little short of lakh of persons. The 72nd, 37th, 22nd, 48th in all 12 Regiments with 14 of the Delhie Regiments are all present but incomplete...'[51] The rebels expected the British to be back in Awadh with reinforcements for the take-over of Lucknow. Their efforts were therefore concentrated on fortifying it. About 15,000 workmen were employed to build fortifications.[52] Moreover, a deep moat was dug around the Kaiserbagh to let in the water from the Gomti and 'every street and lane has been barricaded ... and all the houses are loopholed.'[53]

After the evacuation of Lucknow Colin Campbell had withdrawn to Kanpur, leaving Outram with 4,000 men to control Alambagh. The condition of this latter garrison was vulnerable from the moment of Campbell's departure for Kanpur:

our present position is as follows, we are opposed by a powerful enemy in a hostile country in which we are unable to obtain an adequate supply of provisions in the midst of a disaffected population.[54]

Withholding of provisions from the British at Alambagh seems to have been a deliberate act on the part of the populace of Awadh. No grain dealers or vegetable vendors came forward even though extravagant prices were offered.[55] Forays into villages were no more successful because the villagers were unwilling to part with their grain:

The surrounding villagers still withhold every description of supplies... Yesterday a strong forage party was sent out to Mhow a village 11 villages [sic] off. It was necessary to go so great a distance because the enemy had previously removed all the supplies from the intervening villages. They will now doubtless, take away or conceal grain and other

---

[49]Ibid. Cons. No. 227 (News of 4 Jan. 1857).
[50]Ibid. (News of 7 Jan. 1858). [51]Ibid.
[52]Ibid. (News of 13 Jan. 1858).
[53]Ibid. (News of 7 Jan. 1858).
[54]Couper to Edmonstone, 15 Dec. 1857: For. Dept. Secret Cons., 26 March 1858, Cons. No. 63.
[55]Couper to Edmonstone, 9 Dec. 1857: For. Dept., Secret Cons., 29 Jan. 1858, No. 346.

The Revolt of the People

means of subsistence, in places more remote from our camp, and our chances of obtaining supplies by foraging will consequently grow daily more precarious.[56]

In the context of this attitude of the villagers, Outram, with remarkable prescience, noted how difficult it would be to re-establish British power in the Awadh countryside:

Our advance into the interior should be attended with similar results that the villagers should fly . . . leaving us nothing but their deserted fortresses and dwellings and their neglected cultivation, which so far from being a source of revenue would very likely not suffice for the maintenance of the troops.[57]

The garrison was reduced to virtual inactivity, 'menaced . . . by many thousands of the enemy supported by several guns'.[58] The rebels—

show themselves in great force out of range of our guns, fire their own canon and otherwise insult us. The population are aware of it and also see us insulted. They see too the enemy making active preparations for resisting our re-entry into the capital; they see them erecting batteries in every village garden and enclosure in front of our line: fortifying the Kaisur Bagh and other strong positions: pulling down the Residency buildings. . . They see all this and they also see that we do and can do nothing: that we are insulted in silence, that we can obtain little or no supplies: that we can maintain no uninterrupted communication, that we can induce no man of any rank, caste or grade to come to our assistance and is it strange therefore, if they believe the tales so industriously instilled into their ears that the British rule is at an end and that in spite of rumours of casual reverses the rebel cause will eventually triumph.[59]

Anti-British sentiment ran high, popular opinion had accepted that the British were on the losing side and therefore not worthy

---

[56]Couper to Edmonstone, 15 Dec. 1857; also see Couper to Edmonstone, 9 Dec. 1857: 'A foray which was made on the 7th instant to the large and populous village of Bijnaur about 7 miles distant was unsuccessful although . . . extravagant prices given for the few maunds of grain which they were reluctantly induced to part with and which alone they possessed as the rebels have caused articles of consumption to be carried away from that and from every other village for many miles around. In fact every one from the raja to the pasee is afraid to make any the slightest demonstration in our favour'.

[57]Outram to Canning, 29 Nov. 1857: For. Dept., Secret Cons., 26 March 1858, No. 62.

[58]Couper to Edmonstone, 9 Dec. 1857.

[59]Couper to Edmonstone, 15 Dec. 1857.

of respect or help. Or at least the villagers had realized that the British could not provide permanent protection. Such attitudes were kept agog by the percolation of rumours:

> The rebels industriously give out that the Nana is the Master of Cawnpore that he has driven out the British that he will shortly march on the capital... They also have succeeded in promulgating a belief that Delhi is surrounded will soon be retaken and the Rajah of Puteealah has been plundered by a rebel army.[60]

Very probably such dissemination of rumours to boost morale is indicative of a degree of planning and co-ordination, a possibility generally overlooked in the literature on the subject.

All this while, when Lucknow remained the 'nucleus of the revolt',[61] drawing rebels from all over north India as British forces reconquered area after area, the districts of Awadh had also been activating themselves. Throughout September and October of 1857 the Awadh districts served as 'feeder lines' for the fighting in Lucknow. Men were coming in to join the fight and levies were being raised:

> A tehseeldar has been appointed at Puttee in Pergunnah Belkhur [in Partapgarh], and is said to be raising two or three regiments... Another tehseeldar is at Nawabgunge zillah Pertabghur, raising men for four regiments... Heerwunt Singh with 2 guns and 400 men at Kuriya Bazar [was] on his way to Lucknow. At that place [Kuriya] men were also being enlisted. The Nazim of Salone had returned to Lucknow with 2,000 men, leaving people to enlist 3,000 or 4,000 more. At Shankurpore it was ascertained that Joograj Sing, brother of Rana Banee Madho, had seven days previously gone to Lucknow with 700 men and 2 guns. He was to pick up 1,200 or 1,300 men of Bassunt Sing of Simerpatra [probably Simerpaha], and Ruggonaut Sing of Kujjergam, at Roy Barreilly, and take them with him, as also four guns of theirs. In the fort of Shunkurpore Banee Madho has 1,200 and 8 large guns with him. He is busily employed putting his fort in order; 600 coolies are at work and it will be finished in a month... Beje bahadoor at Shunkerpore... had sent 2 guns and 400 men to Lucknow. Juggernauth Buccus [Baksh], Ram Persand etc., of Nain, have sent 700 men and 2 guns .. to Lucknow... Sheik Ahmed Ali of Allahabad had come as tehseeldar, and was raising men. 200 or 300 men of the old "Doorga Sing Regiment" were with him.[62]

[60]Couper to Edmonstone, 9 Dec. 1857.
[61]Couper to Edmonstone, 15 Dec. 1857; also see the opinion of the government in Calcutta (as given in Ball, *The Mutiny*, ii, p. 243) which described Lucknow as 'the true seat of the rebellion' and as the rebellions' 'central point of union'.
[62]Extracts of Intelligence from Carnegy, 13 Oct. 1857, Inclosure 30 in No. 7,

In November, during the critical days of fighting against Campbell's army in Lucknow, reinforcements were 'pouring in from the districts'.[63] Even in January there were reports of 'levies . . . daily being raised'.[64]

Even when levies raised in the countryside were not sent direct to Lucknow, there was a certain preparedness in the districts to help the rebel cause whenever required. Instructions had been sent to the nazims of Sultanpur and Gorakhpur to help in the collection of talukdars' men.[65] Orders were issued to all talukdars in southern Awadh to join forces and stop the English advance.[66] The talukdars of Gonda-Bahraich were ordered to reinforce the fighting in Gorakhpur; for this purpose eight guns were mounted and Sadan Lall, chakladar of Bahraich, with his own forces and four regiments moved into Gorakhpur.[67] In Dariabad Man Singh's brother, Ramadhin, was ready with reinforcements of 5,000 men and three guns. Around September 1857 there was also in Faizabad a regiment made up of sepoys and *najibs* (militia men) ready to fight.[68] In January two companies of sepoys were at Tanda to join the fighting.[69]

The key figure, at least in southern Awadh, for the organizing of rebel forces in the districts was Mehndi Hussain, the nazim of Sultanpur. Carnegy's reports made it clear that

He [Mehndi Hussain] is . . . a person of some ability . . . he . . . has a considerable force, estimated at from 8,000 to 10,000 men at Hussunpore, a place near Sultanpore, and about twenty miles within the Oude frontier. He is believed to be supported by all the talookdars in Sultanpore and Fyzabad excepting Rostum Shah. There are several guns with this force, and many other guns are scattered at various places along the frontier.[70]

Further Papers (No. 7), p. 74, *Papers Relating to Indian Mutinies* (News of 6 Oct. 1857).

[63]Carnegy's Intelligence, For. Dept., Secret Branch, 26 Feb., 1858, Cons. No. 228 (News of 16 Nov. 1858).

[64]Ibid. No. 227 (News of 1 Jan. 1858).

[65]Ibid. No. 228 (News of 26 Nov. 1857).

[66]Ibid. No. 229 (News of 10 Nov. 1857).

[67]Ibid. No. 227 (News of 8 Jan. 1858).

[68]Ibid No. 228 (News of 27 Sept. 1857).

[69]Ibid. No. 227 (News of 1 Jan. 1858).

[70]Letter from the Secretary to the Government, Central Provinces, to the Secretary to the Government of India, 15 Oct. 1857: Inclosure 25 in No. 7, *Further Papers* (No. 7), p. 71, *Papers Relating to Indian Mutinies*.

100   *Awadh in Revolt*

Under the leadership of Mehndi Hussain rebel forces gathered in Bhadiyan, in Sultanpur district. Table 10 gives a breakdown of that force.

TABLE 10[71]

	No. of men	No. of guns
Mehndie Hussain	900	1
Najib Regiments	2,000	6
Raja Hussain Ali	700	
Kalka Baksh of Rampur	200	
Sogra Bibi of Manyarpur	400	2
Raja Ali Baksh Khan of Mohumedeegaon	400	2
Bachgoti tribe	400	
Udresh Singh of Meopur	400	
Umresh Singh of Meopur	300	
Israj Singh of Meopur	300	
Dalpat Singh of Bhadiyan	200	
Baijnath Singh of Sheogarh	100	
Bakhtwar Khan and others of Umhut	200	
Situla Baksh of Nanemau	100	
Sowars, Noukur Sirkar (government servant)	100	
Arjun Singh and Jugeshur Buksh	50	
Burrear Singh (Brother of Rustam Sah)	300	
	7,050	11

This shows the extent of mobilization in the Awadh countryside: small magnates who could provide a few hundred men were prepared to throw in their lot in the fighting; they did not move to Lucknow but remained in the districts armed, ready to scour the Awadh frontier or to prevent any British advance through the borders of Jaunpur and Allahabad. The mention of 400 members of the Bachgoti clan in the list is significant. It indicates, perhaps, that in the Awadh countryside of the time there were leaderless bands of clansmen who had joined the fight without waiting for the local magnate or clan leader to provide the leadership.

There was a general spirit of belligerence among the rural populace of Awadh, which gave the fighting very much the character

[71]Carnegy's Intelligence, For. Dept., Secret Branch, 26 Feb. 1858, No. 228 (News of 20 Nov. 1857).

of a *levee en masse*. Among Mehndi Hussain's own men there were common villagers. They — especially the members of the Rajkumar clan — as well as the regiments under him, put strong pressure on their leader to cross the Awadh frontier and attack Jaunpur.[72] In Faizabad around mid-October there were 2,000 men under a man called Jafir Ali; in Shahganj, the fort of Man Singh, there were 1,000 men and eight guns in position; at Tanda there was a nazim with 6,000 men inclusive of two regiments of mutineers.[73] At Jagdishpur, in Sultanpur district, there were 2,000 men and two guns and at Amethi 'great preparations have been made and 28 guns of sorts are in position'.[74] And at Koiripur and Chanda 'great battles were fought by the Oude people' to resist the British.[75] By February, when General Frank's columns and the army of Jang Bahadur of Nepal had begun to move into Awadh through the Benares and Gorakhpur frontiers, the rebels tried hard to stop their advance. Despatches were sent to different talukdars to rise and oppose the British.[76] At Faizabad was stationed the '22nd N.I., the "Salamut" Regiment, 40 N.I., and another Regiment . . . numbering 2,000 sepoys'. There were also 5,000 matchlockmen.[77] At Ramghat there were two regiments of infantry, one of cavalry and six guns. In Ajodhya, under Balakram Singh, there was a force of 1,200 men. At Suraj Dooari Ghat there were two regiments of sepoys and two guns. At Mhow two regiments of sepoys, thirty *sowars* and three guns were observed by British spies.[78] At Chanda on the borders of Awadh and Jaunpur, where General Frank met his first opposition, the advance guard of the rebel forces was 6,000 to 8,000 strong with six guns; they were backed up by Mehndi Hussain who at this stage had 10,000 men, 1,200 cavalry and eleven guns. It was ascertained that 20th, 28th, 48th and 71st native regiments were part of this force at

[72]Extracts of Intelligence from Carnegy, 13 Oct. 1857: *Further Papers*, (No. 7), p. 74, *Papers Re. Indian Mutinies*.

[73]Carnegy's Intelligence, For. Dept. Secret Branch, 26 Feb. 1858, No. 228 (News of 16 Oct. 1857).

[74]Ibid., No. 227 (news of 7 Jan. 1858).

[75]Ibid.. No. 228 (news of mid-Nov. 1857).

[76]Newsletters from Carnegy: For. Dept. Political, 30 Dec. 1859, Supplement No. 1137 (News of 26 Feb. 1858).

[77]Ibid., Supplement No. 1135 (News of 9 Feb. 1858).

[78]Ibid., Supplement No. 1137 (News of 23 Feb. 1858).

Chanda.[79] After the defeat at Chanda the rebels fell back on Sultanpur where they were 15,000 strong with twenty guns.[80] In the trans-Gogra region the rebels were opposing the Gurkhas: the raja of Gonda had a force of about 10,000 which included about 500 sepoys, 500 sowars and eight or ten guns.[81] At Faizabad in late February, in spite of desertions, the force pitted against the Gurkhas consisted of 20,000 levies, 100 sepoys and three guns.[82] At Alambagh, near Lucknow, Outram was attacked six times, and at times the attacking force was upwards of 30,000 men.[83] Carnegy received the following information about rebel forces in Lucknow in March:

There are 5 (5,000) or 6,000 sepoys in the 'Martiniere' and there are 30 or 35 guns in position in the neighbouring earthworks. At the Alumbagh entrenchments there are 25 or 30 guns. Ahmed Ali alias Chota Meeah, relieves the different guards daily with 200 men from every sepoy Regiment. At the Palace, 7 Regiments of Nujeebs keep watch. There are not less than 15,000 Cavalry (another account says 13,000), 13,000 old mutineers (one account says, 25,000) besides numberless new sepoys and 100 to 125 guns.[84]

The rebel force both in Lucknow and the districts had thus reached formidable proportions, indicating how widespread the base of the rebellion had become and the extent of anti-British feeling. However, despite the general mobilization in the countryside, the belligerence of the rural populace and the conflux of fighting men in Lucknow, there was a recognition on the part of the rebel leadership that the tide had turned against them. They had failed to take the Residency, stop the relief forces first under Outram and Havelock and then under Colin Campbell, and, subsequently, to defeat Outram at Alambagh. From the rest of north India came the news of one British victory after another: Delhi had fallen, by December the British had secured Kanpur and operations in the Doab had begun. The series of defeats around

[79]Carnegy to Muir, 20 Feb. 1858: For. Dept. Political, 30 Dec. 1859, Supplement, No. 1136.
[80]Newsletters from Carnegy, No. 1137 (News of 23 Feb. 1858).
[81]A.C. Plowden, Military Commissioner, Gorkha Force, to Andrew, 4 Feb. 1858: For. Dept., Political, 30 Dec. 1859, Suppl. No. 972.
[82]Newsletters from Carnegy, No. 1137 (News of 24 Feb. 1858).
[83]McLeod Innes, *The Sepoy Revolt* (London, 1897), pp. 208-9.
[84]Newsletters from Carnegy, No. 1137 (News of 5 March 1858).

The Revolt of the People

Awadh swelled the number of rebels there: they fled to Lucknow, which was still controlled by the rebels and provided a centre and a flag to which they could rally. But these defeats also meant that the net was closing round the province. The rebel leadership realized this and knew, in the light of their past record, that there was little to look forward to. In a meeting of all the chiefs in December the Begum summed up the situation thus:

Great things were promised from the all-powerful Delhie, and my heart used to be gladdened by the communications I used to receive from that city but now the King has been dispossessed and his army scattered; the English have bought over the Seikhs and Rajahs, and have established their Government West, East and South, and communications are cut off; the Nana has been vanquished; and Lucknow is endangered; what is to be done? The whole army is in Lucknow, but it is without courage. Why does it not attack the Alumbagh? Is it waiting for the English to be reinforced, and Lucknow to be surrounded? How much longer am I to pay the sepoys for doing nothing? Answer now, and if fight you won't, I shall negotiate with the English to spare my life.[85]

There is recognition here of the ineptness of the rebel army, of impending defeat, and for the first time of the possibility of a personal reconciliation on the part of a leader. The reply of the chiefs present was also telling:

Fear not we shall fight, for if we do not we shall be hanged one by one; we have this fear before our eyes.[86]

The will to fight still existed but it now derived from desperation, for there was no longer any cause to win. On the subsequent course of the rebellion would fall the intersecting shadows of a desperate fight against all possible odds and of surrender and reconciliation before a superior military power.

In the face of unbroken British successes in the field, a trickle of desertion had already started in February. There were reports of talukdars' men leaving Lucknow[87] and also of talukdars — namely Udres Singh, Umbres Singh, Madho Prasad and Kishan Prasad — deserting Mehndi Hussain.[88] Some of the Rajkumar

---

[85]Carnegy's Intelligence, For. Dept., Secret Branch, 26 Feb. 1858, No. 228 (News of 22 Dec. 1857).

[86]Ibid.

[87]Newsletters from Carnegy: For. Dept. Political, 30 Dec. 1859, Supplement No. 1135. (News of 3 Feb. 1858).

[88]Ibid. (News of 10 Feb. 1858).

chiefs also deserted when faced with the prospect of fighting the Gurkhas.[89] The most important submission and defection at this point of time was that of Man Singh. By the end of February 1858 he had separated himself from the rebels and retired to his fort in Shahganj.[90] By early March, before the fall of Lucknow, he had tendered his submission to the British.[91] Thus was created the first breach between the mass of the rebels and their leaders; Man Singh had defected but the men and sepoys under him still wanted to fight: they cursed Man Singh for refusing to oppose the British.[92]

Despite desertions and ineptitude on the part of the fighting men, Lucknow was not given up without resistance. But resistance was nowhere near what one would expect from the number of fighting men in the city. Colin Campbell began his movement towards Lucknow at the end of February and before the end of March the place was said to be free of the rebels. However the rebels did maintain a constant cannonading on the British, sometimes through the night and day; most of the palaces that were taken had to be breached and Outram's progress from Alambagh to the Chakkar Kothi was halted time and again by rebel forces. Fighting was most intense in the narrow lanes, with intermittent fire from the loopholed houses. The most severe opposition was at the Begum's palace which was surrendered only 'after an obstinate resistance by Pandy'.[93] By 16 March — i.e. within six days of Outram's capture of the Chakkar Kothi — eighty rebel guns had been captured by the British, some 3,000 rebels were dead[94] and some thousands had escaped from the city into the country.

The fall of Lucknow was followed by scenes of loot and plunder which are graphically described in Russell's *Diary*.[95] According to *The Times*, before the army left Lucknow the loot amounted to £600,000 and within a week had shot up to a million

[89]Ibid. No 1137 (News of 24 Feb. 1858).
[90]Ibid. (News of 24 Feb. 1858).
[91]G.H. MacGregor to Secy. to Govt. with Governor-General, 13 March 1858: For.Dept., Political, 30 Dec. 1859, Supplement Nos. 1388-9.
[92]Newsletters from Carnegy, No. 1137 (News of 27 Feb. 1858).
[93]This phrase is from a letter from an officer with Frank's column, 11 March 1858: quoted in Ball, *The Mutiny*, ii, p. 260.
[94]Ball, *The Mutiny*, ii, p. 256.
[95]W.H. Russell, *My Indian Mutiny Diary*, pp. 100-3.

The Revolt of the People

and a quarter sterling.[96]

The victory was also a signal for mass arrests by the British. The arrests indicate the extent of disaffection or at least the contemporary assessment thereof by British officials. Statements of trials held in March of some forty-eight people so arrested are extant[97]. Of them forty-seven were by any definition 'common people', the one exception was a zamindar from a neighbouring village who had come to see his brother in Lucknow. The range of occupations of the remaining forty-seven is significant. There were four 'native' Christians — of whom one had turned Muslim at the time of the revolt, according to one witness — who were drummers in Wajid Ali Shah's band and in two Native Regiments. There were four cultivators who were arrested either in Lucknow, where they had come for a visit, or from their fields. More interesting was the case of two beggars and a couple of fakirs who were arrested from the streets; the two beggars were described as of 'doubtful character' and regarding the two fakirs the Special Commissioner wrote, 'people of this class should not be parted with too easily'. The latter statement is evidently a reference to the role of religious men in the spread of rumours, prophecies and general anti-British sentiment. Among the arrested were also a number of tradesmen — shopkeepers, platemakers, bakers, an oil seller, a cloth merchant and a rice seller cum moneylender. Of these, the oil seller — one Sheikh Damur — was actually found with the 15th *rissala* carrying two guns, and a sword. Among the rest were two sepoys who had failed to escape from the city, a number of domestic servants, labourers, and munshis. A camel man was remanded because an 'English

---

[96]Hibbert, *Indian Mutiny*, p. 366; In a dispatch to *The Times* Russell wrote: 'There are companies which can boast of privates with thousands of pounds worth in their ranks. One man I heard of who complacently offered to lend an officer "whatever sum he wanted if he wished to buy over the captain". Others have remitted large sums to their friends. Ere this letter reaches England, many a diamond, emerald and delicate pearl will have told its tale in a very quiet pleasant way, of the storm and the sack of Kaisarbagh... Some of these officers have made, literally, their fortunes... There are certain small caskets in battered uniform cases which contain estates in Scotland and Ireland...'. Quoted in F. Engels, 'The British Army in India', Marx and Engels, *The First War of Indian Independence*, (Moscow, 3rd repr., 1968), p. 152.

[97]Weekly Statement of Prisoners tried by the Special Comm. from 22 to 27 March 1858: BROG File No. 396.

stocking' was found in his possession. This itself was considered suspicious. Four or five of those arrested were described as having no employment — a phrase which could mean that their occupation was unknown. Among them was one — Jamshid Beg — whose entire family, including his three sons, were killed in the revolt, fighting for the king of Awadh; he himself was involved in the murder of two British officers after the British entered Lucknow.

This sample, however small, does indicate the range of social groups whom the British suspected of connection with the revolt. Arrest by itself was of course no proof of complicity and might well be the result of a conquering army's avenging zeal. What is significant, however, is that to the British any and every Awadhi — tinker, tailor or soldier — could be a suspect and hence liable to arrest. The onus of proving their complicity in rebellion came later, and even then 'proofs' of guilt could be very flimsy, ranging from the possession of arms, being a sepoy of a disbanded regiment, being a beggar or a fakir without an alibi, and even possessing an 'English stocking'. And significantly, with 'native' Christians, passivity was taken as proof enough of complicity.

By March 1858 the writing that the British would ultimately win was fairly clear on the wall. But how long this would take was a moot question. They had gained a most convincing victory in Lucknow against the biggest gathering of rebel forces. They now controlled the imperial city. But control over Lucknow did not mean that the whole of Awadh had been subjugated.[98] The countryside was still armed. The Begum had set herself up in a fort across the Gogra. The talukdars were back in their forts preparing to meet the coming onslaught. The sepoys, now with no reprieve before them, were regrouping. In the follow-up of their success in Lucknow the British had failed to cut off the escape routes, so that the insurgents now swarmed into the countryside.[99]

---

[98] See Ball, *The Mutiny*, ii, pp. 282-3, and also F. Engels, 'The Revolt in India': 'The Capture of Lucknow does not carry with it the submission of Oudh'. Marx and Engels, *First War*, p. 149.

[99] M. Maclagan, *Clemency Canning* (London, 1962), pp. 174-5 argues that this was a military blunder on the part of British generals. For a contrary view that this escape of the rebels was possible because the British army immediately after the fall of Lucknow was rendered inactive by the zeal and greed for looting, and in

Campbell's hope that the pacification of Awadh would automatically follow the fall of Lucknow was thus an illusion. The British had annexed Awadh in 1856, now it remained for them to conquer it, a task that would take at least a year to accomplish, especially since the rebels were no longer in one single body. The rebellion in Awadh had definitely not sounded its last post.

The Last Phase: Episodes in Retreat

One of the first acts of the British government after the fall of Lucknow was the circulation of the celebrated Awadh Proclamation.[100] This perhaps is not the place to discuss the controversy that arose over this proclamation, first between Canning and Outram and subsequently between Canning and the Board of Control in London: Canning's biographer has dealt with such intra-administration controversies at considerable length.[101] For the rebels in Awadh the Proclamation was double-edged, with a deliberate interplay of carrot and stick. In the first instance those that 'have been steadfast in their allegiance to the British' — a total of six talukdars[102] — were rewarded with hereditary possession of their estates, subject to moderate assessment. The stick followed immediately after:

The Governor-General further proclaims to the people of Oude that with the above mentioned exceptions [i.e. the six talukdars] the proprietary right in the soil of the province is confiscated to the British Government which will dispose of that right in such manner as to it may seem fitting.

But things were not left at that. Such a sweeping act of confiscation would hardly have facilitated the re-establishment of British authority, since instead of getting talukdars to help the British it would have forced them to a prolonged and desperate resistance.[103] So a sop was offered to—

fact, for a few days had ceased to be an army at all, see Marx and Engels, *First War*, pp. 136-7 and 152.

[100] The full text of the Proclamation is available in *F.S.U.P.*, ii, pp. 328-30 in Ball, *The Mutiny*, ii, pp. 276-7 and also in Maclagan, pp. 183-5.

[101] Maclagan, Ch. 8.

[102] The six talukdars were Drigbijai Singh (raja of Balrampur), Kulwant Singh (raja of Pudnaha), Rao Hardeo Buksh (of Kutiari), Kashi Prasad (of Sissaindi), Zubr Singh (of Gopal Kher) and Chundi Lall (of Moraon).

[103] This was the opinion of Outram and the Board of Control, see Couper to

those Talookdars, Chiefs and Landholders with their followers who shall make immediate submission to the Chief Commissioner of Oude, surrendering their arms and obeying his orders, the Right Hon'ble the Governor-General promises that their lives and honour shall be safe, provided that their hands are not stained with English blood... To those amongst them who shall promptly come forward and give to the Chief Commissioner their support in the restoration of peace and order this indulgence will be large, and the Governor-General will be ready to view liberally the claims which they may thus acquire to a restitution of their former rights.

The British administration, in March 1858, was probably overestimating the strength of its position in Awadh. The offer of rewards in a proclamation would not automatically induce the talukdars to surrender. Reconciliation would in most cases be based on an assessment of the strength of the British forces in a particular neighbourhood. And such strength was nowhere near being established in Awadh in March 1858 except perhaps in the vicinity of Lucknow. As Russell noted in his diary on 3 April 1858:

At present all Oudh may be regarded as an enemy's country, for there are very few chiefs who do not still hold out, and defy the threats of the Proclamation. The capture of Lucknow has dispersed the rebels all over the country, and reinforced the hands which the rajahs and zemindars have collected around their forts.... All our machinery of government is broken and destroyed. Our revenue is collected by rebels. Our police has disappeared utterly.[104]

On the part of the rebels there was a recognition that they had suffered a crucial defeat, that the British riposte was close on them. They knew that after they had lost their stronghold in Lucknow it was no longer possible to concentrate forces in one particular place, and moreover that the British were too strong for them to attempt a head-on confrontation. Khan Bahadur Khan pointedly expressed this assessment when he formulated the strategy that the rebels should follow:

Do not attempt to meet the regular columns of the infidels, because they are superior to you in discipline and bunderbust, and have big guns; but watch their movements, guard all the ghauts on the rivers, intercept their communications, stop their supplies, cut up their daks and posts, and

Edmonstone, 8 March 1858 and Secret Letter No. 1954 from East India House, London, to Governor-General, 19 April 1858: *F.S.U.P.*, ii, pp. 332ff. and pp. 338ff.
[104]Russell, *My Indian Mutiny Diary*, p. 119.

The Revolt of the People

keep constantly hanging about their camps; give them no rest.[105]

The new strategy then was to harass the British in every possible way and not allow their administration and authority to settle down. Khan Bahadur Khan's advice was taken, for it was noted in June: 'The policy of the rebels has clearly been to harass and drive in all our Thanahs and outposts avoiding as much as possible close contact with any disciplined troops.'[106]

Around April-May 1858 the insurgents were strung out around Lucknow in various groups, all of considerable numerical strength. Table 11 shows the lay out of the main leaders and their men.

TABLE 11

Name	No. of Men	Cavalry	Guns	Where Stationed
Begum's Force	5000		5	44 miles N.E. of Lucknow in Bahraich District
Mumoo Khan	4000			North of Lucknow Nawabganj
Rana Beni Madho	10000	1000	10	Approximately 34 miles S.E. of Lucknow in Purwa and Basiwara areas
The Maulavi	10000			54 miles N.W. of Lucknow in Mohana in Khairabad
Narpat Singh	2000		6	In Royea, near Sandila in Hardoi district
Drigbijai Singh	2800		5	24 miles north of Lucknow in Mahona
Mansab Ali	1500	300	3	At Kushum Ghat on the Gomti
Loni Singh	6000		12	In Muhamdi, 88 miles west of Lucknow
Gurbux Singh	15000		4	36 miles N.E. from Lucknow near Dariabad
Madho Prashad Udit Narain	2000		4	Talukdars of Bishar in Faizabad
Udres Singh and others of Dhoras	5000		5	In Faizabad District
Ghuzuff Hussain Bagun Husain	5000		5	In Faizabad district and

[105]Quoted in ibid., p. 73.
[106]Forsyth to Edmonstone, 5 June 1858: For. Dept., Secret Cons., 30 July 1858, Cons. No. 63.

Name	No. of Men	Cavalry	Guns	Where Stationed
Abbas Ali	500		2	their following included a large number of small talukdars and zamindars, chiefly Rajputs In Tanda, also supplied a strong contingent to Mahomed Husain
Mahomed Husain	5000		4	In Faizabad — has the support of a large number of small Rajput chiefs
Jai Lal Singh Beni Madho of Atraulia	2000		3	In the district of Faizabad
Devi Bux Singh of Gonda	4000		7	In Gonda district
Unnamed rebels	700			Near Nawabganj and Barabanki about 20 miles North of Lucknow
Unnamed rebels	300		3	
Unnamed rebels	1000		2	32 miles N.E. of Lucknow
Unnamed rebels	3000		2	32 miles N.E. of Lucknow

SOURCE: Statement of Faizabad Rebels: For. Dept. Political, 30 Dec. 1859, Supplement No. 951; Summary of Intelligence, 29 May 1858: For Dept. Secret Cons., 25 June 1858, No. 57.

The rebels skirted Lucknow on all sides at a distance of about fifty odd miles, avoiding any kind of direct confrontation. However it is important to note that the table lists their dispositions at a specific time, and that their numbers were liable to vary. Also every British advance outside of Lucknow in Awadh and every British victory outside Awadh added to the numbers of the rebels. It was reported in May that 'some of thousands of rebels, horse and foot, with eight guns, in three divisions' had crossed into Awadh.[107] The news of a British victory near Muhamdi drove 'the insurgents partly to the North and partly to the East where they will endeavour to join the Begam and Beni Madho'.[108]

No post set up by the British had any kind of security; they were always open to sudden raids. The tahsildar of Goshainganj, a

[107] Judge of Fatehpur to the Secretary to the Government with the Governor-General, 30 May 1858: Inclosure 11 in No. 17, *Further Papers* (No. 8), p. 164, *Papers Relating to Indian Mutinies.*
[108] Forsyth to Edmonstone, 5 June 1858.

stone's throw from Lucknow, had to retreat from his position because of such raids. He reported 'that rebels were collecting in groups of two and three thousand men . . . headed by Bainee Madho and Moosahib Allee Chowdree. . .'[109] Similarly, the tahsildars of Bangarmau and Sandila had to evacuate their posts after rebel forays. The police force at Bilgram and Rasulabad mutinied and went over to the rebels.[110] The country was being scoured by bands of armed sepoys and sowars.[111] Just north of Lucknow the main architect of these raids was Raja Drigbijai Singh of Mahona. From April 1858 he gave no rest to the British and their allies. On 8 May, with a force of 4,000 men, he destroyed the entrenchments at Mahona; the next day he plundered carts carrying provisions to Lucknow. By the end of the month he had set up his own *thanas* (outposts) in a dozen villages and was collecting revenue from them in defiance of British orders. June saw further developments, for he 'destroyed the Thanah of Talab Buxee, burnt it and appointed his own Tehseeldar and insisted on the Zemindars presenting themselves to him, also collected the Revenue and prevented provisions from being brought into Lucknow'.[112]

Not only the large talukdars were defying British orders and authority. Even within ten to fifteen miles of Lucknow small zamindars were setting up fortifications and entrenchments with a strength of a few hundreds of men and four to five guns.[113] This is an indication not only of the strength of anti-British feeling in Awadh but also of the weakness of the British position in the first few months after their recapture of Lucknow. Again, not all British efforts to defeat or imprison recalcitrant talukdars met with success at this stage of the operation. Narpat Singh with twenty-two guns inside his extremely strong fort quite surprised Walpole's force with his resistance. He escaped with his men and

[109]S.N. Martin, Dep. Commr. to G. Campbell, Judicial Commr. Oudh, 19 April 1858: BROG File No. 561.
[110]Forsyth to Edmonstone, 5 June 1858.
[111]Martin to Abbott, 17 May 1858: Trial Proceedings, Govt. vs. Raja Drigbijai Singh, Lucknow Chief Court Mutiny *Basta*, F.S.U.P., ii, p. 387.
[112]Extracts from Deputy Commissioner, Lucknow, respecting Raja Drigbijai Singh: Trial Proceedings, Govt. vs. Raja Drigbijai Singh, Lucknow Chief Court Mutiny *Basta*, F.S.U.P., ii, pp. 380ff.
[113]Diary of D.A.V. Thorburn, entry of 12 April 1858: BROG File No. 396.

lived to fight again. This emboldened other talukdars.[114] Drigbijai Singh followed up by sacking the British thana at Mahona,[115] and Loni Singh prepared himself to fight with 12,000 men in his fort at Mithauli.[116]

To the south, in the district of Unao, the Lucknow-Kanpur road marked a clear demarcation between rebel territory and what the British controlled:

South of it [i.e. the Lucknow-Kanpur road] as yet our authority extends but a very little distance. The whole of the Poorwah tuhseel comprising the Poorwah and Morawa Pergunnahs, is in the hands of the enemy, the former pergunnah being held by Baboo Davee Buksh and the latter by Rugbur Singh of Mowai and Oomrao Sing of Kanta. They have collected . . . the whole year's revenue from most of the villages, . . . Davee Buksh has about 2000 men and 3 guns at Poorwah. . .

The whole of the Bhugwant Nugger Tuhseel is in the hands of Baboo Ram Buksh . . and Seorutton Sing of Pathun Behar. . . He [Ram Buksh] has . . . collected his revenue in full. He has been repairing and strengthening his fort at Dhondia Khera and hopes to be supported by the other Bais Talookdars. . .

The Oonam-Hurha Tuhseel is partly in our hands; the Oonam Pergunnah and the northern part of Hurha Pergunnah wholly so. Kalka Persad Kanoongo and Thakoor Sing of Atchulgunge hold the remainder, being about 2/3 of Hurha Pergunnah. . .

The Rusoolabad Tuhseel north of the road is wholly in our hands, excepting Futtehpoor Chowrasie, which is debatable ground. . .[117]

The Lucknow-Kanpur road itself was in danger of being attacked by Beni Madho who was hovering in the neighbourhood.[118] Beni Madho was very much the focus of the resistance to the south-east of Lucknow. He had orders from Birjis Qadr to collect—

an army of Gohars, royal servants, Taluqadars and of others in Baiswara

[114]McLeod Innes, *The Sepoy Revolt*, p. 250.
[115]Translation of petition of Hurssokh Roy, tahsildar of Kursi: Trial Proceedings, Govt. vs. Raja Drigbijai Singh, Lucknow Chief Court Mutiny *Basta: F.S.U.P.*, ii, p. 390.
[116]News of Khairabad and Sitapur from Jhau Lal, Akbar Nawis, to Capt. Orr, 18 April 1858: Lucknow Chief Court Mutiny *Basta: F.S.U.P.*, ii, p. 416.
[117]Evans, Dep. Commr. of Poorwah, to Couper, 31 March 1858: For. Dept. Secret Cons. 28 May 1858, Cons. No. 417.
[118]Forsyth to Edmonstone, 29 May 1858: For. Dept., Secret Cons. 25 June 1858, Cons. No. 56.

The Revolt of the People

and for keeping them ready. In accordance with his royal order I have collected an army of about 10,000 footsoldiers and horsemen of the troops of the Government and of the Taluqadars in Baiswara.[119]

Beni Madho's soldiers were absolutely faithful and prepared for a fight unto death,[120] and they scouted around the countryside keeping a lookout on British troops and movements.[121] In May their leader exulted over a 'crowning victory' he had won over the British.[122]

The British themselves appear to have been in two minds about their own position in April and May 1858. Capt. Barrow, in charge of settlement operations, wrote enthusiastically on 22 May 1858 about the 'great progress' being made in settlement and in the surrender/reconciliation of talukdars.[123] However, on the same date, Forsyth, Secretary to the Chief Commissioner, was writing in his official despatch to the government of India:

The Governor-General's Proclamation to Talookdars and zemindars had been extensively circulated but no landholder of any rank or from any distance save a few petty men in the immediate neighbourhood of Lucknow had come in. . .[124]

British progress in re-establishing authority in Awadh can be gauged from the number of thanas (with the number of men in each) that they had been able to establish in Awadh. Table 12 shows the position.

In the whole of Awadh, outside the city of Lucknow and apart

---

[119]Rana Beni Madho to Peshwa Rao Saheb, Rai Bareli Collectorate Mutiny *Basta: F.S.U.P.*, ii, p. 395. This letter is not dated but it was probably written some time in April 1858. This is evident from the following passage: 'The battle in the Capital city has been lost and the town has been completely vacated. The King has left Lucknow and reached Bahraich.'

[120]As one of them wrote to him 'We are faithful and ready to sacrifice our lives'. Letter from Shankar Lall, Commander of the Shankar Jang Paltan to Beni Madho, 18 Shawwal 1274 A.H. (1 June 1858), Rae Bareli Collectorate Mutiny *Basta, F.S.U.P.*, ii, p. 393.

[121]Ibid.

[122]Rana Beni Madho to Bala Saheb, 6 Shawwal 1274 A.H. (20 May 1858), Rae Bareli Collectorate Mutiny *Basta, F.S.U.P.*, ii, pp. 392-3. It is not possible to place where he had won his victory.

[123]Memo of Capt. L. Barrow, 22 May 1858: For. Dept. Secret Cons. 25 June 1858, Cons. No. 67.

[124]Forsyth to Edmonstone, 22 May 1858: For. Dept. Secret Cons. 25 June 1858, Cons. No. 52.

TABLE 12

Name of District	Tahsil	Thana	No. of Men
Purwa	Saffipur	Futtehpur Chowrasi	30
		Saffipur	30
		Meanganj	30
		2 chowkies	16
	Rasulabad	Rasulabad	200
		Purria	155
		Secunderpur	50
		2 chowkies	30
	Unao	Unao	80
		Harha	300
		Bithur	160
		Bashirganj	184
		chowkies	165
	Nawabganj	Nawabganj	270
		Mohan	68
		Kusorya	70
		Kantha	70
		Sissondi	50
		Purwa	200
Lucknow	Goshainganj	Goshainganj	111
		Arjunganj	12
	Nawabganj	Nawabganj	112
		Chinhat	43
		Murreaon	58
	Lucknow	Chillawan	108
		Kakori	110
	Kursi	Bakshi Talao	35
		Kursi	112
Mullaon	Malliabad	Malliabad	103
		1 chowki	22
		Rahimabad	107
		Ouras	52
	Sandila	Natowa	48
	Mullaon	Bangar Mau	108
	Khyayupur	Khyayupur	51
		Bilgram	108
		1 chowki	49
	Sundiaon	Gopa Mau	54
		Sundiaon	54
		Baurun	54
	Bangur	Lursa	54
Dariabad	Dariabad	Nigoha	91
		Hussainganj	51
		Sidhour	105

The Revolt of the People

Name of District	Tahsil	Thana	No. of Men
		Dariabad	150
	Hydurgarh	Hydurgarh	57
		Radauli	37
Sitapur	Bari	Bari	67
	Biswan	Biswan	33
Salon	Jais	Jais	99
		Mohanganj	55

Total Number of Men 4409
Total Number of Thanas 47

SOURCE: Statement showing thanas and tahsils established in Oude, 22 May 1858: For. Dept.Secret Consultation, 25 June 1858, No. 54.

from military troops, the British had been able to establish forty-seven thanas and a few odd chowkies, and to recruit a total of about 4,500 men who were willing actively to help the British. The pace of operations had been fairly slow — all this had taken a little over two months. And British authority was both geographically constricted and insecure. By early June, many of the posts had to be abandoned:

> Our position at the end of this week is strictly thus: We hold the Lucknow district and the line of road to Cawnpore. Most of our other posts have been abandoned. Towards the North we have a small but efficient force stationed at Chinhut. . . . Throughout the country of Oudh the rebels are complete masters and harass all the followers of the British.[125]

By the middle of June the situation had further worsened. Purwa had to be entirely given up by the British and was immediately re-occupied by the rebels.[126] Mehndi Hussain remained in occupation of Ajadhya and Faizabad, and to the west of Lucknow Narpat Singh was back in his fort at Reoya. This he restored and replenished, and 'joining the Maulvi and Feroze Shah a Delhie prince they have the whole country to within a few miles of the Cawnpore road in their possession'. The last British post to the west was at Malhiabad.[127] Towards the immediate north of Luck-

---

[125]Forsyth to Edmonstone, 5 June 1858: For. Dept. Secret Cons. 30 July 1858, Cons. No. 63.

[126]Forsyth to Edmonstone, 12 June 1858: For. Dept. Secret Cons. 30 July 1858, Cons. No. 70.

[127]Ibid.

now 'a large concourse of sepoys and rebel Rajas' had gathered. They were supposed to join Beni Madho in a co-ordinated attack on Lucknow on 2 June. The rebels took up a position at Nawabganj with 9,000 infantry and cavalry and thirteen guns. But their action was foiled by General Hope Grant cutting off Beni Madho

TABLE 13

Name of Talukdar	Residence	Remarks
Man Singh	Shahganj	Sent Vakil
Madho Singh	Amethi	,,
Rani of Tulsipur	Tulsipur	,,
Raghunath Singh	Tuleray	,,
Basant Singh	Surpahah	,,
Sandarshan Singh	Chandapur	,,
Sheer Bahadur Singh	Duloli	,,
Shankar Singh	Tiloi	Wrote
Maipal Singh	Bari	,,
Shankar Singh	Shahmow	,,
Digbijai Singh	Morarmow	,,
Hanwant Singh	Kalakankur	,,
Ramgolam Singh	Attayah	,,
Seoram Singh	Kitori	,,
Rustam Sah	Derah	,,
Mahesh Narain		
Bijnor Singh	In Sultanpur	,,
Ranjit Singh		
Jaganath Buksh	Simri	,,
Sardar Singh	Chandamah	,,

The following either personally met British officers or were thought to be favourable to British authority:

Hadut Ali Khan	Malhiabad
Bakiral	Rahimabad
Hasu Beg	,,
Fateh Chand	Purwa
Ratan Lall	Hatowrah
Hindpal Singh	Kousilobi
Bisheshur Baksh	Sumrote

SOURCE: BROG File No. 396 and Capt. Barrow's Memo on 20 April 1858: For. Dept. Secret Cons. 25 June 1858, Cons., No. 66.

The Revolt of the People

and then by the defeat of the rebels at Nawabganj on 12 June.[128]

Talukdars willing to respond to the proclamation and submit to the British were few; but they did exist. Table 13 shows the list of talukdars who (around April 1858) had sent in their allegiance either in person, through a *vakil* (agent) or in writing. Most talukdars who were willing to tender their allegiance in Lucknow could not do so because the roads and countryside were infested with rebel bands.[129]

One officer very pertinently noted the dilemmas of the potentially submissive talukdar:

... when they see that to proclaim themselves on the side of the British Government without being prepared for the consequences, is to subject them to the immediate attacks of the rebels, the best affected amongst them are obliged to dissimulate.[130]

Consequently there was a shift of emphasis in the expectations from talukdars:

... in the present state of military affairs, the Chief Commissioner finds it impossible to protect the friendly zemindars from the insults and attacks of the rebels, who now direct all their vengeance against the well wishers of the Government.

The Chief Commissioner therefore modifies for a time his expectation of active aid from isolated zemindars. ... He still expects all those who are well affected to the British Government to give some sign of their allegiance.

This can be done by coming in or sending an agent to the nearest civil authority.[131]

This policy statement recognizes that the British were unable, in

---

[128]Forsyth to Edmonstone, 5 June 1858; and also Forsyth to Edmonstone 19 June 1858: For. Dept. Secret Cons. 30 July 1858, Cons. Nos. 63 and 82 respectively.

[129]See Carnegy to Edmonstone, 16 April 1858: 'When recommended to go [to Lucknow] the Talookdars invariably plead the bad state of the country and the dangerous state of the road infested as it is by large parties of rebels'. For. Dept., Secret Cons. 28 May 1858, Cons. No. 408; also see Memo by Capt. Barrow, 22 May 1858: 'It is not distance but a general insecure feeling, whilst so many armed bands are abroad that prevents men leaving their homes'. For. Dept. Secret Cons. 25 June 1858, Cons. No. 67.

[130]Forsyth to Edmonstone, 12 June 1858: For. Dept. Secret Cons. 30 July 1858, Cons. No. 70.

[131]Memo by R Montgommery, n.d., For. Dept. Secret Cons. 30 July 1858, Cons. No. 71. This memo was probably written around the beginning of June because Forsyth's letter of 12 June (above) forwards it.

the given situation, to offer protection, and also that instances of talukdars willing to offer allegiance were 'isolated'. Both are admissions of the weakness of the British position, or, put differently, indicators of how strong and generalized rebellion was in the Awadh countryside.

The act of sending in a vakil or writing to the Chief Commissioner did not guarantee the loyalty or the allegiance of the talukdars. Quite often there was an element of duplicity involved, an attempt to play off both ends against the middle. Some large talukdars tendered their allegiance in writing and carried on fighting the British. Even Beni Madho sent in his letter of allegiance saying 'he will always obey those who are in power',[132] but he never stopped opposing the British. Lal Madho Singh also carried on opposing the British and Hanwant Singh wrote letters 'full of affection to British Government'[133] and even paid revenue;[134] but these acts did not hinder his firing on a British steamer, for which he received a *khilat* from Fazl Azim, the nazim of Salon.[135] Loyalty and opposition, at this stage of the rebellion, could not always be seen in clear black and white.

The rebels' attitude towards talukdars who actively remained loyal to the British was one of sheer vengeance. They sought to put on as much pressure as they could or to destroy such talukdars and their wealth. The best instance of this is their attitude towards Man Singh. The Begum confiscated Man Singh's estate by a proclamation and proceeded to settle it with other claimants.[136] Man Singh himself, described his plight thus:

I received orders from Major-General Outram to put the Goorkhas across the river and I accordingly expelled the rebels from Oudh and Fyzabad and gathered 200 boats at the Ghat and prepared supplies all through my ilaqa.... I kept up the Oudh ferry, in order that the Bilwa rebels might

[132]Memo of Capt. Barrow, 22 May 1858: For. Dept. Secret Cons. 25 June 1858, Cons. No. 66.

[133]List of Talukdars who have sent in Vakils etc., 19 April 1858: BROG File No. 396.

[134]Forsyth to Edmonstone, 12 June 1858: For. Dept. Secret Cons. 30 July 1858: Cons. No. 70.

[135]Forsyth to Edmonstone, 1 Oct. 1858: For. Dept. Political Proc. 22 Oct. 1858, No. 262; also 7 Aug. 1858: For. Dept. Secret Cons. 27 Aug. 1858, Cons. No. 37.

[136]Forbes to Secy. of Chief Commissioner, 24 July 1858: For. Dept. Secret Cons. 27 Aug. 1858, Cons. No. 36.

not be able to reach Bustee. It happened . . . that these Bilwa rebels wrote to the Begum complaining. . . . They procured (from her) orders to all zemindars, Talooqdars and mutineers to join them and made preparations for my ruin so far that about a week ago all the Talooqdars from Gonda-Bahraitch, Buttanpore [sic] collected to the number of 30,000 and 40,000 men and crossing by other ferries arrived near Shahganj. . . . The rebels first invested my thana of Bindowlee. . . . Mehndee Hussain's men brought 25 boats from Tanda . . . and about 1,000 rebels crossed the river. . . . Then Mehndee Hussain himself joined these from Tanda. Orders were issued to all the Talookdars by the Begum for aiding Mehndee Hussain. Talookdars of Budhapur, Peerpur and Lummipoor and others are gradually coming in to his assistance in compliance with the order . . . in consequence of my being known as the well-wisher of the British Government all the Talookdars have become my enemies and wish my destruction. They intend soon to besiege Shahgunge . . . Raja Debi Buksh Sing and Gujadhur Captain accompanied by Mutineer sepoys and sowars have crossed the river . . . Wazeer Ally Bhuttee appointed by the Begum as the 'Moonsurrum' of Durriabad is also with the Raja. Now I do not know what to do. . . there being enemies on two sides of me. The receipt of the Begum's order . . . has changed the minds of all both high and low and every one is elated with pride. . . My mokuddums too have already and are every day turning from me.[137]

Man Singh abjectly pleaded for British help — but in vain since they were in no position to enter Faizabad.[138] The rebels besieged him in his fort and pressed him to sue for terms. The price demanded for immunity from further molestation was 'the gift of 3 lakhs of Rupees to the Begum, 4 months pay to the rebels, 15 guns and his personal presence with the Army'.[139] Man Singh was quite willing to buy his way out, but he was not willing to risk the last clause.[140] The war that ensued began with the burning of Man Singh's villages but soon became a full scale onslaught with Man Singh and his men inside the fort and the rebels trying to breach it. Operations lasted more than a month and a half, and over a thousand lives were lost.[141] The British were apprehensive

[137]Man Singh to Chief Commissioner, n.d. and Petition of Rajah Maun Singh, 26 May 1858: For. Dept. Secret Cons. 30 July 1858, Cons. Nos. 72 and 65, respectively.
[138]Forbes to Secy. to Chief Commissioner, 3 July 1858: For. Dept. Secret Cons. 27 Aug. 1858, Cons. No. 27.
[139]Forsyth to Edmonstone 3 July 1858: For. Dept. Secret Cons. 30 July 1858, Cons. No. 89.
[140]Ibid.
[141]A day-to-day account of the battle was prepared by a munshi in the employ of

that they would lose Shahganj together with its eight or ten lakhs of revenue.[142] But the old fort was strong enough and the rebels had to disperse because of the news that British troops were making tracks into Faizabad.[143]

The raja of Tiloi was similarly invested by the rebels for twenty-six days and the British were unable to help their loyal ally. Describing his plight, the raja squarely blamed the British:

No answers have been received to my urzees and I feel in great dismay, like a fish out of water, twisting round in distraction. The fight has now gone in Tiloe for 26 days. . . . I have received no help from you. . . . The rebels after a lengthened siege have employed Raja Sheo Darshan Singh to treat with me and have called on me to pay revenue according to the rate of 1262 and to promise and swear never to treat with or hold any communication with the English and to call on me to aid them in fighting the English . . . the enemy are systematically burning every hamlet, village, ganj and bazar in my territory, and plunder every person in it, reducing me to the depth of distress.

I shall now perish. The whole country is against my life, and no one helps me. . . . Your name is the cause of all my misery.[144]

Forced by circumstances the raja had to sue for terms with Fazl Azim, the nazim of Salon.[145] Rustam Sah of Dera in Sultanpur, the other staunch supporter of the British, also had his estate confiscated by orders from the Begum.[146] His ilaqa was also plundered by rebel talukdars who sought revenge because Rustam Sah had waited upon General MacGregor and facilitated the movement of British reinforcements.[147] The estates of some other talukdars willing to favour the British were similarly plundered.[148] Even the

Man Singh. For. Dept. Cons. 27 Aug. 1858, Cons. No. 39.

[142]Forbes to Sec. to C.C., 3 July 1858.

[143]A British relief force was sent off to Shahganj on or before 24 July 1858, Forbes to C.C., 25 July 1858: For. Dept. Secret Cons. 27 Aug. 1858, Cons. No. 36. There is no reason to believe that the rebels did not know of such movements on the part of the British. On the contrary, given the efficiency of the grapevine, there is every reason to conclude that they did and wanted to avoid a confrontation with the British force and so dispersed from Shahganj around 26 July.

[144]Tiloi Raja to Barrow, 27 June 1858: For Dept. Secret Cons. 30 July 1858, Cons. No. 91.

[145]Ibid.

[146]Forbes to Secy to the C.C., 24 July 1858.

[147]Carnegy to Bowring, 31 March 1858: For Dept. Secret Cons. 28 May 1858, Cons. No. 397.

[148]See for example Translation of a letter from Rajah Indur Bikram Singh to Barrow, 2 July 1858: For Dept. Political Cons. 3 Sept. 1858, Cons. No. 84.

raja of Balrampur, Britain's strongest ally in Awadh, was threatened by the Begum in co-operation with talukdars, the Nana, and a force of 12,000 men.[149] The once-recalcitrant talukdar realized after the fall of Lucknow that the days of the rebellion were numbered and wanted to win favour with the British. But he was frightened because even in the middle of 1858 the British could not protect their allies, and was therefore in a quandary. His predicament was summed up rather eloquently by the raja of Amethi:

Every soul likes to preserve his life and honour, and just now the war is going on between the King's government and the British Government. Every one can see that the King's Government army, never has, and never can overcome the British army, but all the people are getting ruined and destroyed while victory still remains undecided, for the King's army destroys all the friends of the British and the servants of the British Government destroy all who remain quiet, considering them enemies; in fact the people are ruined in every way.

Maun Sing and the Tiloe Rajah have been ruined by the enemy and I beg you will consider what we are to do when the Government does not protect its own friends. This is the reason, the friends to the British Government hang back from sending in their allegiance to the British Government. We cannot resist or disobey the Government. . . . If Government will not help us, we perish for nothing. . . . I earnestly wish to present myself before some British officer as a loyal subject . . . but I dare not for fear of consequences.[150]

This fear of reprisals from the rebels not only kept men like Lal Madho Singh and those of his ilk from submitting to the British but also often forced them to return to the fold of rebellion.

In a sense, perhaps, this turning upon loyal talukdars by the rebels was a symptom of disarray, of a growing awareness among the rebels that faced against a superior well-organized military force their side was falling apart. But the rebellion still mustered considerable strength of numbers and maintained large though dispersed pockets of resistance. The enclaves of resistance were concentrated in the south and south-east of Lucknow, in areas roughly corresponding to the districts of Unao, Rae Bareli, Sultanpur, Partapgarh and Faizabad; west and north-west of Luck-

---

[149]Forsyth to Edmonstone, 24 July 1858, For Dept. Secret Cons. 27 Aug. 1858, Cons. No. 33.

[150]Raja Lal Madho Singh to Barrow, 22 June 1858: For. Dept. Secret Cons. 30 July 1858, Cons. No. 90.

now (in Muhamdi and Sitapur) and in the far-flung north in Gonda-Bahraich.

To the south the major figure in the resistance was Beni Madho. As the British columns entered Sultanpur and Faizabad around August 1858, Beni Madho set about preparing to oppose them, collecting his forces in the directions of Partapgarh and Sultanpur. Forsyth commented that, 'Benee Madho has a large force estimated at 25,000 men and 28 guns, scattered all over Salone District and he is constantly moving about'.[151] He was so swift of foot that he was able to strategically spread out his force: in July he left five of his guns with Ram Baksh, and five spread all over Baiswara, and with the other seven marched towards Rae Bareli, changed his plan and marched towards Salon via his fort in Shankarpur.[152] His followers were willing to encounter the British, sometimes even without his leadership. They fought the British troops at a place called Jabraoli in Baiswara.[153] Beni Madho himself fought Lieutenant Chamberlain and Major Bulwer in the vicinity of Purwa. He had about 10,000 men with him and was repulsed after five hours of fighting.[154]

There was an attempt on the part of the talukdars of southern Awadh to make a united effort to rekindle the dying embers of revolt. The talukdars of Nain, of Atcha (in Partapgarh), Lal Madho Singh of Amethi and even Hanwant Singh agreed to join the cause.[155] In fact the raja of Amethi issued a call to all the talukdars of Baiswara to oppose the British columns.[156] Lal Madho Singh made strenuous efforts to keep together the large rebel force, consisting of 6,700 sepoys, 8,900, levies 1,500 cavalry and 11 guns, that had gathered in Sultanpur to meet the British

---

[151] Forsyth to Edmonstone, 23 Oct. 1858: For. Dept. Political Cons. 12 Nov. 1858, Cons. No. 195.

[152] See Forsyth to Edmonstone, 24 July 1858, 31 July 1858 and 7 Aug. 1858: For. Dept. Secret Cons. 27 Aug. 1858, Cons. Nos. 33, 35 and 37. Also see Forsyth to Edmonstone, 28 Aug. 1858: For. Dept. Political Cons. 17 Sept. 1858, Cons. No. 120.

[153] Salar of Shankar Jang Paltan to Rana Saheb, 16th Rabiul Awwal 1275 A.H. (25th Oct 1858), Rae Bareli Collectorate Mutiny *Basta: F.S.U.P.*, ii, pp. 466-7.

[154] Forsyth to Edmonstone, 30 Oct. 1858: For. Dept. Political Cons. 12 Nov. 1858, Cons. No. 196.

[155] Forsyth to Edmonstone, 7 Aug. 1858: For. Dept. Secret Cons. 27 Aug. 1858, Cons. No. 37.

[156] Telegram from Edmonstone to Reade, 22 Aug. 1858: *F.S.U.P.*, ii, p. 464.

army.¹⁵⁷ However, Sultanpur fell on 13 August and many talukdars and zamindars submitted. Lal Madho Singh remained refractory and with the other rebels, fell back on his fort.¹⁵⁸

Just before the onset of Lord Clyde's final campaign in Awadh, the situation in the south and south-eastern theatre of the province was roughly thus: Baiswara remained largely unsubdued with Beni Madho intermittently threatening the British, his activities foreboding a stiff resistance.¹⁵⁹ Lal Madho Singh held out in Amethi, refusing to come to terms; Partapgarh was still very much under rebel influence. In Unao and Dariabad things were still on a see-saw, though the British had a definite edge.¹⁶⁰ Faizabad, after the withdrawal of the rebel siege on Shahganj and the arrival of the British reinforcements, was practically clear of the rebels.¹⁶¹ As the British columns had marched into the region, more talukdars recognizing their inability to oppose the British military juggernaut and also quick to perceive the rewards of submission had laid down their cudgels.¹⁶² Battles had been won, but the denouement was yet to be.

In the west and north-west Narpat Singh had repaired his fort gathered his forces again, and—

¹⁵⁷Forsyth to Edmonstone, 21 Aug. 1858: For. Dept. Political Cons. 17 Sept. 1858, Cons. No. 119.

¹⁵⁸Forsyth to Edmonstone, 18 Sept. 1858; For. Dept. Political Cons. 8 Oct. 1858, Cons. No. 196 and Forsyth to Edmonstone, 23 Oct. 1858: For. Dept. Political Cons. 12 Nov. 1858, Cons. No. 195.

¹⁵⁹'in Baiswara . . . a vigorous stand may be expected', so Forsyth to Edmonstone, 7 Aug. 1858: For. Dept. Secret Cons. 27 Aug. 1858, Cons. No. 37.

¹⁶⁰Dariabad became clear enough of the rebels by end July 1858 to admit to British civil administration (Forsyth to Edmonstone, 31 July 1858, For. Dept. Secret Cons. 27 Aug. 1858, Cons. No. 35), but in October the rebels were back 1,200 strong with two guns, led by Abid Khan, and had to be repulsed. Forsyth to Edmonstone, 9 Oct. 1858: For. Dept. Political Cons. 22 Oct. 1858, Cons. No. 267. For Unao see Forsyth to Edmonstone, 14 Aug. 1858: For. Dept. Secret Cons. 27 Aug. 1858, Cons. No. 40.

¹⁶¹Forsyth to Edmonstone, 7 and 14 Aug. 1858.

¹⁶²For example, with the advance of British forces Udres Singh of Miapur 'one of the largest and most powerful zemindars of the Dist. (Fyzabad) came in and offered his submission'. Forsyth to Edmonstone, 24 July 1858, For. Dept. Secret Cons., 27 Aug. 1858, Cons. No. 33. After the occupation of Faizabad Mullick Tuffzul Hussain of Dimampur, Raja Abbas Ali of Tanda and Raja Hussain Ali of Hussunpur, all opponents of the British submitted. Forsyth to Edmonstone, 7 Aug. 1858.

assumed offensive operations far greater than he ever before attempted . . attacked Sandeela and is looked upon throughout that part of the country as the Chief leader of the rebels. . . . Narpat Singh stands in the way of peace and the zemindars who had showed a desire to submit have been intimidated and maltreated by Narpat Singh.[163]

Raja Drigbijai Singh still continued his activities around the region of Bakshi-ki-Talao in the immediate north-west of Lucknow. In the immediate north of Lucknow, Abdul Wali Khan and Khoda Baksh were appointed collectors by the Begum and they kept the British constantly under threat in the country around Dewa and Mahona, twenty-six miles north of Lucknow.[164] Throughout August and September the Mullaon district was scoured by Prince Feroze Shah who had about three thousand men and five guns with him. In August they were repulsed from Sandila after two and a half hours fighting, but still remained strong in the district.[165] But a large number of talukdars and zamindars in Mullaon had submitted with the initial thrust of the British forces. The most notable were Hashmat Ali, Bhopal Singh, Baml Singh, and Mahomed Ashraf. According to one count fifty-six talukdars had been settled with in Mullaon.[166]

However, further to the north things were completely outside British control:

The District of Mohomdee and the North of Seetapoor District are so entirely in the hands of the rebels that anything like general communication with the inhabitants of those districts is impracticable and I learn . . . that . . . no influences but that of an army can at present operate in our favour in that direction, the rebels there under Hurpershad chukladar being free from the pressure of the immediate proximity of British Troops have more power and the well-affected see no alternative but to yield. . .[167]

[163]Forsyth to Edmonstone, 3 July 1858: For. Dept. Secret Cons. 30 July 1858, Cons. No. 79.

[164]Forsyth to Edmonstone, 9 Oct. 1858: For. Dept. Political Cons. 22 Oct. 1858, Cons. No. 267.

[165]Forsyth to Edmonstone, 18 Sept. 1858: For. Dept. Political Cons. 8 Oct. 1858, Cons. No. 196; and also Telegram from Edmonstone to Reade, 15 Aug. 1858: F.S.U.P., ii, p. 487.

[166]Forsyth to Edmonstone, 17 July 1858: For. Dept. Secret Cons. 27 Aug. 1858, Cons. No. 30.

[167]J. Clarke, Commissioner Khairabad Division to Forsyth, 18 Aug. 1858: For. Dept. Political Cons 17 Sept. 1858, Cons. No. 121.

These districts being adjacent to Rohilkhand, the rebels from there spilled over. The rebel leaders in the region, and their strength around August, is set out in Table 14.

TABLE 14

Name	Stationed at	Strength
Khan Ali Khan	Naurangabad (near Muhamdi)	8,000 cavalry, 4,000 sepoys 3,000 matchlockmen and 15 guns
Khan Bahadur Khan	Pipri (near Naurangabad)	2,000 cavalry, 2,000 sepoys and 11 guns
Wilayat Shah	Alipur (near Mithauli)	600 cavalry, 400 sepoys and 3 guns
Qazi (a rebel tahsildar)	Haidarabad (in Kheri District)	100 cavalry, 800 or 900 sepoys and 3 guns
Loni Singh	Mithauli	100 cavalry, 4000 matchlockmen and 19 guns
Namadar Khan	Berpara (near Sandila)	100 cavalry, 400 sepoys and 1 gun at least
Gulab Singh Chandrika Buksh Lakkar Shah Jat Bahadur Raja Parbandawala	Fort Purwa (near Sandila)	3,000 matchlockmen and sepoys and 11 guns
Baldeo Singh	Deorhi (near Sandila)	300 matchlockmen and 2 guns

SOURCE: Newsletter from Munna Lall Pandey to Capt. A. Orr, 4 Sept., 1858: Lucknow Chief Court Mutiny *Basta: F.S.U.P.*, ii, pp. 492ff.

Apart from this force there was a host of petty leaders with bands of men ranging from 100 to 1,000 in number, and a few guns, scattered all over Muhamdi and Sitapur.[168]

The trans-Gogra region was the territory where the Begum operated. The whole of Gonda and Bahraich remained completely outside British influence and control till late in the year. The rajas of Gonda and Churda remained with the Begum, and she was also supported by the Nana and Bala Rao who had moved in from Kanpur. The British anticipated, quite logically, that once their columns had covered southern and central Awadh the

---

[168] Newsletter form Baldeo Bux, 17 Oct. 1858: Lucknow Chief Court Mutiny *Basta: F.S.U.P.*, ii, pp. 511ff.

rebels would move northwards, and that this area would then become the main arena of conflict.[169] The Begum was ensconced in the fort of Baundi (Bahraich district), strongly supported by the rajas of Churda and Payagpur. Her army and following were considerable:

> ... a force is encamped on all sides of the Fort, numbering about 15 or 16,000 including followers. Among these, there are 1,500 cavalry and 500 mutineer sepoys, the rest are nujeebs and followers. There are also about 60 or 70 shutre sowars [soldiers on camels]... and 17 guns; 13 are outside the Fort of which only 5 are large...[170]

The Begum issued orders for the plunder of 'loyal' (i.e. to the British) talukdars.[171] Even in this stage of nearly total disarray the Begum's camp functioned as the headquarters of rebel activities. Often major plans of attack and defence were made here and then circulated. For example, in late September plans were drawn up for a co-ordinated movement of rebel forces throughout Awadh and northern and eastern Rohilkhand. These plans are of considerable significance[172] for they show that even in the face of almost certain defeat there was enough life in the rebellion to generate detailed schemes of co-ordinated and sustained resistance. Given the presence of the British army in Lucknow and Faizabad their implementation was of course enormously difficult. Yet the entire conception was by no means pure fantasy. According to a British despatch 'many of the movements have been made and foiled'.[173] It was as a result of these plans that the British encounter with Beni Madho at Purwa took place.[174] Also similar in origin was Harprashad's crossing of the Gomati early in October with 12,000 men and twelve guns; strengthened by the adhesion of several zamindars he attacked Sandila and took partial possession of the

---

[169] '... in this corner of Awadh [i.e. Bahraich Division] the greatest resistance may be expected': so Forsyth to Edmonstone, 17 July 1858, For. Dept. Secret Cons. 27 Aug. 1858, Cons. No. 30.

[170] Forsyth to Edmonstone 3 July 1858, For. Dept. Secret Cons. 30 July 1858, Cons. No. 89.

[171] Translation of a newsletter from Thakoor Gurnam Singh, talukdar of Rampore Moherah, 21 July 1858: For. Dept. Political Cons. 3 Sept. 1858, Cons. No. 84.

[172] See Appendix to this chapter.

[173] Forsyth to Edmonstone, 11 Oct. 1858: For. Dept. Secret Cons. 26 Nov. 1858, Cons. No. 38.

[174] See above, p. 122.

town for four days before he could be driven off.[175] Harprashad's advance was the signal for the rebels under Mansab Ali and Willayat Ahmed to move from Banarmau and Mianganj for a combined attack. But they had to withdraw in the face of British opposition.[176] These plans and their attempted implementation show the extent of the strength the rebels could still muster; they also demarcate the regions where they were entrenched, and identify the principal leaders. The very fact of their formulation and circulation proves that even in October 1858 the channels of information and co-ordination were still open. Most important they show that the rebel leadership believed that one combined, well-planned attack could still dislodge or shake the growing British hold over Awadh. In that sense at least the British control over Awadh, before the beginning of Lord Clyde's winter campaign, was not an accomplished fact. A map shows how few were the stations that the British securely held before the onset of the winter campaign. There is a need to underscore this since it is held far too often that Lord Clyde's final campaign only rendered a *coup de grace* to a languishing rebellion.[177]

The British crackdown under Lord Clyde began in the middle of October. Lord Clyde's tactics reflected the fragmentation of the rebel forces. The rebels in the cis-Gogra regions were to be dealt separately with the Lucknow–Kanpur road acting as the divide. Rebels on both sides of the road were to be pushed across the Gogra with the British forces in Rohilkhand and Azamgarh not only holding the western and eastern flanks but also advancing into Awadh, beginning at the southern end. This pressure from the flanks, as well as that from Lucknow and Sultanpur, would leave the rebels nowhere to flee except the north, where they could be herded off into the Nepal terai.[178]

In the western theatre, i.e. in the Hardoi-Sitapur area, events moved swiftly after Sandila had been re-taken from Harprashad.

---

[175]Forsyth to Edmonstone, 9 Oct. 1858: For. Dept. Political Cons. 22 Oct. 1858, Cons. No. 267.

[176]Ibid.

[177]For a statement that there was nothing very serious left in the rebellion after the fall of Lucknow see J. Pemble, *The Raj, The Indian Mutiny and The Kingdom of Oudh, 1801-1859*, pp. 233ff.

[178]The most lucid exposition of Lord Clyde's winter campaign is to be found in Innes, *Sepoy Revolt*, pp. 260ff.

The flanking movement from Rohilkhand began in the middle of October, with Colonel Hale moving in from Farrukhabad in the south and Brigadier Troup from Shahjhanpur. The region was quickly subjugated.[179] However, the major figures in the rebel camp put up a resistance and a number of them did not submit. Narpat Singh and Feroze Shah combined forces to resist the British at a place called Minaoli on 9 November.[180] Defeated there the two of them disappeared in the jungles of Shahbad. Narpat Singh later appeared in the Begum's camp and Feroze Shah moved on to Khairabad where he joined up with Harprashad. At Khairabad the rebels numbered eight or nine thousand.[181] This force was defeated at Biswa early in December but the leaders could not be captured. Feroze Shah with 1,500 men (900 of them well mounted) dodged and escaped through the British forces across the Doab to join the Central Indian rebellion.[182] Drigbijai Singh offered a resistance at his fort in Umeria, early in December, and escaped with his followers across the Gogra to the Begum.[183] In Sitapur the major opposition was the large force collected near Mithauli under Loni Singh, Khan Bahadur Khan and Khan Ali Khan.[184] They were dispersed from Mithauli early in November and driven by Brigadier Troup toward Aliganj, where after another encounter on 17 November they disappeared across the river with the Begum. The rebels, though large in number, found it difficult to confront the British army; and with pressure on them from the flank as well as from Lucknow, they could either submit or resist and try to escape. Most submitted, but many remained recalci-

[179] By 12 November 1858 the following areas were free of rebels. Bangarmau, Bilgram, Roeya, Mallanwan, Banosa, Sandi, Pali, Saromannagar, Shahabad, Naktora, Muhamdi, Pasgawan, Padora, Barora, Aurangabad, Pihani, Mithauli, Saadatnagar, Gopamau: Newsletter from Chedi Lal, resident of Shahabad, 12 Nov. 1858: Lucknow Chief Court Mutiny, *Basta: F.S.U.P.*, ii, p. 543.
[180] Ibid.
[181] Newsletter from Munna Lal Pandey to Capt. A. Orr, 18 Nov. 1858: Lucknow Chief Court Mutiny, *Basta: F.S.U.P.*, ii, p. 557.
[182] Edmonstone to Dep. Commr., Hamirpur, 6 Dec. 1858 and Newsletter sent for information of Magistrate and Collector of Hamirpur, 8 Dec. 1858: *F.S.U.P.*, ii, pp. 562-3.
[183] Forsyth to Edmonstone, 4 Dec. 1858: For. Dept. Political Cons. 17 Dec. 1858, Cons. No. 254.
[184] Forsyth to Edmonstone, 13 Nov. 1858: For. Dept. Political Cons. 26 Nov. 1858, Cons. No. 248.

trant and unrepentant.

In Baiswara the British campaign, under the personal supervision of Lord Clyde, was not so smooth. There were more encounters and more hurried marches and chases.[185] Operations began with Colonel Kelly moving in from the Azamgarh frontier to capture Akbarpur and Tanda. Meanwhile Hope-Grant had to encounter the Kanhpuriah clan at Rampurkasaia early in November.[186] Lord Clyde began at the fort of Amethi where a mini drama was enacted. Lal Madho Singh was asked repeatedly to surrender. After much ado he appeared in the British camp at the dead of night. He could not guarantee the behaviour of the men in his fort, and he was unwilling to tell the rebels of his personal surrender for fear of life. His men remained rebellious and instead of confronting the British at Amethi escaped to join Beni Madho at Shankarpur.[187] In one view the incident epitomized the extent of popular resistance in Awadh; the common rebel, as distinct from the magnate, was still willing to fight. The magnates themselves were now calculating more carefully the pros and cons of alternative courses of action. Some surreptitiously changed sides, leaving the men to their own fate. The other possibility (which emerges from a very close reading of Charles Ball's account) is that the personal surrender of Lal Madho Singh was a well-planned ploy. The rebels, quick to comprehend that the British were willing to guarantee the safety of the raja, planned his personal surrender as a diversion to give themselves time to escape through the jungles. Lord Clyde tended to believe that this was the case:

The Commander-in-chief was rather disappointed. . . . The rajah, indeed, had surrendered, and, so far, had complied with the terms granted to him; but his fort was still in the hands of those who might turn out to be dangerous; and some of whom were certainly guilty sepoys, whose escape it was most desirable to prevent. Besides, they might be making use of this time to drag away the guns and to desert through the dense jungles.[188]

[185]Russell's *Mutiny Diary*, pp. 209ff., provides the best firsthand account of this part of the campaign.
[186]Innes, *Sepoy Revolt*, p. 265.
[187]The Amethi episode is described in detail in Ball, *Mutiny*, ii, pp. 530ff., in Russell, *Mutiny Diary*, pp. 216 ff., and in Shadwell, *Life of Colin Campbell, Lord Clyde*, 2 vols (London 1881), ii, pp. 332ff.
[188]Ball, *Mutiny*, ii, p. 532.

That the raja's surrender could be part of a ploy was further suggested by his later pretence that he was unaware about how many guns there were in his own fort.[189] The truth is probably a mixture of both interpretations. The raja was willing to surrender to save himself, the rebels suspecting this may have used him to gain time and make good their own escape. What is important, however, in this case is that a certain disjunction had appeared between the rebels in general, who were still willing to fight, and magnate leaders who were keen, even if belatedly, to submit and seek rewards.

From Amethi Lord Clyde moved through Baiswara, establishing military and civil posts, to meet Beni Madho at Shankarpur. Beni Madho was asked to surrender, and the raja of Tiloi also made a special effort to make him submit. The wily talukdar got his son to write to the British saying that he (the son) was willing to throw out the father, provided the British settled the estate with him. To the raja of Tiloi Beni Madho was more forthright. He wrote that 'one king was all he could serve and that he had pledged his fealty to Birjees Kuddr, and should not desert him or his cause'.[190] While the British mustered forces to cordon off Shankarpur, Beni Madho escaped in the night with his entire following; when the British entered the fort the following morning an old and sick Brahmin was the sole human occupant.[191] The chase of Beni Madho across the plains of Baiswara was one of the most exciting episodes of the revolt. For seven days four British columns — under Lord Clyde, Hope Grant, Evelegh, and Horsford respectively — scoured the country to locate him. The rebel leader had become as elusive as the proverbial Pimpernel. As Russell remarked:

We have 'certain' intelligence that he is at all points of the compass of exactly the same hour of the same day, and we have not thirty-one columns to spare to verify these reports.[192]

Beni Madho seems to have first proceeded towards Rae Bareli and then doubled back and moved south-west consistently harassing

---

[189]Ibid. p. 532.   [190]Ibid. p. 538.
[191]Ibid., Russell, *Mutiny Diary*, p. 226: 'Not a soul was left, except a few feeble old men, priests, dirty fakirs, and a mad elephant. . .'
[192]Russell, *Mutiny Diary*, p. 231.

British troops. To the British it seemed 'as if the country were swarming with rebels'.[193] Evelegh was attacked by a strong body of men as he passed through a narrow village,[194] he was attacked again by Beni Madho on 17 November at Bera.[195] The inevitable confrontation took place at Daundiakhera on the banks of the Ganges on 24 November 1858.[196] Beni Madho suffered a defeat but escaped once again with his men and considerable treasure, snatching from his enemies the satisfaction of a complete victory.[197] He then moved off towards the Gogra with the British at his heels. He crossed over on 4 December to join his king in Bahraich. Even at this time he had as many as 5,000 men with him.[198] The disappearance of Beni Madho and his followers from southern Awadh — the nucleus of the rebellion in the region — was the signal for the establishment of British authority.

With western, southern and eastern Awadh cleared of rebels the rest was easy game. The rebels in Gonda-Bahraich were hemmed in from three sides. Yet there were some fierce encounters. On 25 November 1858, Hope Grant encountered a large body of rebels under the raja of Gonda and Mehndi Hussain, and at Tulsipur another band under Bala Rao. Lord Clyde himself had to defeat a considerable body of insurgents at Bargadia and could only capture the fort of Masjidia after three hours of fighting. The Nana was defeated at Banki near Nanpara at the end of the year.[199] Mehndi Hussain submitted to Lord Clyde early in 1859.[200] Table 15 is a list of important rebel leaders who went with the Begum into Nepal.

The total following of these rebel leaders was said to be in the region of 8,000 men.[201] The subsequent history of these men is

---

[193]Ibid. p. 226.   [194]Ibid. p. 227.
[195]Shadwell, *Lord Clyde*, ii, p. 340.
[196]A detailed reconstruction of the battle is given in Shadwell, pp. 342ff.
[197]'So far the whole affair had been a failure. Beni Madho had gone. . . . Our only gain was the possession of a useless stronghold. No one liked this, except possibly Bene Madho himself, and those who escaped': so Russell, *Mutiny Diary*, p. 238.
[198]Forsyth to Edmonstone, 4 Dec. 1858: For. Dept. Political Cons. 17 Dec. 1858, Cons. No. 250.
[199]Lord Clyde to Governor-General, 7 Jan. 1859: quoted *in extenso* in Ball, *Mutiny*, ii, pp. 563ff.
[200]Ibid.
[201]Forsyth to Sec., Govt. of India, 27 June 1859: For. Dept. Secret Cons. 22 July 1859, Cons. No. 223.

TABLE 15

Names	Remarks
Hazrat Mahal and Birjis Qadr	
Nawab Mumoo Khan	former daroga of the Begum; Chief of the rebels
Bakht Khan	subahdar in the Company's army, mutinied at Bareilly, made rebel commandor in Delhi and came into Lucknow after the fall of Delhi
Yusuf Khan	a relative of Mumoo Khan
Khan Bahadur Khan	the famous Rohilla Chief
Abid Khan	a relative of Mumoo Khan
Ganga Singh	subahdar of 41st N.I. commanded a division of rebel troops in Lucknow relative of Mumoo Khan
Ahsan Ali Khan	relative of Mumoo Khan
Dalganjan Singh	not known
Tilak Ram Tiwari	not known
Rana Beni Madho	talukdar of Shankarpur
Umrao Singh	brother of the raja of Ikauna fought at Gorakhpur
Drigbijai Singh	talukdar of Mahona
Raja Narpat Singh	talukdar of Roeya
Chowdhree Narpat Singh	son of rebel leader Jussa Singh of Unao district, a firm friend of the Nana
Gulab Singh	karinda of Chandrika Baksh
Hardat Singh	talukdar of Rampurkasaia
Dabi Baksh Singh	talukdar of Gonda
Mir Muhammad Hussain	nazim of Gorakhpur
Khan Ali Khan	a resident of Shahjahanpur; fought throughout the rebellion
Raghubir Singh	a rebel from Baiswara
Umrao Jan	formerly a munshi; during the rebellion a chief adviser of Mumoo Khan
Bhagwan Baksh	one of the thakurs of Nain
Miftah Ud Dowlah	a Brahmin convert who was the king's treasurer
Mir Mehndi	tutor to Birjis Qadr, in charge of intelligence during the rebellion
Udit Praksh Singh	talukdar of Ekona in Bahraich
Hakim Raza	tutor to Shurfuddowlah who was prime minister during the rebellion
Jyoti Singh	talukdar of Churda in Bahraich
Gopal Singh	not known
Umrao Singh	subahdar in the 6th Awadh Irregular Force
Raghunath Singh	was in 2nd Oude Military Police
Sangram Singh	
Suraj Singh / Ram Singh	subahdars of the regular native infantry

Names	Remarks
Ausan Singh	havildar in the artillery of Capt. Bunbury's Regiment
Madho Singh	havildar in 2nd Oude Military Police
Drigpal Singh	sepoys
Shivdat Singh	
Ganga Singh	a subahdar in the Company's army; took a leading part in the rebellion at Lucknow
Nazar Ali	not known
Sardar Singh	subahdars in the Company's service,
Ranjit Singh	rebels in Lucknow
Kochuk Sultan	son of Bahadur Shah
Khuda Baksh	a rebel zamindar of the Dariabad district
Khan Ali	chakladar of Sultanpur and Khairabad, inhabitant of Lucknow
Jwala Prashad	a Brahmin from Baiswara; instigated the Kanpur rising

SOURCE: Forsyth to Sec., Govt. of India, 6 April 1859: For. Dept., Political Cons. 30 Dec. 1859, Supp. No. 550.

lost in obscurity, but it is known that Beni Madho died in November 1859 fighting the gurkhas led by Jang Bahadur, an ally of the British.[202] In a sense, the swan song of the rebellion was heard in the hills of Nepal.

It has been the aim of this chapter to show that the rebellion in Awadh, through all its stages, mustered considerable support. Even after they were driven out of Lucknow the rebels sustained their resistance in the countryside. At this stage there was a brief weakening of morale when some talukdars actually submitted and others gingerly sent in letters of submission. But once it became evident that British authority outside Lucknow was fragile and incapable of protecting its allies, activities again gained in momentum. The fragility of British authority outside Lucknow and the rebel hold over the Awadh countryside were of

---

[202]Martin, *Indian Empire*, p. 498n. The deaths of the raja of Gonda, Narpat Singh, Bala Rao, Khuda Baksh and Harprashad were also reported in early 1860. Khan Bahadur Khan was captured by Jang Bahadur towards the end of 1859. Mummoo Khan surrendered. Till the end of 1859 the Begum was still in Nepal with about 1,500 followers. (Ibid., p. 500).

course interrelated: the strength of the one fed on the weakness of the other.

It has sometimes been suggested that the rebels were powerful in the countryside throughout 1858 because Lord Clyde held his hand throughout the hot and rainy seasons.[203] The rebels realized the advantages of the Indian summer. Khan Bahadur Khan urged them to keep fighting since the British, he thought, would not be able to withstand the summer.[204] But, in reality, Lord Clyde's decision to delay his operations in Awadh were based on his understanding that strategically it was not possible to subdue two rebel strongholds, adjacent to one another, simultaneously. In his letter to Canning (dated 24 March 1858) he openly admitted the surviving strength of the resistance in Awadh:

The province of Oudh being still in a state of active rebellion, it becomes a matter of doubt whether any mere garrison could take care of itself — that is to say whether it might not be liable to be blockaded and cut off from supplies, unless the country within a certain radius be thoroughly reduced and held.... I have observed that wherever our columns have marched they have literally walked over the insurgent bodies; but that directly they had passed, the rebels again formed in their rear, cut off their communications, and intercepted their supplies. The respective marches of the Maharajah Jung Bahadoor, of Brigadier-General Franks, and Brigadier-General Sir James Hope Grant, are all convincing instances of what has been advanced in point of fact, until the country shall have been thoroughly reduced, we can almost say that, as far as the garrison of Lucknow is concerned, the enemy is as formidable after he has been beaten as he was before.[205]

Contemporary British observers, more than modern day analysts, perceived clearly the power of the revolt in Awadh. It is necessary to underscore this in view of the common presumption that the revolt had run its course by the fall of Lucknow. For the rebels, doom came only when Lord Clyde overran Baiswara; till then the issue was still undecided and the rebellion retained much of its robustness and manpower, and even elements of planning and co-ordination.

[203]'Having held his hand during the hot weather and rains of 1858, in order to save his troops, Sir Colin had determined that during the coming winter, the Province of Oude should be thoroughly subjugated': Innes, *Sepoy Revolt*, p. 260.
[204]Translation of a letter arrived from Lucknow, 15 Feb. 1858: For. Dept. Political, 30 Dec. 1859, Supplement No. 952.
[205]Quoted in Shadwell, *Lord Clyde*, ii, pp. 177-9.

CHAPTER 5
ORGANIZATION AND IDEOLOGY

In the previous chapter I have emphasized the elements of co-ordination and organization in the revolt of 1857. Certain questions arise in this connection. The rebels' efforts at organization do suggest aims which went beyond overthrowing the Raj, and the rebel leaders' mental horizon was probably less narrow than it is made out to be. But how crucial was the magnates' leadership role and how important the linkages with events outside Awadh? These are some of the questions which the present chapter attempts to answer.

A Rebel State?

The first efforts to organize and bring some order to the activities of the rebels were made immediately after the battle of Chinhat when the rebels swarmed into Lucknow. As already noted, Jailal Singh was made the rebels' chief spokesman. Birjis Qadr was crowned King of Awadh mainly at his instance. There seems to have been a feeling here that the presence of a king would provide legitimacy and also facilitate the enforcement of the orders and directives required to fight a war. The seal of a monarch was important. The coronation of Birjis Qadr was also, however, an act of consensus. All the begums of Wajid Ali Shah were asked for their consent and the ceremony took place in the presence of most of the rebel leaders.[1] The king being a minor it was obvious from the beginning that Begum Hazrat Mahal held the strings. The rebels, however, having begun proceedings, were not willing to relinquish control completely. They laid down their conditions:

---

[1] See Statement of Mir Wajid Ali Darogah, taken on 8 July 1859: Trial Proceedings, Govt. vs. Raja Jai Lal Singh Lucknow Collectorate Mutiny *Basta: F.S.U.P.*, ii, 81ff., and statement of Mata Din taken on 5 July 1859: Trial Proceedings, Govt. vs. Raja Jai Lal Singh, Lucknow Collectorate Mutiny *Basta:* ibid., pp. 90ff.

1. That orders from Delhi were to be obeyed and that whatever orders were received should be final.
2. That the Wazir should be selected by the army.
3. The officers of the Regiment should not be appointed without the consent of the army.
4. Double pay was to be issued from the date of the sepoys' leaving the English service.
5. No interference should take place respecting the treatment and disposal of those who are friends of the English.[2]

The rebel army, in the very act of crowning Birjis Qadr, was making out certain autonomous spheres of activity for itself. With the progress of the rebellion such distinctions would be difficult to maintain.

What is more important is the fact that, despite the claims of royalty on the part of the Awadh royal family, the overall sovereignty of the Mughal emperor was imposed and accepted. Awadh nawabi was to maintain its autonomy but in a subsidiary position to the monarch in Delhi. The rebellion was to be carried through in the name of the Mughal emperor. As one of the rebels told a British officer, 'we will only receive our orders from the King of Delhi as he is the only person who can grant summons.'[3] The faith in the legitimacy of the Mughals as the suzerain rulers of India had evidently survived the demise of their effective power. However, what the rebels invoked was not the imperial splendour of *pax Mughalia*, which recognized no autonomies of provincial overlords, but the eighteenth century empire wherein regional powers flourished under Delhi's suzerain authority and carried over the Mughal tradition.[4] The coronation of Birjis Qadr was thus a throwback to the preceding century, an attempt to wipe out an unpleasant interregnum — the years of firanghi rule. The rebels were reviving old traditions, following an antique drum. The carry-over of Mughal traditions is witnessed by the pomp and ceremony that accompanied the coronation of Birjis Qadr, in the offer of nazranas, the gift of khilats, and the establishment of

---

[2] Statement of Mir Wajid Ali, ibid., p. 85.

[3] Colonel Gordon (surname illegible) to Outram, 2 Sept. [1857] reporting the interrogation of a rebel subahdar: Mutiny Papers of Outram, Havelock and Campbell.

[4] Barun De, 'Some Implications of Political Tendencies and Social Factors in Eighteenth Century India', Bhatnagar (ed.), *Studies in Social History*.

Organization and Ideology

the durbar.[5] Birjis Qadr reportedly also sent an ambassador to Delhi bearing his petitions to Bahadur Shah, asking for confirmation. The Mughal emperor bestowed on him the title of Wazir and asked him to rule in Awadh as his representative.[6] Birjis Qadr also struck and issued coins that bore the name of the Mughal emperor and predated those issued by Ghazi-ud-din Haidar, the first king of Awadh.[7] A recent historian of Awadh has noted:

For Birjis Qadr guided by his mother and the Awadh courtiers and notables who supported him, the traditions of the Mughal Empire seem to have been regarded as stronger than the imperial pretensions of the Awadh *padshahs*, that had been intended to replace them. He apparently believed that his rule in Lucknow would be legitimized more effectively by an appeal to the Mughal Emperor than by recourse to the four decade old assertions of his predecessors in the Awadh Court.[8]

For the conduct of the rebellion itself the executive structure that was set up and the people who manned it were more important than the imperial myth. It appears that two separate decision-making bodies were established. One looked after organization, payments, etc. and consisted mostly of old nawabi bureaucrats or Court officials:[9]

Shurufuddowlah Naib
Mummoo Khan Darogah Diwan Khana (in charge Hall of Audience)
Meer Wajid Ali Naib of Diwan Khana
Meer Kasim Ali Darogah of Magazine
Maharaja Bal Kishan Diwan (Finance Minister)
Munshi Thakur Dayal Household Munshi and Paymaster
Meer Mehndi Chief of Intelligence Department
Ahmed Hussein Darogah of Nazul (**Government** Land)
Sewak Ram Naib of Thakur Dayal
Munshi Amir Hyder Sahib-e-Duskut (**in charge** of royal letters)
Muzaffar Ali Khan General

---

[5]Statement of Mir Wajid Ali describes in some detail the ceremony of coronation and the granting of khilats etc.

[6]A.C. Bose, *Hazrat Wajid Ali Shah, King of Oudh* (n.p., n.d.), cited in M. Fisher, 'The Imperial Court and the Province: A Social and Administrative History of pre-British Awadh (1775-1856)' (D. Phil Dissertation, University of Chicago, March 1978), p. 91.

[7]See Fisher, p. 91.

[8]Ibid.

[9]Statement of Daya Krishna, 24 June 1859: Trial Proceedings Govt. vs. Raja Jai Lal Singh: Lucknow Collectorate Mutiny *Basta:*, *F.S.U.P.*, ii, pp. 107ff.

Raja Jai Lal Sing Collector[10]

The other body was the 'military cell' which took decisions 'to assault the Bailee Guard to send forces to Cawnpore or in any other direction.'[11] This 'cell' was composed mostly of sepoys or rebel soldiers with a few of the above officials:[12]

Sheikh Sukun Rissaladar Weston's Horse
Wajid Ali Khan Rissaladar 1st Oudh Irregular Cavalry
Jehangir Khan Captain Artillery
Ghamandi Sing Captain Orr's Regiment
Rajmund Tiwari Bole Regiment
Raghunath Sing Captain Police Battalion
Umrao Sing Police Battalion
Burkat Ahmed Rissaladar 12th Irregular Cavalry
Mummoo Khan
Muzuffur Ali Khan
Meer Kasim Ali
Sangum Sing Captain of Begum's New Regiment
Surjoo Sing
Raja Jai Lal Sing

Raja Jailal Singh seems to have been the most important and powerful figure on both bodies. He also acted as the link between these bodies and the Begum.[13] He also had a crucial role in co-ordinating supplies and in general planning:

The making, repairing, digging entrenchments, mines, supplies, labourers, scaling-ladders were all under Jyelall Sing; he used also to go to superintend the attacks and neither court nor assault could take place without Jyelall's consent.[14]

It is significant that at this very early stage — July 1857 — of the rebellion in Awadh no talukdar was in any of the decision-

---

[10]In Nawabi times this appointment (Collector) was given to the Commandant of forces that went out to collect revenue from recalcitrant subjects. Presumably Jailal Singh's appoitment meant that he was in charge of the collection of revenue.

[11]Statement made by Mahmud Ali Munshi on 23 June 1859: Trial Proceedings, Govt. vs. Raja Jai Lal Singh: Lucknow Collectorate Mutiny *Basta: F.S.U.P.*, ii, p. 110.

[12]Ibid.

[13]Ibid.

[14]Statement of Munshi Wajid Ali, 4th Police Infantry taken on 29 June 1859: Trial Proceedings, Govt. vs. Raja Jai Lal Singh: Lucknow Collectorate Mutiny *Basta: F.S.U.P.*, ii, p. 98.

making bodies. This reinforces the point made earlier that no important talukdar (the only exception being the raja of Mahmudabad) had appeared on the scene till the battle of Chinhat, though some talukdars' men had joined the rebel forces. This is further borne out by the fact that a number of *hukumnamajats* (orders) were issued to talukdars and zamindars asking them to join the flag:

> . . . as God has given us back our hereditary dominions to us [*sic*] we must extirpate those English heathens and work together to kill their remnants at the Bailly Guard. Therefore exhibit your bravery. God willing you will be endowed with jagirs and rewards even better than in the old days. All those who will kill them will be allowed a half of the Jama of their jagirs free.[15]

An appeal was being made by the monarch to landed magnates to show their valour and join hands against a common enemy. The rewards on offer were connected with land and revenue. The oppression that zamindars had often suffered at the hands of the chakladar (and other state officials) in former Nawabi times was to be counteracted by invoking the huzur tahsil system:

> . . . those Zemindars who may feel aggrieved at any violence or exaction committed upon them by any Amil, Chakladar or Tehsildar should wait upon the Huzoor and apply for permission to pay their revenue direct to the latter so that such prayer may be immediately granted. . .[16]

The aim was to unite the landed classes with the rest of the King's subjects to fight a common enemy:

> It is incumbent on all the Zemindars, Talookdars and all other subjects of this gracious sarkar to unite together and earnestly employ their best exertions in exterminating the evil disposed infidels. In reward for this meritorious service they the Malgoozars, will obtain a remission of 4 annas in the Rupee on account of the revenue of their Zemindarees payable to the Sarkar. It therefore behoves them to put a speedy end to the existence of the infidels and thereby to exhibit their firm attachment to the Sarkar.[17]

The talukdars responded to the appeal on an impressive scale and many were duly rewarded with khilats and appointments. Raja

---

[15]*Qaisar-ut-Tawarikh*, ii, pp. 228-9, quoted in *F.S.U.P.*, ii, p. 107.
[16]Translation of A Proclamation dated 11 Rajab 1274 A.H. (25 Feb. 1858): For. Dept. Political Proc. 30 Dec. 1859, Supplement No. 1693.
[17]Ibid.

Man Singh, for example, became head of the field force.[18] He was helped by 150 other chiefs who managed military matters.[19]

This administrative arrangement, if it can be called that, was loose and precarious. Obedience to orders was not always forthcoming; talukdars and other rebel leaders often acted independently and in accordance with their personal direction. Loni Singh, the rebel talukdar from Mithauli, handed over Captain Orr and Mr Jackson (whom he had sheltered) to the Lucknow court on pain of a heavy fine and the loss of his ilaqa to Man Singh.[20] He had paid no heed to earlier hukumnamahs issued to him.[21] Yet he was a well-known rebel leader who fought against the British till the very end and had welcomed the coronation of Birjis Qadr with a gun salute.[22] Similarly Harprashad, the chakladar of Khairabad, another rebel leader who fought till the very last, disregarded orders to surrender the belongings of some Englishmen that he had with him.[23]

However, the most serious rift in the administrative set-up was the challenge to the Begum's authority by the Maulavi.[24] Around

---

[18]Carnegy's Newsletter (News of 15 Dec. 1857): For. Dept., Secret Cons., 26 Feb. 1858, Cons. No. 228.

[19]Carnegy's Newsletter (News of 7 Jan. 1858): For. Dept. Secret Cons., 26 Feb. 1858: Cons. No. 227.

[20]Translation of the Hukumnamah of Birjis Qadr to Loni Singh dated Safar 5 1274 A.H. (25 Sept. 1857): Lucknow Chief Court Mutiny *Basta: F.S.U.P.*, ii. p. 133; Loni Singh pleaded in his trial that he handed over the Englishmen because he received a hukumnamah (dated 22 Safar, 1274 A.H., 12 Oct. 1857: *F.S.U.P.*, ii, p. 134) from Birjis Qadr saying that the two Englishmen were needed to treat with the English at the Bailee Guard (*F.S.U.P.*, ii, pp. 128ff). He also pleaded he was in danger of being attacked by the rebels. Whatever might be the truth the fact remains that Loni Singh refused to comply with a number of previous hukumnamahs.

[21]Loni Singh had hukumnamahs issued to him on 27 July 1857, 11 August 1857, 2 September 1857, 10 September 1857 and 19 September 1857 ordering him to surrender the Englishmen. *F.S.U.P.*, ii, pp. 130-2.

[22]Hutchinson. *Narrative*, p. 201.

[23]See Raja Jai Lal Singh's letter to Rameshwar Baksh, talukdar of Mallanwan d. 12 Zilhijja 1273 A.H. (3 August 1857): Lucknow Collectorate Mutiny *Basta: F.S.U.P.*, ii, pp. 134-5.

[24]The Maulavi — Ahmadullah Shah — is one of the best-known characters in the annals of the revolt of 1857. He appears in practically every book on the subject.
The most succinct account of the Maulavi and his activities is in Majumdar,

Organization and Ideology 141

December 1857 and early January 1858 serious dissension broke out among the rebel leaders, splitting, them into two camps. The Maulavi threatened to set himself up as King and wished the Begum and Birjis Qadr to acknowledge him as such and become his disciples.[25] He based his claim on divine will.[26] The sepoys and insurgents from Delhi and other places who were in Lucknow, as well as the inhabitants of that city, were said to be on the side of the Maulavi. But the Awadh regiments, especially the contingent corps and the Najeebs, espoused the cause of the Begum and Birjis Qadr.[27] The two factions were reportedly reconciled, but the amity proved short-lived and by mid-January they actually clashed:

The exact cause is not clearly known. Some say that the Maulvee commenced to form a bridge of boats across the river near his residence at Ghaoghat and that Mummoo Khan sent a force to compel him to desist... Others again state that the Moulvee issued a 'hidayah Namah' to the boy King whose mother then desired the soldiers to declare either for him

Sepoy Mutiny, pp. 169ff. Majumdar's account is based on his reading of Ball, Malleson and Holmes and not on any archival sources. The following account draws on the Deposition of Wazir Khan, late Sub. Asstt., Surgeon of Agra Dispensary: For. Dept. Political Proc., 30 Dec. 1859, Suppl. No. 312. The Maulavi gave himself out to be a disciple of Mehrab Shah, a holy man from Gwalior, where Ahmadullah Shah said he had resided for a long time. Ahmadullah Shah preached as a fakir in Agra and in other parts of N.W.P., propagating a holy war against the British. He was around forty at the time of the outbreak; a man of little learning, having a smattering of Persian and Arabic and some English. Apparently he had been to England and spoke with 'great apparent familiarity' regarding places in England. After the annexation of Awadh he went to Faizabad, carried on preaching and started collecting men to revenge the death of Maulavi Amir Ali who had died during the disturbances at Hanumangarhi. For this he was arrested by the British. When the mutiny occurred in Faizabad, he was released from jail by the mutineers. He was present at the battle of Chinhat and in Lucknow in the subsequent months. His hold over the popular mind was enhanced by the temporary success of the rebels which seemed to fulfil his prophecy about the end of the Raj. He carried on fighting in western Awadh after the fall of Lucknow and died fighting in June 1858 in Shahjahanpur district.

[25]Carnegy's Intelligence (News of 7 Jan. 1858): For. Dept. Secret Cons. 26 Feb. 1858: Cons. No. 227. This news probably pertains to December as it was brought in by Chandika Pandit who was in confinement in Lucknow for three and a half months.

[26]Couper to Edmonstone, 24 Jan. 1858: For. Dept. Secret Cons. 26 March 1858, Cons. No. 70.

[27]Ibid.

or for the Maulvee and on their declaring for him[i.e. Birjis Qadr] she ordered them to seize the Moulvee and hence the origin of the disturbance. However may be it this is certain that a fight did take place and that a large number of men, probably not less than 200 were killed and wounded.[28]

The Maulavi also interfered with the Begum's orders to send off twelve regiments to stop the advance of the Gurkha troops from the Gorakhpur side. The regiments left the city but halted on receiving a message from the Maulavi pointing out—

> that the object of the begum, Shurf-ood dowlah and others ... in sending them out was to get rid of them in order that they might give up the city to the British whose rule they were anxious to see reestablished. He added that nothing would go well until they made up their minds to slay Shurf-ood dowlah.[29]

The last objective the Maulavi accomplished during Colin Campbell's entry into Lucknow in March 1858 on the plea that Shurufuddowlah was a traitor.[30] Little more is known of this faction fight, but it should be noted that according to Outram the British position around the end of 1857 was so precarious that 'even if dissatisfaction became universal and ended in an absolute rupture between the Queen Mother and the Moulvee our situation would not be materially benefitted thereby.'[31]

Perhaps the opposition of the Maulavi represented a certain tension within the rebel camp between a religious leader at the grass roots level and a leadership entrenched in the upper echelons of the royal court. But be that as it may, once Lucknow had fallen and the rebels dispersed into the country, the Maulavi carried on the revolt around the borders of Awadh and Rohilkhand till his death in June 1858. The Begum's authority on the other hand remained unbroken till the last days of the retreat.

Even in retreat when the Begum had fled from Lucknow and was at Baundi she tried to maintain at least a facade of administration. Naturally, through death and the pressure of the fighting things had changed: new factions and new people had replaced

---

[28]Ibid.   [29]Ibid.

[30]Deposition of Wazir Khan, late Sub. Asstt. Surgeon of Agra Dispensary: For. Dept., Political Proc., 30 Dec. 1859, Supplement No. 312.

[31]Couper to Edmonstone, 9 Dec. 1857: For. Dept. Secret Cons. 29 Jan. 1858, Cons. No. 346.

the old. It was now no more possible to hold court. But there was still a decision-making body, at least in name, and Birjis Qadr was still the legitimizing authority — indeed more so after the removal of Bahadur Shah. A man called Syed Abdul Hakim who worked as an Extra Assistant in the British bureaucracy was taken prisoner by the insurgents. On his release he gave an account of the set-up in Baundi.[32] According to him orders were still issued under the name of Birjis Qadr and collections were received from nazims and chakladars appointed by him. Mumoo Khan acted as the Agent. But with Mumoo Khan there was a coadjutor, Bakht Khan, a subahdar of artillery from Bareilly. There was an element of tension, rivalry and suspicion between the Begum's camp and the sepoys. The latter were led by Bakht Khan, and Syed Abdul Hakim felt that it was Bakht Khan who called the shots in most matters. Apart form these there was also another body of men who were described as 'the Parliament'. This body, according to the report, discussed and conducted all business and consisted of:

1. Maulavi Fuzl Haq, a former *serishtadar* (head officer in a court) at Delhi, who was always 'most violent in preaching a crusade against the British.'
2. Maulavi Mahomed Hussain, formerly employed in the district of Agra.
3. Kasim Ali.
4. Raja Imdad Ali Khan of Kuntoor.
5. Maulavi Ahmad Hussain.
6. Hakim Hussain, Raza of Bilgaon.

The predominance of religious men is worth noting, especially as it was reported that 'these men are bitter in their hostility to the Government and spread the most absurd and incredible reports'.[33] It is conceivable that these religious leaders used their hold over the populace to stir up anti-British feeling and, in the later stages, whip up flagging zeal.

The existence of these various cliques notwithstanding, there was an effort to maintain a semblance of order and organization. And the organization as well as the chain of command and tacti-

[32]Enclosure to Forsyth to Edmonstone, 14 Aug. 1858: For. Dept. Secret Cons., 27 Aug. 1858, Cons. No. 42.
[33]Ibid.

cal decisions all depended on the legitimizing power of royal sanction. The detailed plan of September 1858 discussed in the previous chapter was accompanied by a proclamation under the name of Birjis Qadr laying down guidelines for sepoys and commanders:

> Every man should . . . now try to do his best to maintain the authority of the Sircar in the Country. . . . It is therefore the wish of the Sirkar that the 22nd Suffer [1 Oct. 1858] every Sirkaree fauz which is close to the British troops shall make an attack on them at the fixed time and give them no quarter. During the engagement every Sepoy shall follow the advice of his Officer and act accordingly. . . .
> Every officer should also not act selfishly and should obey the orders of the Officer in Command whether the latter be a Nazim, Chukladar, Sipah Salar or Markh Salar and making it one common cause would commence operations on the fixed day.
> They should be very careful that no mistake or misconception occurs regarding the day fixed for the campaign and the Troops, Nazims, Chukladars, Talooqdars and Zemindars should all commence at once.[34]

Factions could be revived but without the royal approval no orders had any authority, nor any plans any chance of execution. Here was the source of Begum Hazrat Mahal's power.

Since a large number of the insurgents were former sepoys, one of the primary concerns of the leadership was to arrange for their regular payment. This was one, if not the most effective, way to keep the striking force of the revolt intact. As the fighting spread there was a desperate shortage of cash: revenue collections were almost impossible in the circumstances even though district appointments had been made.[35] Gold and silver ornaments were made into coins to pay the sepoys.[36] At one point money had become so scarce that—

> Mummoo Khan and Rajah Jeylal Sing went and dug up rupees etc from Aly Nukee Khan's House, and brought them into the expenses [exchequer] and disbursed in pay whatever was absolutely necessary. . . Once Jeylal Sing, Meer Hussoo, a Mutsuddee and Chobdar of the Dewan Khana. . . went to the Arghai's [probably Agaie] house in Narkass and

---

[34]Translation of a Proclamation issued by Birjis Qadr for the information and guidance of his Army dated 10 Suffer 1275 Hijree, corresponding with 18 Sept. 1858: For. Dept. Political Cons. 12 Nov. 1858, Cons. No. 194.

[35]Carnegy's Newsletter (News of 15 Dec. 1857): For. Dept. Secret Cons. 26 Feb. 1858 Cons. No. 228.

[36]Ibid.

Organization and Ideology 145

dug up 1,000 gold Mohurs, 29 or 30,000 rupees, one khasdan, 1 gold spitoon.[37]

Chandi Shah and Dinanath Mutsuddi — probably two wealthy men of Lucknow — gave five lakhs and two lakhs of rupees respectively.[38] Again, just before the final British assault on Lucknow, money was in short supply there and Jailal Singh had to proceed to Dariabad to arrange for some collection.[39] In December 1857 the talukdars received remission of revenue so that they could pay their fighting troops.[40] The old sepoys of the Awadh army received twelve rupees per month while the regiments which had come in from Delhi got only seven — the difference was said to be the reason why the Delhi troops supported the Maulavi.[41] It was also ordered that the families of sepoys who were killed in action should receive a hundred rupees each and wounded sepoys fifty rupees each.[42] As the odds turned against the insurgents the rates of pay could no longer be maintained. In July 1858 it was reported that the cavalry and the infantry under Khan Bahadur Khan were receiving four annas and one anna per day respectively.[43] In the Begum's camp at Baundi around September 1858 the sepoys received one anna eight pi per day. And at Bala Rao's camp near Bahraich the troops were being paid two annas per day.[44] In the later stages, as the fighting spread to the country-

[37]Statement by Mata Din, Munshi of Raja Jai Lall Singh taken on 5 July 1859: Trial Proceedings, Govt. vs. Raja Jai Lal Singh: Lucknow Collectorate Mutiny *Basta: F.S.U.P.*, ii, p. 93.

[38]Carnegy's Newsletter (News of 3 Nov. 1857).

[39]Statement by Mata Din: *F.S.U.P.*, ii p. 96. Statement by Munshi Wajid Ali, 29 June 1859: Trial Proceedings, Govt. vs. Jai Lal Singh: Lucknow Collectorate Mutiny *Basta: F.S.U.P.*, ii, p. 101.

[40]Carnegy's Newsletter (News of 3 Dec. 1857).

[41]Couper to Edmonstone, 9 Dec.1857: For. Dept. Secret Cons. 29 Jan. 1858, Cons. No. 346.

[42]Carnegy's Newsletter (News of 19 Dec 1857), Cons. No. 227. Even in September 1858 this promise to look after the heirs of the dead and the wounded was repeated, presumably to keep up the spirits of the sepoys: 'Every sepoy should know that the heirs of those who fall will be maintained by the Sirkar and those who are wounded will get compensations for their wounds.': Translation of A Proclamation issued by Birjis Qadr for the information and guidance of his Army dated 18 Sept. 1858: For. Dept. Political Cons. 12 Nov. 1858, Cons. No. 194.

[43]Forsyth to Edmonstone, 17 July 1858: For, Dept. Secret Cons. 27 Aug. 1858, Cons. No. 30.

[44]Enclosure to Forsyth to Edmonstone, 14 Aug. 1858: For. Dept., Secret Cons. 27

side and the British troops gradually moved in, paying the troops became a very serious problem. Rana Beni Madho noted this in his petition to the chief munshi:

> The conditions obtaining here are not very encouraging. The troops stationed at Salon demand their arrears of pay from the Chakledar, Muhammad Fazl Azim Khan Bahadur and the Taluqadars, who make professions of loyalty, harbour designs of the non payment of half of the government dues as allowed to them by the Sarkar. Under such conditions it is not possible to pay the daily allowance to the troops, as sanctioned by the Government. . . . The affairs here being all topsy-turvy there is every likelihood of the enemy's intervention. I, therefore, out of my anxiety beg to submit that if the persons at the helm of affairs in this Sarkar intend to continue the administration of this ilaqa in the hands of Muhammad Fazl Azim Khan, they should issue an order of censure to the army strictly enjoining upon them not to demand anything more than the daily allowance from the Chakledar, nor to disobey him but to discharge their duties faithfully. They should also issue letters of remonstrance to the Taluqddars holding out threats of punishment in case of failure to pay up the Wasil Baqi of 1262 Fasli. . . . Another letter confirming confidence in him be issued to Muhammad Fazl Azim Khan stipulating therein, that after realizing the arrears from the Taluqadars and making the payment of daily allowance to the troops, he should send the balance to the Sarkar and that he should do all he can to curb the power of the wicked. But if the men in authority there think of entrusting this work to some one else, immediate orders may kindly be issued to the Taluqadars and to the army, pending which the ilaqa is likely to lapse into chaos.[45]

Incidentally, the above statement highlights features of the revolt other than its problems of cash. The appeal to the sarkar to order talukdars not to stop payments to troops and the sepoys to maintain discipline indicates that only the king's word carried legitimate authority. Even in the face of imminent defeat that authority survived. The emphasis on administration, revenue collection, and maintenance of order shows that these were the underpinnings, albeit weak, of the revolt, and that all was not chaos and disorder once the insurgents had taken over.

To overcome the scarcity of money and provide for themselves and their followers, many rebel leaders took to plundering. Often the conspicuously wealthy or the mahajan became the victims, but

---

Aug. 1858, Cons. No. 42.

[45] Rana Beni Madho's petition dated 9 Zilhijja 1274 A.H.(21 July 1858) addressed to the Chief Munshi: Rae Bareli Collectorate Mutiny *Basta: F.S.U.P.*, ii, pp. 454-5.

innocent villages also did not escape the rapine. In July 1858 Kalka Parshad plundered a wedding festival in a village in the district of Unao.[46] Raja Drigbijai Singh became a master in the art of plundering the wealthy. In the middle of May he robbed one Haider Hussain Khan of a lakh of rupees and also seized the mahajan of Tickaitganj (between Lucknow and Mahmudabad) and his property valued at 76,000 rupees. He also plundered a number of villages.It was reported that in Kursi, near Lucknow, he had levied a tax of one rupee per house.[47] In October 1858 the rebel infantry and cavalry were said to be collecting their pay in 'any way', but food supplies were being sent by ilaqadars.[48] Such plunder would obviously have been detrimental to any popular and united support for the rebels. Yet plundering the rich, Robin Hood-fashion, is a familiar expression of popular discontent.[49] Scarcity of money was a natural concomitant of the diffusion of fighting and also of the financial bankruptcy of the Awadh court and monarchy. Yet this scarcity was not all that different from the one that haunted the Mughal state in its declining years — the political and administrative model invoked by the rebels.

A War of Religion?

I have so far tried to show that the rebellion had a wide range of support, and continued over a considerable period of time, and that its leadership tried to set up some kind of administration. The question that naturally arises is what motivated this fighting. What held the movement together, and what was its rallying cry? Also, what was the self-image of the insurgents themselves, and how did they visualize their struggle? To find the answers is difficult, if only because the rebels themselves provided little writ-

---

[46]Forsyth to Edmonstone, 17 July 1858: For. Dept. Secret Cons., 27 Aug. 1858, Cons. No. 30.

[47]Extracts from Reports of the Deputy Commissioner, Lucknow, respecting Raja Drigbijai Singh: Trial Proceedings, Govt. vs. Raja Drig Bijai Singh: Lucknow Chief Court Mutiny Basta: F.S.U.P., ii, pp. 380-3.

[48]Newsletter from Baldeo Baksh, 17 October 1858: Lucknow Chief Court Mutiny Basta: F.S.U.P., ii, p. 517.

[49]See M. Keen, *The Outlaws of Medieval England* (London, 1977 edn.), Chs. 11, 13 and 14; also see R. Hilton (ed.), *Peasants, Knights and Heretics* (Cambridge, 1976), contributions by Hilton, Holt and Keen.

ten evidence of what they thought. A sketchy reconstruction is possible from a few proclamations of the rebel leadership, mostly issued in the name of either Birjis Qadr or Begum Hazrat Mahal, some in that of the Delhi princes who were fighting in Awadh, such as Prince Feroze Shah. One letter sets out the views of the sepoys; there is also a rather firebrand pamphlet. The salient feature of the proclamations is their virulent anti-British character. One proclamation, probably issued in the early stages of the revolt, used the most insulting language to describe the British, especially Queen Victoria, and urged people to fight the British in every conceivable way:

It has become the bounden duty of all the people, whether women or men, slave girls or slaves, to come forward and put the English to death. The adoption of the following measures will lead to their destruction, viz: all the Moulvees and the Pundits should explain in every village and city the misfortunes which the success of the English will entail on the people and the advantages and spiritual benefit which will accrue from their extirpation. The Kings, Wazeers, Rajahs and Nawabs ought to slay them in the field of battle, the people should not leave their city in consequence of the entrance of the English therein, but on the contrary should shut up their doors and all the people whether men, women or children. . . ought to put these accursed English to death by firing guns, carbines and pistols, from the terraces, shooting arrows and pelting them with stones, bricks. . . and all other things which may come into their hands. They should stone to death the English in the same manner, as the swallows stoned the Chief of the elephants. The sepoys, the nobles, the shopkeepers, the oil men etc. and all other people of the city, being of one accord, should make a simultaneous attack upon them, some of them should kill them by firing guns. . . and with swords, arrows, daggers. . . some lift them up on spears. . . some should wrestle and through stratagem break the enemy to pieces, some should strike them with cudgels, some slap them, some throw dust in their eyes, some should beat them with shoes. . . . In short no one should spare any efforts, to destroy the enemy and reduce them to the greatest extremities.[50]

It is precisely this method of fighting, the mass resistance of an entire population, that made Havelock's entry into Lucknow in September 1857 so difficult and cumbersome.[51] The attempt to rally everybody to participate in some way or other in the cause

---

[50]Proclamation enclosed with translation of a pamphlet entitled *Fateh Islam:* For. Dept. Political Proc., 30 Dec. 1859, Suppl. No. 1135-1139: *F.S.U.P.*, ii, pp. 160-2 (hereafter Proclamation).
[51]See Ch. 4

was a running theme. Prince Feroze Shah, in a proclamation issued in early 1858, exhorted that—

all of us must conjointly exert ourselves for the protection of our lives, property and religion and to root out the English from the country. . .
Those that are old should offer their prayers. The rich but old should assist our sacred warriors with money.
Those in perfect health as well as young should attend in person.[52]

The preservation of religion emerged as the dominant rallying cry of the rebellion. The revolt was seen as a war of religion. It was a firm conviction among all sections of the rebels that the British 'wish to deprive the Hindoos and Mahomedans of their religion and wish them to become Christians.'[53] Feroze Shah informed the people that—

Within the last few years the British commenced to oppress the people in India, under different pleas and continued to eradicate Hindooism and Mahomedanism and to make all the people embrace Christianity.[54]

He circulated a list of the 'real intentions' of the British. Among these were[55]: (1) burning all the books of every other religion (2) making eating and drinking with Europeans compulsory for Indians seeking employment (3) destroying mosques and temples (4) forbidding Maulavis and Brahmins to preach (5) administering all law courts according to English law (6) compelling all marriages to take place according to English customs under the supervision of English priests (7) prohibiting all prescriptions made out by Hindu and Muslim physicians, and substituting these with English medicine (8) disallowing Hindu and Muslim

---

[52]Proclamation issued by Prince Mirza Mahomed Feroze Shah on 3 Rujib 1274 (17 Feb. 1858): For. Dept. Secret. Cons., 30 April 1858, Cons. Nos. 121-122 (hereafter Proclamation: Feroze Shah). The famous proclamation of Bahadur Shah issued on 25 Aug. 1857 known as the Azamgarh Proclamation analyses the grievances of different sections of the population — the rich, zamindars, merchants, public servants, sepoys, artisans, pundits, fakirs and other learned persons — and appeals to them to join the struggle. The full text of the Proclamation is given in C. Ball, *The Mutiny*, ii, pp. 630-2 and in *F.S.U.P.*, i, p. 453-8 (hereafter Azamgarh Proclamation).

[53]Proclamation issued under the seal of Birjis Qadr Walee of Lucknow to all zamindars and inhabitants of the country of Lucknow: For. Dept. Secret Cons., 25 June 1858, Cons. No. 69 (hereafter Proclamation Birjis Qadr).

[54]Proclamation: Feroze Shah.

[55]Ibid.

fakirs from converting people without the permission of Christian missionaries (9) allowing only European doctors to assist Indian women at childbirth.

Deliberately the most sensitive issues, and those lying closest to the Indian heart, were picked to rouse people and show that 'the real purpose of this war is to save religion', and to make 'every Hindoo and Mussulman to render assistance to the utmost'.[56] In a different version of the same proclamation Feroze Shah saw himself as God's servant and urged others to join him:

Placing my trust in God; devoting myself solely to God's service; observing the precepts of religion; strengthening my determination . . . my sword taken in my hand, the sword of religious zeal, I arise in the name of God. We shall obtain victory through the grace of God, who promises victory to those who put their trust in him. Therefore again I urge you, and urge you one and all, join me prompted solely by the desire of doing God's work.[57]

A group of sepoys, while retreating into Nepal set out, in a tone of impotent despair, why they had fought. Here again the defence of faith comes into the limelight:

For a century ago the British arrived in Hindoostan and gradually entertained troops in their service, and became masters of every state. Our forefathers have always served them and we also entered their service. . . . By the mercy of God and with our assistance the British also conquered every place they liked, in which thousands of us, Hindoostani men were sacrificed, but we never made any excuses or pretences nor revolted. . . But in the year 1857 the British issued an order that new cartridges and muskets which had arrived from England were to be issued; in the former of which the fats of cows and pigs were mixed; and also that attah of wheat mixed with powdered human bones was to be eaten; and even distributed them in every Regiment of infantry, cavalry and artillery. . . . They gave these new cartridges to the sowars of the 3rd Light Cavalry, and ordered them to bite them; the troopers objected to it, and said that they would never bite them, for if they did, their religion and faith would be destroyed. . . . Upon this the British Officers paraded the men of the 3 Regiments and having prepared 1400 English soldiers, and other Battalions of European troops and Horse Artillery, surrounded them, and placing 6 guns before each of the infantry regiments, loaded the guns with grape and made 84 new troopers prisoners, and put them in jail with irons on them. . . . The reason, that the sowars of the said Canton-

[56]Ibid.
[57]This version of the proclamation is in Abstract N.W.P. Narrative, Foreign, 1858: *F.S.U.P.*, i, pp. 459-63.

ment were put into jail, was that we should be frightened into biting the new cartridges; on this account we and all our country-men having united together, have fought here and there with the British for the preservation of our faith. . . . we have been compelled to make war for two years and the Rajahs and Chiefs who are with us in faith and religion, are still so, and have undergone all sorts of trouble; we have fought for two years in order that our faith and religion may not be polluted. If the religion of a Hindoo or Mussalman is lost, what remains in the world?[58]

The growing belief that there was a conspiracy to despoil cherished religion and caste, and the fear that coercion would be used if necessary to break the faith, acted as the motors of collective hatred. Talukdars and rebel leaders in the countryside also believed that the fight was in defence of the faith. Beni Madho referred to his enemies as 'heathens';[59] in the period when British troops were moving into the Awadh countryside and many talukdars were wavering, they were urged to carry on fighting by these words:

they [the British] have decided to make all Christians; some villagers have deserted their religion and gone over to the British. . . . We have given up our means of livelihood and stand by our religion, we have accepted hanging, we have been fighting a whole year. . .
This is a religious war. . . . If you are fighting for your religion, say so before the evening.[60]

The classic anti-British invective occurred in the Begum's reply to the Queen's proclamation which promised non-interference in religious matters. The counter proclamation of the Begum retaliated with:

In the Proclamation it is written, that the Christian religion is true, but no other creed will suffer oppression, and that the laws will be observed towards all. What has the administration of justice to do with the truth or falsehood of a religion? That religion is true which acknowledges one God, and knows no other. Where there are three Gods in a religion,

---

[58]Abstract Translation of an Arzi from the rebel camp on the part of all the rebel officers, sepoys to Maharaja Jang Bahadur, no date: For. Dept. Political Cons., 13 May 1859, Cons. No. 326: *F.S.U.P.*, ii, pp. 603-5. A party of prisoners were individually asked before their execution why they had fought and what was the object of the war. And each one of them replied: 'The slaughter of the English was required by our religion. . .', Ball, *The Mutiny*, ii, p. 242.

[59]See Beni Madho's letters in *F.S.U.P.*, ii, pp. 392ff.

[60]Translation of letter from Naipal Singh to Thakurs Balkuri Singh, Sital Singh: For. Dept. Secret Cons., 25 June 1858, Cons. No. 57.

neither Mussulmans nor Hindoos — nay, not even Jews, Sun-worshippers, or Fire-worshippers can believe it true. To eat pigs and drink wine, to bite greased cartridges, and to mix pigs fat with flour and sweetmeats, to destroy Hindoo and Mussulman temples on pretence of making roads, to build churches, to send clergymen into the streets and alleys to preach the Christian religion, to institute English schools and to pay people a monthly stipend for learning the English sciences, while the places of worship of Hindoos and Mussulmans are to this day entirely neglected; with all this, how can the people believe that religion will not be interfered with? The rebellion began with religion, and for it, millions of men have been killed. Let not our subjects be deceived; thousands were deprived of their religion in the North-West, and thousands were hanged rather than abandon their religion.[61]

Everything connected with the British had *ipso facto* become suspect. The liberal zeal of the era of reform had come home to roost with a vengeance; every act was now interpreted as a deliberate attack on indigenous religious practices and traditions. It had forged a unity between two causes: the defence of religion and the fight against the British. The civilizing mission of Bentinck and Macaulay was now paying its dues and more: the belief in Indian inferiority and the 'pacific triumphs of reason over barbarism'[62] had recoiled into a veritable crusade. This is not to say that religion was all that there was to the revolt of 1857. However, it did form a vital component of the tradition that determined the circumstances in which the insurgents tried to reshape their own history. In the Indian world of the nineteenth century, religion was a part of the ordinary business of common life, symbolizing human trust and vitality — the 'general theory of this world, its encyclopaedic compendium, its logic in a popular form, its spiritualistic *point d'honneur*, its enthusiasm, its moral sanction, its solemn complement, its universal source of consolation and justification.'[63] In such a context, religion not only became the sigh of the oppressed, but in a cataclysmic moment like 1857 it also

[61]Translation of a proclamation issued by the Begum in the name of Birjis Qadr: For. Dept. Political Cons. 17 Dec. 1858, Cons. No. 251 (hereafter Proclamation: Begum).

[62]These words are Charles Trevelyan's, quoted in T.R. Metcalf, *The Aftermath of Revolt: India, 1857-1870* (London, 1965), p. 12.

[63]K. Marx, *A Contribution to the Critique of Hegel's Philosophy of Right*, Introduction, in Marx, *Early Writings*, ed. L. Colletti (Harmondsworth, 1975), p. 244.

coloured the articulation of all grievances. It helped create a unity, in opposition to the British, which covered a broad spectrum of society.

It is remarkable that even though many of the leaders who issued proclamations were Muslims, no divisive issues between Hindus and Muslims were invoked. The rebellion was seen as a war in which both Hindus and Muslims had equally to lose or gain. The emphasis was always on pre-British Hindu-Muslim coexistence within the Mughal imperial framework. Bahadur Shah's proclamation emphasized the standard of Mohammad and the standard of Mahavir.[64] Every proclamation mentioned Hindus and Muslims and their respective religions in the same breath. Even a pamphlet called *Fateh Islam* (Victory of Islam) emphasized this coexistence and co-operation:

The Hindoos should join the Chief with a view to defend their religion, and should solemnly pledge themselves; the Hindoos and the Mahomedans, as brethren to each other, should also butcher the English, in as much as formerly the Mahomedan Kings protected the lives and property of the Hindoos with their children in the same manner as protected those of the Mahomedans, and all the Hindoos with heart and soul were obedient and loyal to the Mahomedan Kings. . . . The Hindoos will remain steadfast to their religion, while we will also retain ours. Aid and protection will be offered by us to each other.[65]

This opposition to the British was not merely politic: it had an unmistakable stamp of spontaneity and harked back to the Mughal traditions with which the insurgents identified. The communal unity could survive considerable strain: witness the British failure to raise the Hindu population of Bareilly against the Muslims in 1858.[66] The prevalent spirit of harmony was

---

[64]The relevant passage runs: 'I, who am the grandson of Abul Muzuffer Serajuddin Bahadur Shah Ghazee, King of India, having in the course of circuit come here to extirpate the infidels. . . and to liberate and protect the poor helpless people now groaning under their iron rule, have by the aid of the Majahdeens, or religious fanatics, erected the standard of Mohammad, and persuaded the orthodox Hindoos who had been subject to my ancestors, and have been and are still accessories in the destruction of the English, to raise the standard of Mahavir'. The Azamgarh Proclamation.

[65]Proclamation.

[66]Couper to Edmonstone, 1 Dec. 1857: '. . . [Chief Commissioner] had authorized the sum of Rs 50,000 to be expended in an attempt to raise the Hindoo population of Bareilly against the Mahommedan rebels. . . the attempt was quite

expressed most convincingly when the rebels hailed the young Muslim prince Birjis Qadr as Lord Krishna.[67]

A War of Restoration?

The other major theme of rebel propaganda harped on disaffection created by British annexations. According to Feroze Shah they did not intend to leave a *biswa* of land with the Indian rulers.[68] Birjis Qadr noted how dishonourably the Company had acted towards Awadh:

It is known to everyone that my ancestors brought the British into Hindostan; but Bulvant Sing, the Rajah of Benares, was cause of much annoyance to them, and therefore the province of Benares was given to them. A treaty was then signed by the British, in which they wrote that they would never act treacherously as long as the sun and moon should exist. But they have broken that treaty, and dethroning my father, Wajid Ali Shah, have sequestered his state, palaces, and everything he had.[69]

The Begum, as the sole spokesman of the rebels at the time, in her retort to the Queen's proclamation condemned every single act of annexation in north and central India. Her broadside summed up the Indian reaction to such annexations:

In the Proclamation it is written that all contracts and agreements entered into by the Company will be accepted by the Queen. Let the people carefully observe this artifice. The Company has seized on the whole of Hindoostan and if this arrangement be accepted, what is then new in it. The Company professed to treat the Chief of Bhurtpore as a son, and then took his territory. The Chief of Lahore was carried off to London, and it has not fallen to his lot to return, the Nawab Shumshoodeen Khan on one side they hanged, and on the other side, they took off their hats and salammed to him, the Peswah they expelled from Poonah Sitara and imprisoned for life in Bithoor, their breach of faith with Sultan Tippoo is well known, the Rajah of Benares they imprisoned in Agra. Under pretence of administering the country of the Chief of Gwalior they introduced English customs, they have left no name or traces of the Chiefs of Behar, Orissa and Bengal; they gave the Raes of Farruck-

---

unsuccessful and has been abandoned. . .': For. Dept. Secret Cons., 27 Aug. 1858, Cons. No. 25.

[67]See Ch. 4.   [68]Proclamation: Feroze Shah.

[69]Abstract Translation of a letter from Birjis Qadr to Maharaja of Nepal, 7 Jeth Samvat 1915 (9 May 1858): For. Dept. Secret Cons., 27 Aug. 1858, Cons. Nos. 97-108: *F.S.U.P.*, ii, pp. 444-5.

abad a small monthly allowance and took his territory. Shajenhanpore, Bareilly, Azimgurh, Jounpore, Gorruckpore, Etawah, Allahabad, Futtehpore etc. our ancient possessions they took from us on pretence of distributing pay and in the 7th article of the Treaty, they wrote on oath, that they would take no more from us, if then the arrangement made by the Company are to be accepted what is the difference between the former and present state of things? These are old affairs, but recently, in defiance of treaties and oaths, and notwithstanding that they owed us millions of Rupees, without reason, and on the pretence of the misgovernment and discontent of our people, they took our country and property worth millions of Rupees. If our people were discontented with our Royal predecessor, Wajid Ally Shah, how come they are content with us? And no ruler ever experienced such loyalty and devotion of life and goods as we have done? What then is wanting that they do not restore our country?

Further it is written in the Proclamation that they want no increase of territory but yet they cannot refrain from annexation. If the Queen has assumed the Government why does Her Majesty not restore our country to us when our people wish it?[70]

Each act of annexation was a grievance, an act of treachery. Consequently the British could no longer be trusted. The emphasis on property was reiterated in Birjis Qadr's proclamation, where it was noted that under native governments property, being 'dear to every man', was never confiscated, whereas under the British it was not sacrosanct.[71]

Such sentiments not only tie up with the grievances of dispossessed talukdars but are also a pointer to the order of things visualized by the rebel leadership. Here was an almost automatic and perhaps inevitable affiliation with the viewpoint of the magnates and the propertied classes. Hierarchy, status based on lineage, and honour were important. All pre-British Indian sarkars had preserved the people's izzat and had allowed every man—

to possess his honour according to his worth and capacity, be he a person of good descent, of any caste or community Syud, Sheikh, Moghul or Pathan, among the Mahomedans or Brahmin, Chhuttree, Bais or Kaith among the Hindoos. All these retain their respectability according to their respective ranks, and no person of a lower order such as sweeper, chamar, Dhanook or Pasee can claim equality with them.[72]

But under the *angrez* sarkar—

The honour and respectability of the higher orders are considered by

[70] Proclamation: Begum.
[71] Proclamation: Birjis Qadr.
[72] Ibid.

them equal to the honour and respectability of the lower orders, nay, comparatively with the latter they treat the former, with contempt and disrespect; and at the instance of a chamar force the attendance of a Nawab or a Rajah and subject him to indignity.[73]

In the immemorial pattern of society as a hierarchy in which some ruled and some obeyed, where patronage and deference were important, the move from status to merit and contract was an assault which had to be resisted. But even in the resistance, hierarchy must be maintained; a chief must be appointed to lead and guide the fighting, and his leadership must be accepted as an article of faith:

Common sense and a regard for faith point out that servitude under the Mahomedan Chiefs and such Rajahs as are dependents of the Mahomedan Kings is infinitely better than that, under the infidel Victoria and the English, the enemies of our faith.[74]

The magnates or lords of the land had a prerogative to lead. This was reinforced by promises to talukdars of lighter jama, preservation of honour and complete autonomy in one's ilaqa.[75]

This espousal of hierarchy, property and honour was in conformity with Mughal tradition, the ideal generally accepted by the leadership. The British had undermined the traditional world of lineage, lordship, patronage, service and deference. The primordial loyalties asserted themselves in rebellion. In a sense perhaps the revolt was voicing the viewpoint of an older political, economic and cultural order that had lost its viability in the previous century. This emerged also in the fact that the rebel leadership, trammelled as it was by Mughal vestiges, could not think about artisan production beyond exclusive employment 'in the services of the Kings, the rajah and the rich', although they showed a remarkable awareness of the ruin of artisans and weavers under the impact of foreign commerce.[76] However, it would be wrong to

[73]Ibid. [74]Proclamation.
[75]See the Azamgarh Proclamation: '. . . in the Badshahi Government. . . the Jumas will be light, the dignity and honour of the zemindars safe, and every zemindar will have absolute rule in his own zemindary'. Also, proclamations were issued to talukdars which announced that 'half the Jama of the Ilaqas will be allowed free to all those Taluqdars and Zemindars who fight and kill the English': Letter of a talukdar to Ahmad Ullah Shah: Lucknow Collectorate Mutiny *Basta: F.S.U.P.*, ii, p. 379.
[76]The Azamgarh Proclamation.

deny the validity and strength of rebel aims simply because they harked back to a previous order. Their pertinence lies in what the rebels thought were the shortcomings of British rule and in what they considered the British had destroyed or attempted to destroy. To them Britain's work in India was an onslaught on their traditional, familiar world, and on cherished values. Theirs was not a struggle to establish a new social order. British rule had turned their world topsyturvy; their aim was to restore that world, and all therin. Their essential sentiment was indignation, their essential aim restoration.

Talukdars and Peasants: A Popular Resistance?

An appendix to this chapter gives a list of the talukdars of southern Awadh and a description of how they behaved during the revolt. The number of men these talukdars could provide is given in the appendix to Chapter 2, which shows the distribution and strength of talukdars' forts. This important item of information has been overlooked in the extant literature on the subject.

The talukdars' multiple roles in the rebellion covered a wide spectrum. There were consistent loyalists like Rustam Sah; others like Man Singh were loyal in the beginning and later fought actively, but as the wind changed became turncoats. Hanwant Singh steered a middle course. First a protector to the British, later a participant in the rebellion, he submitted as soon as British troops entered his ilaqa but always maintained his dignity and honour. Lal Madho Singh was a shade different from Hanwant Singh as he was more involved in the fighting and only submitted at the last moment while his men were still intent on fighting. And finally there was Beni Madho a rebel from the beginning till his death in Nepal.

The talukdars, both big and small, participated in the revolt wholeheartedly, and their action was not necessarily related to the losses they suffered under the British revenue settlement. This near-universal participation by the talukdars was widely noticed Outram noted in a letter to Canning about the Awadh Proclamation that among the chief rajas of Awadh one would find only a dozen who were loyal to the Raj.[77] S.B. Chaudhuri's researches reinforce such a conclusion.[78] In southern Awadh—i.e. in the districts of Unao, Salon, Sultanpur, Faizabad and Dariabad — nearly seventy-four per cent of the talukdars fought or opposed the British. The extent of the talukdars' participation is emphasized in the comment of a British revenue officer who noted that to exclude from settlement talukdars who had carried the flag of revolt outside Awadh would result in a major upheaval:

> It would have the effect of changing more than half the land tenures of the Byratch division; one third of Faizabad, two-thirds of Sultanpur, nearly the whole of Salone, and similar results in Seetapore and Mahomdee.[79]

The above calculation is based only on one criterion — the invasion of the North-Western Provinces. The picture would be even more staggering if rebellion *per se* was taken as the yardstick. In Salon only 12 out of 40 talukdars were loyal; in Sultanpur 11 out of 37; in Unao 1 out of 11; in Faizabad 3 out of 8 and in Dariabad 8 out of 30. If detailed lists were available for Gonda, Bahraich, Sitapur and Muhamdi, where talukdars held the major chunk of the villages before annexation[80] and where the revolt did acquire a measure of intensity and durability, they would almost certainly reveal a similar pattern.

The only possible debate refers to the question of motives — a controversy dating back to the events themselves. British officers in Awadh saw a clear linkage between the Company's revenue policies and the talukdari revolt. Reid, who was an officer in Faizabad, wrote in June 1857 that the revolt was to be expected since 'Our settlement operations created such a social revolution'.[81] Another officer thought that the disaffection of the talukdars was 'natural enough as we have deprived them of part of their income.'[82] Outram also located the reasons for the talukdars' support to the rebel cause in the unjust treatment they had

---

[77] Couper to Edmonstone, 8 March 1858: *F.S.U.P.*, ii, p. 333.

[78] Chaudhuri, *Civil Rebellion*, pp. 309ff.

[79] Letter to Sec. to Chief Commr., no name, no date: BROG File No. 1037. The contents of the letter make it obvious that the writer was a high official.

[80] See Table 3.

[81] Reid to Edmonstone 29 June 1857: For. Dept. Secret Cons., 25 Sept. 1857, Cons. No. 517.

[82] (Illegible) to Outram, 17 Sept. 1857: Mutiny Papers of Outram etc.

received in the settlement operations.[83] Some officers even suggested that the quickest way to quell the rebellion in Awadh was to cancel the settlement with the village proprietors and to engage in settlement with talukdars.[84] Canning, however, was quick to perceive that the causes of rebellion were not so straightforward. He noted that talukdars who had lost as well as those who had benefited were both involved in the rebellion:

> No chiefs have been more open in their rebellion than the Rajah of Churda, Bhinga and Gonda. The Governor-General believes that the first of these did not lose a single village by a Summary Settlement, and certainly his assessment was materially reduced. The second was dealt with in a like liberal manner. The Rajah of Gonda lost about thirty villages out of 400 but his assessment was lowered by some 10,000 rupees.
>
> No one was more benefited by the change of government than the young Rajah of Naunpara. His estates had been the object of a civil war with a rival claimant for three years, and of these he was at once recognized as sole proprietor by the British government, losing only six villages out of more than a thousand. His mother was appointed guardian, but her troops have been fighting against us at Lucknow from the beginning.
>
> The Rajah of Dhowrera also a minor was treated with equal liberality. Every village was settled with his family; yet those people turned upon Captain Hearsay and his party. . . .
>
> Ashruf Bux Khan, a large talookdar in Gonda, who had long been an object of persecution by the late Government, was established in the possession of all his property by us; yet he has been strongly hostile.
>
> It is clear that injustice at the hands of the British government has not been the cause of the hostility which, in these instances at least, has been displayed towards our rule.
>
> The moving spirit of these men and of others amongst the Chiefs of Oude must be looked for elsewhere; and in the opinion of the Governor-General, it is to be found mainly in the repugnance which they feel to suffer any restraint of their hitherto arbitrary powers over those about them, to a diminution of their importance by being brought under equal laws, and to the obligation of disbanding their armed followers. . . .[85]

A distinguished historian has, in recent times, agreed with the general line of Canning's argument: what mattered was not the extent of loss or the more material dimension but the 'subjective attachment to a traditional status and way of life', military lord-

---

[83]Couper to Edmonstone, 8 March 1858.

[84]Tucker to Canning, 12 July 1857: For. Dept. Secret Cons., 18 Dec. 1857, Cons. No. 73.

[85]Edmonstone to Outram, 31 March 1858: *F.S.U.P.*, ii, pp. 337-8.

ship and jurisdiction.[86] It is true that loss of status angered the talukdars; according to Hanwant Singh, British rule in Awadh was unpopular because 'to rich and poor we mete out even justice; a Talookdar cannot buy an acquittal'.[87] This loss of status and honour was also emphasized in various proclamations. Charles Wingfield also noted that the talukdars disliked British rule 'because it reduced them to disband their armies, pay their revenue regularly, and not oppress their ryots.'[88] However, to separate the loss of status from the impact of British revenue policy is to introduce an artificial distinction. It has to be stressed that from the outset British policy was consistently anti-talukdar. This led to large-scale dispossession in some areas, as has been noted in Chapter 2, and also to loss to status. Material loss and status-dissonance were not always separate, watertight compartments. Both occurred in the more general context of an anti-talukdar policy. Individual losses suffered by each and every talukdar are not possible to quantify; the losses of some of the important rebels like Loni Singh, Lal Madho, Beni Madho, Hanwant Singh, Man Singh have been noted. Those of some small talukdars are recorded in the appendix.[89] Their importance is not in question. Hanwant Singh emphasized it in his statement to Barrow.[90] During the later stages of the rebellion, when overtures were being made to the talukdars, Beni Madho 'expressed fears that Government will as before make a summary settlement for three years and then take his estate. . .'[91] Lal Madho Singh was ready to submit to Lord Clyde provided his estates were guaranteed to him.[92] In fact more and more talukdars submitted when they realized that the British were intent on restoring them to

[86]Stokes, *Peasant and the Raj*, pp. 133 and 135.

[87]Memo by Carnegy, 21 Sept. 1858: B.R. Partapgarh File No. 385 Part 1, also available in For. Dept. Political Proc., 22 Oct. 1858, No. 263.

[88]Quoted in Metcalf, *Land Landlords and the Raj*, p. 175 Metcalf cites two memos by Wingfield dated 6 Feb. 1858 and 17 May 1858. The quoted sentence does not occur in the latter.

[89]It may be noted that the Raja of Baundi in whose fort the Begum lived after the fall of Lucknow had been excluded from the terms of the Summary Settlement: Wingfield's Memo of 17 May 1858: BROG File No. 1037.

[90]See Ch. 3.

[91]Forsyth to Edmonstone, 24 July 1858: For. Dept. Secret Cons., 27 Aug. 1858, Cons. No. 33.

[92]Ball, *The Mutiny*, ii, p. 530.

their lands; if their estates were to be restored resistance could be sacrificed.[93] Where it occurred, dispossession (whether absolute or relative) and the loss of status and overlordship had a shattering impact on the world of rural Awadh. Together they created the basis for disaffection and revolt. It is an otiose exercize in disaggregation to assess which of the two grievances was of paramount importance.

Other concerns also motivated the talukdars. Hanwant Singh emphasized the general unpopularity of the annexation — 'every one wishes to see the King restored, if not to the throne, at least to the country'.[94] He himself was a personal friend of Wajid Ali Shah and wished that the British would not tax his loyalty to his king.[95] The plight of the king and his family had moved him:

... with tears in his eyes the old man appealed to me 'is it justice' said he 'to turn a deaf ear when the King has sent his very women to plead at the very foot of your throne? Surely not.'[96]

Such traditional loyalties asserted themselves in the rebellion, drawing people out to resist an alien government. Beni Madho remained firmly committed to the king he had chosen to serve: 'Now if I were to swerve from his [Birjis Qadr's] directions I shall be faithless, and in my disposition there is no grain of faithlessness toward anyone'.[97] Mehndi Hussain, the former raja of Farrukhabad and the famous rebel of Sultanpur, announced while submitting to Lord Clyde, 'I was twenty-five years in the service of the King of Oude', implying, according to Ball, that 'he could not, as a man of honour, help fighting in the cause of one he had served so long'.[98] Evidently a varied and complex set of motives was at work.

This aspect of the rebellion is often underplayed. Metcalf plays down the talukdars' opposition to the British by emphasizing

---

[93]'I have reason to know that many Talookdars expressed themselves highly pleased on hearing that hopes had been held out to one of their number, that he might retain certain of his villages, while a rehearing would be granted in regard to other villages': so Carnegy to Bowring, 31 March 1858: For. Dept. Secret Cons., 28 May 1858, Cons. No. 397.
[94]Memo by Carnegy.
[95]Ibid., and Memo by Barrow 25 Oct. 1858: BROG File No. 1037.
[96]Memo by Carnegy.
[97]Quoted in Metcalf, *Land, Landlords and the Raj*, p. 179.
[98]Ball, *The Mutiny*, ii, p. 562.

that they were basically fighting out old clan or family rivalries: 'The Mutiny was simply an arena in which old rivalries could be fought out anew.'[99] The example he chooses to illustrate his case is the rivalry between the raja of Balrampur and his enemy on the neighbouring Tulsipur estate, these representing the Janwar and Raikwar clans respectively. He argues that once the rani of Tulsipur and her followers had thrown in their lot with the rebellion and out of their old enmity had turned against the raja of Balrampur, the latter had to remain loyal to the British. Quite possibly some talukdars did try to settle old scores during the general upheaval. But at the same time some bridges were in fact mended, and ancient enemies fought together on the same side and against the hated firangi. One could counter Metcalf's example of the Balrampur-Tulsipur conflict with that of Chaudhuri Raghunath Singh of Jabrowli, a Janwar Rajput, who was a bitter foe of Beni Madho but yet made up his quarrel through the mediation of the raja of Daundiakhera and fought actively for Beni Madho.[100] Similarly Fateh Bahadur (No 13 in the Appendix) joined Beni Madho even though the latter had once imprisoned him under Nawabi rule. In the rebellion many clans and families, with competing and divergent past histories, fought together against a common enemy. It is this unified opposition, rather than the odd exception, that strikes the historian of the revolt.[101]

Concerning the talukdars' participation there remains one more ghost to lay. This is the view that the revolt was basically compartmentalized, with very few linkages. To quote Stokes:

Only a small handful of these [the leaders of the revolt] were fit or willing to look beyond their local horizon, even in Oudh where the magnate levies formed the bulk of the rebel forces compartmentalism remained the order of the day. Only when a local magnate was forcibly tipped out of his district by British military action was he constrained to enlarge his political horizon.[102]

[99]Metcalf, *Land, Landlords and the Raj*, p. 177.
[100]See Appendix (No. 16).
[101]Metcalf (p. 177, note 25) cites Elliott, *Chronicles of Oonao* (p. 51) for more instances of 'family feuds determining behaviour during the Mutiny'. What Elliott describes is the feud between Runjeet Singh and Oomrao Singh and Buljor Singh and also states that the two sides took opposing sides in the revolt. Elliot does not imply or state that their old feud had a *determining* influence on their choice of sides in the revolt.
[102]Stokes, *Peasant and the Raj*, p. 132.

It has already been noted how even before any kind of British victory in Awadh many talukdars had moved away from their own locality into Lucknow or had at least sent their fighting men there. In a sense, until the fall of Lucknow a large number of talukdars considered the defence of Lucknow, and therefore the defence of Awadh, top priority; at this time their political horizon was certainly not restricted to their own ilaqa. In fact this widening of linkages had begun earlier. Kaye records that many of the chiefs and Lucknow 'soukars' — he mentions Man Singh by name — were in correspondence with Nana Sahib about the revolt.[103] Some of the talukdars of southern Awadh fought for the Nana or sent help to him.[104] Beni Madho's brother Jograj Singh went to Kanpur to assist Nana Sahib. (See Appexdix No. 9). The Kanpur uprising itself was said to have been instigated by one Jwala Prasad, a Brahmin from Baiswara. (Table 15). Jailal Singh personally welcomed the Nana, on Birjis Qadr's behalf, when he came to Awadh in August 1857.[105] Birjis Qadr's links with the Mughal court and traditions have also been noted.

It is true that men like Khan Bahadur Khan, Feroze Shah or Kunwar Singh came into Awadh only after they had been 'tipped out' from their own region. Yet Khan Bahadur Khan was aware of the close connections between the Awadh and the Rohilkhand rebellions.[106] Kunwar Singh may have been drawn into the Awadh rebellion because of his near relation Beni Madho, and also because he wanted to ally himself to Man Singh.[107] It is significant that the rebel court in Lucknow gave a farman for Azamgarh to Kunwar Singh.[108] This not only shows the linkages of Kunwar Singh with the revolt in Awadh but also reinforces the thesis that the Lucknow court was harking back to its pre-British

---

[103]Kaye, *Sepoy War*, i, p. 579n.
[104]See Appendix (Nos. 82 and 85).
[105]*F.S.U.P.*, ii, p. 116.
[106]See Ch. 4.
[107]Beni Madho's son had married the granddaughter of Kunwar Singh. See K.K. Datta, *Biography of Kunwar Sing and Amar Sing* (Patna, 1957), p. 143, note 2. That Kunwar Singh was seeking an alliance with Man Singh is mentioned in ibid.
[108]Ibid., p. 142.

authority, i.e. the kingdom of Awadh before its truncation in 1801 by Wellesley. The reactions of talukdars could often be influenced by factors operating from outside their locality. Barrow thought that Hanwant Singh's initial hesitation in joining the rebellion was influenced by the loyalty of his near relation, the raja of Rewa.[109] He felt pulled in two opposite directions by the raja of Rewa and his personal friendship with Wajid Ali; these two demands on his loyalty — both operating from outside his local world — were evident in his behaviour. A number of letters[110] from various talukdars to the Maulavi indicate that they were willing to ally themselves to forces and persons extraneous to their locality. Rebel leadership, whether magnate, court bureaucrat or religious fakirs and dervishes, was not always confined to, and concerned with, localities. The rebels' vision may not have been national, yet they were open to influence from outside their ilaqa and their political horizons could extend beyond their locality to encompass more general causes and movements.

The real strength of the talukdars' resistance, and indeed of the revolt in Awadh, sprang from the unhesitating and complete support received from the peasantry and the general populace of the Awadh countryside. Beni Madho had claimed to Sleeman that when required his entire peasantry would fight with him.[111] This was not a vainglorious boast: in the uprising, according to Barrow, there was 'hardly a village in Bainswara' which had not furnished its quota for the huge force under Beni Madho.[112] And in his own estate Beni Madho received the support and sympathy of the village zamindars and peasants because of the latters' 'attachment' to the talukdar.[113] In the revolt the talukdars did provide the bulk of the fighting force. Their levies far exceeded the number of their retainers. For example Rana Raghunath Singh of Khajurgaon had 1,500 retainers, but within a few hours he could

[109]Memo by Barrow, 25 Oct. 1858: BROG File No. 1037.
[110]These letters will be found in *F.S.U.P.*, ii, pp. 367-79.
[111]See Ch. 1.
[112]Barrow's Memo of 9 Apr. 1859 cited in Metcalf, *Lana, Landlords and the Raj*, p. 182.
[113]Commr. Lucknow to Sec., C.C., 17 June 1859: cited in Metcalf, *Land, Landlords and the Raj*, p. 183.

provide three to four thousand men.[114] These must have been his peasants and clansmen. In the context of Awadh agrarian relations, with their mutual dependence and interpenetrations, such support and joint resistance came naturally. Resistance to the British was greatest and most prolonged in southern Awadh; and after this had been reduced, fighting moved onto Gonda-Bahraich, i.e. resistance was most concentrated in those areas which have been delineated as the axis of talukdar-peasant interdependence.[115] Man Singh noted the importance of southern Awadh when he wrote that the rebellion was continuing because of the 'delay which has occurred in chastising Bainswarah'.[116]

The large-scale participation of the peasantry emerges from the character of fighting in rural Awadh. An officer reporting from the Awadh-N.W.P. border noted:

... the Oude people are gradually pressing down on the line of communication from the North. . . . The Oude people are villagers. . . these villagers are nearly intangible to Europeans melting away before them and collecting again. The Civil Authorities report these villagers to amount to a very large number of men, with a number of guns.[117]

Talukdars were convinced that theirs was 'an army composed of men of every village'.[118] Outram perhaps implied the popular and peasant character of the resistance when he commented that the British were faced with an enemy 'ever able to move two miles to our one'.[119] The Chief of Staff himself noted how 'the *population of the country* rose and closed in on its rear' when the British army had advanced into Awadh.[120] Moreover, the general populace did not indulge in random fighting:

---

[114]See Appendix (No. 10).

[115]See Ch. 1.

[116]Man Singh to C.C. n.d.: For. Dept., Secret Cons. 30 July 1858, Cons. No. 72. The letter was probably written in July 1858 because Man Singh says he has just been besieged.

[117]O'Brien to G.G. and C-in-C, 21 Aug 1857: For. Dept., Secret Cons., 18 Dec. 1857: Cons. No. 596.

[118]Translation of letter from Naipal Sing to Thakur Bulkri Sing, and Situl Sing: For. Dept., Secret Cons. 25 June 1858, Cons. No. 57.

[119]Couper to Edmonstone 18 Jan. 1858: For. Dept., Secret Cons., 29 Jan. 1858, Cons. No. 361.

[120]Chief of Staff to Edmonstone, 19 June 1858: For. Dept., Secret Cons., 30 July 1858, Cons. No. 76 (emphasis mine).

It is very true that according to our notions of regular armies the insurgents have the appearance of a rabble but those who have dealt most with the Insurgents know that this rabble fights on a system. . . when the late Sir Henry Havelock tried in the first instant to force his way into Oudh, he was obliged to retreat before the 'rabble' enemy.[121]

The people of Awadh had fought the British. This is clear from the number of ordinary and common weapons — the armoury of a 'peasant' army — that were recovered or surrendered. By the beginning of February 1859 there had been collected 29,941 spears, 427,932 swords and 129,414 firearms.[122] Bows and arrows were counted at 6,418.[123] Firearms could be recovered even from the house of an ordinary peasant.[124] The total strength, in numbers, behind the rebellion is impossible to determine. According to official British estimates—

the approximate number of rebels who have taken advantage of the Amnesty and returned to their homes without reporting themselves is according to reports received form District Officers Twenty thousand one hundred and twenty. I am however directed to observe that no reliance is to be placed on this return, as the number is quite inadequate and 200,000 is more likely to represent the number who have actually come in.

But it would be impossible to do more than guess the numbers that have returned to their homes under the Amnesty. Probably *three fourths of the adult male population of Oudh, had been in rebellion*. . .[125]

After this statement it would be labouring the obvious to emphasize the popular, widespread character of the resistance.

It is a common assumption in 'mutiny' literature that the peasantry participated only under magnate leadership.[126] It is true that talukdari leadership was dominant in the revolt in the countryside. But the peasantry did not have a completely subaltern role, merely following where the magnate led. The best illustration comes from the ilaqa of the raja of Balrampur, Britain's most steadfast ally in Awadh. While the talukdar remained loyal, only

---

[121]Chief of Staff to Edmonstone, 20 June 1858: Ibid., Cons. No. 77.
[122]Collection to Political Despatches 33 Pt. 2, Collection No. 21.
[123]List of Arms surrendered 16 Dec. 1858: For. Dept. Political Cons. 31 Dec. 1858, Cons. No. 244.
[124]Capt. Thomas to Commissioner of Ordnance. 1 June 1858: BROG File No. 754.
[125]Forsyth to Secy., Govt. of India, 27 June 1858: For Dept., Secret Cons. 22 July 1859, Cons. No. 223, (emphasis mine).
[126]Stokes, *Peasant and the Raj*, pp. 131 and 185.

300 of his men were willing to side with him, 'the sympathies of the rest and of all about him are with the rebels'.[127] Digbijai Singh of Morarmow, one of the major chiefs of Baiswara, himself saved British fugitives and did not join the revolt, but his men fought at Lucknow.[128] A large number of the Bachgoti talukdars of Sultanpur — in fact the majority of them[129] — remained loyal to the British, but 400 leaderless Bachgoti clansmen were present at Bhadiyan.[130] In Dariabad, Syed Rahamat Ali (No. 111 in the Appendix) did not participate in the rebellion but his ilaqa contained 'rebels in strength'. Rani Talamund Koer (No. 108 in the Appendix) sent her *karinda* to surrender, but her ilaqa was full of rebels and a large number of them were her own villagers. As late as October 1858, after most talukdars had started coming in, Barrow noted that the village communities had not rendered any assistance to the British forces when they entered a district and gradually assumed control.[131] Lal Madho Singh's peasantry and retainers were still intent on fighting and went off to join Beni Madho while the raja walked into Lord Clyde's camp. Hanwant Singh had to abandon his initial vacillation and join the fighting because of growing pressure around him.[132] Resistance in Awadh was not always elitist in character. The revolt there had a mass and popular base — peasants and clansmen could and often did act outside the magnates' initiative.

The participation and initiative of the peasantry assume greater significance if it is recalled that the sepoys were, in their origins, peasants with close ties with their kinsmen in the villages. To use a cliche, the sepoys were really peasants in uniform. The importance of the sepoys stands in no need of greater emphasis. Their part in the revolt is well chronicled. Even loyal sepoy

---

[127]Wingfield's Memo of 17 May 1858: BROG File No. 1037. It has to be pointed out that Metcalf (*Land and Landlords*, p. 176) on the evidence of the same memo says that the Balrampur raja had 3,000 supporters. This is evidently a mistake on the part of a very meticulous historian. I have checked the document and it clearly says: 'of his own men there are not 300 on whom he could rely, the sympathies of the rest and of all about him are with the rebels'.

[128]Appendix (No. 22).

[129]Appendix (Nos. 61-68).

[130]See Ch. 4.

[131]Barrow's Memo of 25 October 1858: BROG File No. 1037.

[132]Ibid.

families could throw up a rebel: Sitaram's son was a rebel.[133] There was a report that the Begum was in correspondence with certain 'loyal' regiments and the agreement was that 'when they engage the rebels the Regiments are to fire blank ammunition.'[134] The sepoys sparked off the rebellion; in Lucknow they also tried to keep a hand in the affairs of administration. In a sense therefore, given the sepoy-peasant linkages, the role of the peasantry was not really subordinate. In many cases their influence could be decisive. Even the arch rebel Beni Madho seems to have been pressurized by the sepoys and his men to keep on fighting. According to Hanwant Singh it was clear —

> that the rebellion was now kept up by the Sepoys who looked for no mercy and that Banee Madho and other Talookdars who had attached bodies of Mutineers to themselves found. . . [that] if they thought of joining the British the Sepoys would shoot them. . .[135]

The sepoy element persisted in fighting towards the end of 1858 because sepoys doubted the sincerity of the promises of pardon. There had been incidents in which sepoys promised a pardon had been killed without trial after surrender.[136] And such incidents were reported far and wide in Awadh.[137] Whereas talukdari elements in the revolt could be sure of a certain pardon, the peasant-sepoy element ran the risk of being butchered on surrendering.

It is of course an impossible task to assess precisely the motives that led the peasant to rebel. To be sure the heavy overassessment laid the material basis of their disaffection. The settlement, by removing the talukdar — whom the peasant often saw as his protector — left him in a no-man's land. The revenue demand disturbed his 'subsistence ethic'. The removal of the king had an

---

[133]Sitaram, *Sepoy to Subedar*, p. 168.

[134]Carnegy's Newsletter (News of 21 Feb. 1858): For. Dept., Political Proc. 30 Dec. 1859 Suppl. No. 1137.

[135]Carnegy's Memo 21 Sept. 1858: B.R. Partapgarh, File No. 385, Part 1.

[136]Russell, *Mutiny Diary*, p. 215 describes such a scene.

[137]These men [i.e. the rebel leadership in the Begum's camp at Baundi]. . . spread the most absurd and incredible reports in order to deter the wavering from submission. One story told and credited is that the British Officers enticed 1,000 sepoys to come in on promise of forgiveness and having secured them, put the whole body to death in one night. . .': Enclosure to Forsyth to Edmonstone 14 Aug. 1858: For. Dept., Secret Cons. 27 Aug. 1858, Cons. No. 40.

emotional impact which left its imprint on folk memory.[138] The entire range of fears about religion and caste that stirred the sepoys must have found echoes in the minds of the villagers. In fact the imposition of British rule and the subsequent policies caused an upheaval in the rural world. The Raj assaulted the traditional view of social norms and obligations, the realms of mutual interdependence between the raja and the peasant that constituted its moral economy. In the revolt of 1857, in the uprising of the entire agrarian population, this moral economy, the world of paternalism and beneficence, reasserted itself. Together the talukdar and peasant resisted intervention in their cherished world. The passionately held notions of the common weal, and the world of patronage and deference expressed themselves in such scenes of voluntary tendering of allegiance as Barrow witnessed in Hanwant Singh's courtyard,[139] in the talukdar's visualization of himself as a leader of protectors (*rakhwars*),[140] and in the united resistance and opposition the agrarian body presented. In a sense it was the revolt of a people trying to redeem their own past.

A whole amalgam of issues, an entire complex of emotions, traditions and loyalties worked themselves out in the revolt of 1857. Here was a military mutiny, sparked off by certain fears about caste and religion, merging itself with disaffection created by interventions in the traditional rural world of Awadh, using the loss of land, loss of a king and threats to religion as a rallying cry, seeking its identity in the traditions of a former despotism and finding its popular base among a rural confraternity held together by bonds of mutual interdependence. The multiplex issues and the popular bases were noted already in 1858:

Suddenly the people saw their King taken from amongst them and our

[138]See the folk songs about Wajid Ali and the annexation in W. Crooke, 'Songs About the King of Oudh', *The Indian Antiquary*, Vol. XL, 1911.

[139]'. . . within one week of the dissolution of Govt in the District, the District Officers witnessed Hanwant Sing's Courtyard crowded with the very Proprietors [i.e the proprietors who had been settled with] tendering their allegiance to the Talooqdar': Barrow Memo of 25 Oct. 1858: BROG File No. 1037.

[140]Gulab Singh, the talukdar of Tirowl, was charged in his trial with having been a leader in the rebellion; he retorted that 'he was leader of Protectives (Rakhwars) not of rebels; that his people protected and did not destroy'. George Tucker to Barrow, 1 March 1859, Report as to the conduct of Gulab Sing: B.R. Partapgarh, File No. 105.

administration substituted for his, which however bad, was at least native, and this sudden change of government was immediately followed by a Summary Settlement of the Revenue, which in a very considerable portion of the Province, deprived the most influential landholders of what they deemed to be their property, of what certainly had long given wealth and distinction and power to their families.

We must admit that, under these circumstances, the hostilities which have been carried on in Oude, have rather the character of legitimate war than that of rebellion.[141]

It is probable that the revolt was so intense because the people of Awadh thought they were fighting in a just and legitimate war. In Awadh the opposition to the British in 1857 was truly universal, a 'people's' resistance.[142] It represented not a revolutionary challenge but a popular rejection of an alien order.

---

[141] Secret Letter from East India House, London to Governor-General, 19 April 1858: F.S.U.P., ii, p. 340.

[142] Even Canning for all his disagreement with the Secret Letter of 19 April had to admit that 'the rising against our authority in Oude has been general, almost universal': Canning to Secret Committee of Court of Directors, 17 June 1858: F.S.U.P., ii, p. 353.

EPILOGUE

The world of rebels and insurgents is always one where suppression and defeat lurk in the shadows. The revolt of 1857 also suffered its ultimate doom in spite of the popular and widespread support that it received in Awadh. By the beginning of 1859 the triumph of the Raj was complete. The reasons for the revolt's failure concern the historian. Reasons such as disunity, lack of leadership, inferior generalship and military expertise have been noted elsewhere.[1] The argument of this book questions the importance of some of these — such as lack of unity — at least in the case of Awadh. That the British were superior in military and tactical matters cannot be denied. Contemporary observers noted, for example, that most of the talukdars' forts in Awadh lacked a 'bomb-proof cover' and were therefore easy to besiege.[2] There was also the greater effectiveness of grapeshot.

What does not figure in any account of the rebellion is how the rebels themselves perceived their defeat. There is some stray evidence of their reactions which may be of interest. Hanwant Singh confessed to Carnegy that most rebels had been amazed by the resources of the British. They had expected that the British would need the help of France to quell the conflagration.[3] However, Hanwant Singh thought that the British success was mainly due to the fact that the revolt 'belonged to Oude and was not participated in by the men of influence throughout the rest of India'.[4] This contention invites further enquiry. For one thing it focuses on the strength of the rebellion in Awadh, i.e. its popular base as distinct from the rather narrow support it received in other areas. There is need for more detailed studies of other areas — e.g. Rohilkhand and the Doab — if we are to assess the validity of

---

[1] Majumdar, *Sepoy Mutiny*, pp. 270 ff.
[2] Lord Clyde to Lord Canning, 7 Jan. 1859: quoted *in extenso* in Ball, *The Mutiny*, ii, p. 565.
[3] Carnegy's Memo of 21 Sept. 1858: B.R. Partapgarh File No. 385, Part 1.
[4] Ibid.

Hanwant Singh's view. The other issue to which this statement draws attention is the inevitability of suppression and failure of popular resistance if it is confined only to one region in a large country. Given the fact that Britain was the master of practically the whole of India and could concentrate its forces on north India (where the rebellion was located) it was easy to cast a net around the core of popular resistance (i.e. Awadh), mop up the rebellion in Delhi, the Doab and Rohilkhand by the end of 1857, and then concentrate on Awadh. It is a measure of its power that despite such severe handicaps the revolt in Awadh could hold out for nearly a whole year and that the insurgent bodies had to be broken up by promises of land to magnates.

It is interesting that another leader, Feroze Shah, thought that the rebellion failed because the sepoys had started it somewhat prematurely.[5] He also thought that the killing of innocent women and children had worked against the insurgents.[6] Hanwant Singh had noted in his statement the lack of fighting prowess and courage among the sepoys.[7] A group of them, when asked about this, ascribed their lack of pluck to the killings that had taken place during the mutinies. In their words —-

Sahib, it has been all the work of fate. After what we had done, we never could fight. No matter whether your troops were black or white, native or European, we could not stand against them; *our salt choked us.*[8]

In a world where loyalty mattered, a loss of loyalty, an act of *namakharami*,[9] could haunt and rankle; and lack of courage, leading to defeat, could be seen as retribution for one's sins. In pragmatic terms the sepoys' sense of guilt undermined their morale.

I have emphasized that the sepoys' actions were often motivated by 'irrational' fears. Similarly, as in the instance just noted, in their defeat certain 'irrational' influences may be observed. The appear-

[5]'I had not the least intention to announce war before I had everything in order, but the army became very enthusiastic and commenced fighting with the enemy the English:' Proclamation Feroze Shah.
[6]Ibid.
[7]Carnegy's Memo.
[8]Quoted in Ball, *The Mutiny*, ii, p. 550.
[9]Literally 'going against one's salt,' i.e. going against one to whom gratitude is due; transgression.

ance of a comet in 1858 gave rise to superstitious fears that destruction was inevitably at hand.[10] All this, however, is not to gainsay the tremendous military and tactical superiority of the British. Only, it is worthwhile taking note of certain aspects of the revolt's failure that are always ignored.

The failure of the rebellion had certain important consequences.[11] The triumphant Raj saw itself now in a halo of permanence, ruling India by right of conquest.[12] To the major participants in the popular resistance in Awadh — talukdars and peasants — the failure of the revolt marked a crucial turning point. The old paternalism-deference equation was finally broken. The raja was transformed into a landlord, a cog in the socio-economic structure that the Raj engendered in North India. He was secure in his estate with a special *sanad* from the Raj and with laws governing succession.[13] The village proprietors and peasants had to remain as underproprietors or as tenants-at-will striving to improve their own positions. And the talukdars' position *vis-a-vis* the peasantry was consistently strengthened by the British government.[14] The moral economy of the Awadh countryside was finally broken by the process of violent rebellion and its suppression. The British destroyed the talukdar-peasant interdependence by conquering Awadh militarily and then buying over the talukdars with rewards of land. It was only then that talukdars became subordinate allies of the Raj, representing the politics of order and collaboration. Defeat led to subordination and loyalty. The peasantry now faced a landlord without the former frills of paternalism and 'rajadom'. It perhaps came into its own as a class through a series of sporadic agrarian disturbances directed against the exploitation of talukdars in the countryside.[15] It had

[10]Forsyth to Edmonstone, 2 Oct. 1858: For Dept., Political Cons., 15 Oct. 1858, Cons. No. 279.

[11]For an exhaustive analysis of the aftermath see Metcalf, *Aftermath*, and *Land, Landlords and the Raj*.

[12]'When we go, if we are ever to go': so Gladstone to Northbrook, 15 Oct. 1872, quoted in S. Gopal, *Jawaharlal Nehru: A Biography*, Vol. 1 (London, 1975), p. 13.

[13]Metcalf, 'The Oudh Talukdar: from Raja to Landlord,' in Frykenberg (ed.), *Land Control and Social Structure*, pp. 127 ff.

[14]Ibid, p. 134.

[15]S.T. Jassal, 'Agrarian Contradictions and Resistance in Faizabad District of Oudh,' *Journal of Peasant Studies*, Vol. 7, No. 3, April 1980, pp. 312-37.

been their lot to lose and serve even though their grievances found expression at certain times in India's national movement.[16] Yet the events of 1857, the year in which traditional loyalties asserted themselves, when many talukdars and peasants fought and died together, retain a place in men's hearts. It is thus that a Rana Beni Madho could become a folk hero and be exalted in rustic songs at carnival time.[17]

---

[16]See M.H. Siddiqi, *Agrarian Unrest in North India;* and G. Pandey, *The Ascendancy of the Congress in Uttar Pradesh, 1926-34* (Delhi, 1978).

[17]P.C. Joshi 'Folk Songs of 1857', in P.C. Joshi (ed.), *Rebellion: 1857* (Delhi, 1957), p. 276.

APPENDIX TO CHAPTER 2
List of Talukdars' Forts in Awadh

(SOURCE: Proclamation for the surrender by the Chiefs and Rajas of Oudh of their forts, Foreign Political Consultations. 31 Oct 1856, Nos. 135-52; F.S.U.P., i, pp. 115-120; and BROG File No. 395.)

The Foreign Political Consultations provide an aggregative description of the number of forts in the various districts. But the Board of Revenue Oudh General File gives details of which talukdar held what kind of fort with how many guns the fort had. This detailed information is available only for the districts of southern Awadh, i.e. the area I have demarcated as the area of talukdar-peasant co-operation where the talukdars' strength was concentrated. Set out below is a general description of the number of forts in the districts of Lucknow, Sitapur, Mullaon, Bahraich, Gonda, and a more detailed account of the forts in Salon, Faizabad, Sultanpur and Dariabad and Unao.

LUCKNOW: Total number of forts: 92. Tahsil-wise break up: Lucknow 8, Dewan 35, Nawabganj 23, Ramnagar 19, Gossaingunj 7. Of these only the fort of Bijnour in tahsil Gossaingunj had guns.

SITAPUR: According to the Commissioner, this district had no strong forts, but some had guns.

MULLAON: Small forts were said to be more numerous than in Sitapur but there were only three forts with guns — Guri-Rehmanpur, Dharmpur, Surtipur in Bangur.

BAHRAICH: Total number of forts 13. The fort of Banki belonging to the raja of Tulsipur had two guns. The fort of Churda was described as being very strong, it had three guns. Tepraha fort was very formidable but had no guns, instead it was defended by broad deep moats.

GONDA: Total number of forts 29. The fort of Gonda was very strong, so was Dhanapur. The latter was the stronghold of Raja Kissen Datt, who also owned Sunowli and Mattipur which were also strong forts. The fort at Kindaha in Tulsipur was described 'as a naturally strong position.'

SALON:

Locality of the fort	Description of the fort	Name of Talukdar	Guns	Sowar	Foot
Morarmau	A kutcha fort of middling size, surrounded by jungle on all sides, covering 1 mile	Dirgbijai Singh Bais	3	25	400
Shankarpur	A kutcha and extensive fort surrounded by a deep trench and an immense jungle to the extent of 8 miles	Beni Madho Buksh, Bais	12	1,200	12,000

Jagatpur	A kutcha fort of middling size surrounded by a jungle	Narpat Singh Bais	2		300
Bhikh	A kutcha fort of middling size surrounded by a jungle	Jugraj Singh	1		150
—do—	—do—	Sheogopal	1		100
Rampur	A small kutcha fort on the banks of the Ganges surrounded by a jungle	Beni Madho			100
Mulkegaon	A great kutcha fort surrounded by a jungle	—do—	1		200
Umbawaon	—do—	—do—	1		100
Chunaimyan	—do—	Sardar Singh	3	12	200
Alumpur	A small kutcha fort in brushwood	—do—			50
Churuhar	A kutcha fort in a jungle of Bubul trees on the northern bank of the Ganges	Ajadhyabuksh Bais	3	15	300
Gourah	A great kutcha fort a jungle on the east	Bhopal	4	25	400
Hajeepur	A great kutcha fort	Rana Raghunath Singh Bais	18	50	1,500
Khajurgaon	A small kutcha fort on the south bordered by the Ganges	—do—			50
Jahangirabad	A small kutcha fort	—do—			10
Dhoolah	—do—	—do—			50
Seeonurpi	A great fort surrounded by jungle	Wife of Busunt Singh	16	25	600
Saitaon	A small kutcha fort	Futeh Bahadur Bais	3	8	210
Porasi	A great kutcha fort surrounded by a deep trench and jungle	—do—			8
Pohusna	A great kutcha fort in a jungle	Sheodarshun Singh Kanhpuriah	8	30	600
Pikremau	A small kutcha fort in a jungle	—do—	1		100
Tiloi	A kutcha fort in a jungle	Jugpal Singh Kanhpuriah	12	40	800
Tokasi	A small kutcha fort in a jungle	Surjit Singh Kanhpuriah	2		100
Nain	A great kutcha fort in a jungle bordered by the river Sai on the north and west	Jaganath Buksh, Basant Singh Bhagwan Buksh Kanhpuriahs	12		2,500

Appendix to Chapter 2

Kumoli	A great kutcha fort in a jungle	—do—			300
Bhawanshahpur	A small kutcha fort	Hunman parshad Kaith			50
Rampur Kashia	A small fort in a jungle	Ramzulam Singh Kanhpuriah	8	25	1,500
Rajapur	A small kutcha fort in a jungle	Shambur Singh Kanhpuriah		5	100
Kaithola	A small fort in a jungle	Jageshur Buksh Kanhpuriah	1	3	200
Pahu	A great kutcha fort in a jungle	Bhup Singh Bais	1		200
Kalakankar	A great kutcha fort surrounded by a ditch with the Ganges on the south and west and a jungle on the north and east	Hanwant Singh Bissein	13	15	1,515
Dharupur	A kutcha fort with jungle on 2 sides	—do—			200
Bhudri	A great kutcha fort with double ditches on all sides	Sannath Koer Bissein		5	600
Shumspur	A great kutcha fort bordered by the Ganges on the south and by a *nullah* on the north	Chattarpal Singh Bissein		3	600
Benti	A small kutcha fort on the northern bank of the Ganges	—do—			200
Dhugurh	A small kutcha fort in a thick jungle	Sitalbuksh Bissein		5	800
Dhyangura	A small kutcha fort in a jungle	Mardan Singh Bais		2	100
Bhiturgaon	A small kutcha fort	Koili Singh		2	50
Dhingwis	A small kutcha fort	Kublas Koer Bissein		1	400
Shahmau	A kutcha fort in a jungle	Sheomber Singh Kanhpuriah		3	1,200
Bhagirathpur	A small kutcha fort near a thick jungle	—do—			100
Seewun	A kutcha fort	Rudraparshad Kanhpuriah		1	300

Kytari	A small kutcha fort surrounded by a jungle on the south and east and by a *nullah* in the north	Susnam Singh Kanhpuriah	2		500
Reisi	A small kutcha fort in brushwood	Arjun Singh Kanhpuriah			100
Barrah	A small kutcha fort	Mahiput Singh Gautam			50
Shekhpur	A small kutcha fort in brushwood	—do—			100
Duhiyan	A kutcha fort in a jungle	Sheodutt Singh Bissein	1		200
Rusulpur	—do—	Isree Buksh Kanhpuriah		2	100
Konsah	—do—	Jaganath Buksh	4	30	300

SULTANPUR:

Tirowl	A kutcha fort in a jungle	Gulab Singh Sombansi	6		500
Baispur	—do—	Sultan Bahadur Sombansi	4		300
Domipur	A kutcha fort in a jungle circled by a ditch	Hanman Buksh Sombansi	5		400
Tejurh	A kutcha fort encircled by a ditch surrounded by a jungle on the south west	Sreejit Singh Sombansi	2		400
Deoli	A kutcha fort encircled by a ditch with a jungle on the east and north	Bijrai Bahadur Singh	3		700
Pithrigunge	A kutcha fort encircled by a deep ditch surrounded by a jungle	Baniparshad Sombansi	1		250
Sujakhur	—do—	Balbahadur Singh Sombansi	3		300
Purulgaon	A small kutcha fort encircled by a deep trench with a jungle on the west	Bhagwan Singh Sombansi	2		150
Urmusri	—do—	Mahipal Singh Bachgoti			100
Untoo	—do—	Surbdour Singh Bachgoti			200
Duherah	A kutcha fort encircled by a deep ditch; jungle on the south east	Madhoparshad Bachgoti	1		150

Appendix to Chapter 2

Dariapur	A small kutcha fort encircled by a ditch	Lal Bhagwant Singh Bachgoti			100
Ramnagar (commonly called the fort of Amethi)	A great kutcha fort with jungle on the east and south and west with a deep moat encircling the jungle	Raja Madho Singh	25	400	10,000
Bhitgaon	A small kutcha fort encircled by a ditch and jungle	—do—			50
Jangowli	—do—	—do—			200
Amethi	—do—	—do—			100
Sitigurh	—do—	—do—			50
Kunkwah	A kutcha fort in the village	Durga Bachgoti	1		58
Kohrah	A small kutcha fort encircled by a ditch and a jungle	Bhup Singh Bandhalgoti			40
Sutuha	—do—	Hanwant Singh Bandhalgoti			50
Muhownah	A large kutcha fort surrounded by a jungle and a deep *nullah*	Ali Buksh	2		1000
Benetigurh	A kutcha fort surrounded by a jungle and nullah	Mohommed Hossein	2		400
Piralirrh	—do—	Dulip Singh			100
Kunjas	—do—	Golab Khan			150
Rampur	A kutcha fort surrounded by a ditch, and immense jungle in the south	—do—		2	402
Shahpur	A kutcha fort with a jungle on three sides	Sheokoor			200
Dihlah	A kutcha fort with the Gomti on the east and jungle on the three sides	Ishraj Singh Bachgoti			600
Pakurpur	A small kutcha fort with the river Gomti and a jungle on the east	Birj Buksh Bachgoti			400
Kudurah	An insignificant kutcha fort	Ranjit Singh Bachgoti	3		1000
Daudpur	A great kutcha fort with a *jheel* on the north, a jungle on 3 sides	Pirthipal Singh Bachgoti	4		1000
Mudhpur	A great kutcha fort 3 sides jungle and on the east a large jheel	Dina Singh	1		400
Ispur	A great kutcha fort	Ganesh Singh Bachgoti			200

Bodeya Diah	A great kutcha fort surrounded by a jungle	Sheomangul Singh Bachgoti			400
Bhadayan	A kutcha fort encircled by a ditch and jungle in the west and north				400
Jamu	A small kutcha fort jungle on all sides	Jaganath Buksh Kanhpuria			310
Burulea	A small kutcha fort	The son of Pirthipal Singh	1		200
Ramgurhi	—do—	—do—			400
Sireundah Ali	A small kutcha fort	Hossein Ali Khan			200
Kurdurar	A kutcha fort with the Gomti on the west	(illegible)			
Mireanpur	A small kutcha fort	Daughter of Busaori Khan Khauradah			
Ainhut	—do—	Bakhtwar Khan			
Khupradih	A great kutcha fort encircled by a very deep ditch	Ramsarup	1		400
Dera	A great kutcha fort in a jungle encircled by a ditch	Rustum Sah Rajkumar	3	25	1500
Lumborah	A small kutcha fort on the northern bank of the river Gomti	—do—			50
Shewgurh	A small kutcha fort within the village	Kalka Buksh Rajkumar			
Jumkhuri	A small kutcha fort with the river Gomti on the north and encircled by a ditch				
Harumaon	A small kutcha fort in brushwood	Ali Buksh	1		200
Jagdishpur	A small kutcha fort in a fortified village				
Katchnao	A small kutcha fort in brushwood	Mohomed Hussein			50
Deogaon	A great kutcha fort in a jungle	Jamshed Khan	1		100
Huthgaon	A small kutcha fort in a jungle	Madho Pratap Singh Bachgoti			30
Beharpur	A small kutcha fort in brushwood	Joghra Bibi			30

Appendix to Chapter 2

Hoyatnagar	—do—	—do—			25
Sonara	A small kutcha fort in a jungle				30
Jalalpur	—do—	—do—			50
Kythowli	A small kutcha fort in brushwood	Dhowkul Singh Rajkumar			30
Bahadurpur	A small kutcha fort with the river Gomti on the west	Hosein Ali Khan			50
Kurno	A small kutcha fort in brushwood	Raja Madho Singh			50
Banermau	A small kutcha fort	Partap Singh			30
Shaffipur	A small kutcha fort in a jungle	Ajeet Koer, wife of Ranjit Singh Bachgoti			500
Moryni	A small kutcha fort in brushwood	Kalka Buksh Bachgoti			10
Mukondpur	A small kutcha fort				10
Aurangabad	—do—				
Chandah	—do—				
DARIABAD:					
Asah	A great kutcha fort in a jungle	Sheoumber Singh	4	15	200
Shewgurh	A small fort in a jungle	Daljit Singh	2	25	400
Rubowri	A kutcha fort with the Gomti on the north and east	Sahajram	4	4	600
UNAO:					
Sangrampur	A kutcha very extensive fort on the banks of the Ganges surrounded by a jungle on the east	Ram Buksh, Bais	8	70	2570
Somasi	A great kutcha fort surrounded by a jungle of Bubul trees	Jaganath Buksh a minor Bais, Dhowkal Singh and Zalim Singh are his Karindas	4	15	315
Dubai	A small kutcha fort surrounded by a jungle	Durga Buksh Bais			20
Banpur	—do—	Shoamber Singh and Shewraj Singh Bais	1		15

Naraingarh	—do—	Hindpal Singh	6	50	600
Pachiwar	A kutcha dilapidated fort	Barjone Singh Bais			25
Malowli	A small kutcha fort				
Purwa	A small kutcha fort in a village	Debi Buksh Bais	1	10	125
Buldupur	A kutcha fort in brush wood	Thakur Buksh, Bais	2	7	200
Bhilwul	A small fort on the southern banks of the river Sai, surrounded by a jungle, and a nullah on three sides	Musahib Ali	2	300	3000
Mallownah	A new fort	Duma Singh Bais			100
Chandersena	A small kutcha fort in a jungle of bamboos	—do—			25
Lukhdemau	A small fort in a jungle	Ram Baksh, Gautam			40
FAIZABAD:					
Sidheepur	A great kutcha fort surrounded by a jungle	Ramsurup Singh, Nihal Singh	3		400
Daslawan	—do—	—do—			
Shahganj	A great kutcha fort encircled by a very deep ditch with a little jungle on the east	Man Singh	25	50	5000
Paharpur	A kutcha fort encircled by bamboo	—do—			200
Bhurtipur	A fort of middling size in a jungle	—do—			300
Tundowli	A fort of middling size with a jungle on the south and west	—do—			150
Raipur	A small kutcha fort encircled by a deep ditch	—do—			50
Kutargarh	A fort of middling size on the southern bank of the Ghagra	Abbas Ali	1		200
Jalalpur	A fort of middling size partly kutcha and partly *pukka*	—do—	2		200
Utnear	A fort of middling size				100
Man-Jadbanspur	—do—	Jailal Singh Kurmi	5	800	5000
Ghatimpur	A small kutcha fort encircled	Tilydil Singh Chauhan			60

Appendix to Chapter 2

	by a deep ditch and a jungle of bamboo, in the north a jheel			
Khajurhat	A great kutcha fort encircled by a new deep ditch and a jungle on the south and west	Abhaidatt Singh Bachgoti		200
Bhagujelapur	A small kutcha fort encircled by a deep ditch and jungle of brushwood	Raghunath Kooer	1	400
Jalaluddin	A small kutcha fort surrounded by a jungle	Jailal Singh		
Bhiti	—do—	Jaidatt Singh Bachgoti	2	500
Ferapur	—do—	Rustum Sah		100
Mowrahpara	—do—	Raja Madho Pratap Singh Bachgoti		
Showruah	A great kutcha fort	Udres Singh Rajkumar	20	1500

Total Number of forts in Salon, Sultanpur, Dariabad, Unao and Faizabad: 147

Total Number of Guns: 303
Total Number of **Sowar**: 3,313
Total Number of Foot Soldiers: 78,211

APPENDIX TO CHAPTER 3

1. *Mutinies in North India*

Date	Place	Corps
10 May	Meerut	3rd Light Cavalry, 11th Native Infantry, 20th Native Infantry
11 May	Delhi	5th Light Field Battery, Foot Artillery, 3rd Battalion 2nd Company, 38th Native Infantry, 54th Native Infantry
20 May	Aligarh	9th Native Infantry
22 May	Mainpuri	9th Native Infantry
	Bulandshahr	9th Native Infantry
23 May	Etawah	9th Native Infantry
25 May	Nawshera	55th Native Infantry
28 May	Nasirabad	15th Native Infantry, 30th Native Infantry, 6th Light Field Battery
30 May	Lucknow	7th Light Cavalry, 13th Native Infantry, 48th Native Infantry, 71st Native Infantry
31 May	Bareilly	18th Native Infantry, 68th Native Infantry, 15th Light Field Battery, 8th Irregular Cavalry
	Shahjahanpur	28th Native Infantry
1 June	Moradabad	29th Native Infantry
2 June	Saharanpur	5th Native Infantry
3 June	Nimach	1st Light Cavalry, 4th Troop 1st Brigade Horse Artillery, 15th Light Field Battery, 72nd Native Infantry
	Azamgarh	17th Native Infantry
	Sitapur	41st Native Infantry
4 June	Kanpur	2nd Light Cavalry, 1st Native Infantry, 74th Native Infantry, 56th Native Infantry
	Benares	37th Native Infantry
5 June	Kanpur	53rd Native Infantry
	Jaunpur	Regiment of Ludhiana
6 June	Jhansi	12th Native Infantry
	Azamgarh	4th Company, 9th Battalion Artillery
	Allahabad	6th Native Infantry

Appendix to Chapter 3

7 June	Jullundur	6th Light Cavalry, 36th Native Infantry, 61st Native Infantry
8 June	Phillour (Jullundur)	3rd Native Infantry
	Faizabad	22nd Native Infantry, 13th Light Field Battery, 5th Battalion, 2nd Company
10 June	Rohtak	60th Native Infantry
	Nowgong	4th Company 9th Battalion Artillery
18 June	Fattehgurh	10th Native Infantry
25 June	Sialkot	35th Native Infantry
1 July	Saugor	42nd Native Infantry, 3rd Regiment Irregular Cavalry
	Mhow (Indore)	1st Light Cavalry, 23rd Native Infantry
2 July	Mhow	2nd Co. 6th Battalion Artillery
7 July	Jhelum	14th Native Infantry
9 July	Sialkot	9th Light Cavalry
12 July	Jaghadri (Ambala)	5th Native Infantry
25 July	Dinapur	7th Native Infantry, 8th Native Infantry, 40th Native Infantry
30 July	Lahore	26th Native Infantry
	Hazaribagh	8th Native Infantry
2 August	Dorundah (Ranchi)	Ramgarh Battalion
14 August	Bhagalpur	5th Irregular Cavalry
19 August	Ferozepur	10th Light Cavalry
29 August	Peshawar	51st Native Infantry
16 Sept	Nagode (in Central India)	50th Native Infantry
18 Sept	Jabalpur	52nd Native Infantry
19 Oct	Deoghar and Rampurhat	32nd Native Infantry
22 Nov	Dacca	73rd Native Infantry, 4th Company, 9th Battalion Artillery

2. Disarmed Regiments

15 May	Mian Mir	8th Light Cavalry
16 May	Kangra and Hoshiarpur	4th Native Infantry
22 May	Peshawar	64th Native Infantry
		27th Native Infantry
		24th Native Infantry
		5th Light Cavalry
28 May	Ambala	5th Native Infantry
		4th Light Cavalry
31 May	Shahjahanpur	44th Native Infantry
	Etawah	67th Native Infantry
10 June	Multan	69th Native Infantry
		62nd Native Infantry
14 June	Barrackpur	2nd Native Cavalry
		43rd Native Cavalry
		70th Native Cavalry

22 June	Jhelum	39th Native Cavalry
7 July	Rawalpindi	58th Native Cavalry
9 July	Amritsar	59th Native Cavalry

3. Other Corps That Mutinied

Benares	13th	Irregular Cavalry		
Jhansi	14th	"		
Sultanpur	15th	"		
Sitapur				
Faizabad				
Sicrora (Bahraich)	Oude	Irregular Force	No 1	Artillery
	"	"	1st	Cavalry
	"	"	3rd	"
	"	"	No 2	Infantry
Lucknow	"	"	2nd	Cavalry
Partapgarh	"	"	3rd	"
Gonda	"	"	No 3	Infantry
Dariabad	"	"	No 5	"
Faizabad	"	"	No 6	"
Sultanpur	"	"	No 8	"
Sitapur	"	"	No 9	"
Mullaon	"	"	No 10	"

This list is not absolutely exhaustive. Some odd corps might have been missed.

SOURCE: Memo of Native Regiments which have mutinied: BROG File No. 1229; List of Corps that have Mutinied: BROG File No. 919; Return of the Name or Number of each Regiment in India which has Mutinied: P.P., vol. xviii, 1859.

APPENDIX TO CHAPTER 4
Begum's Plan for a Co-ordinated Attack

Intizam-ood-dowlah (this I suppose is the title of Khan Ali Khan) is requested to concentrate a sufficient force including artillery for the defence of Pilibheet on the Bheera and Jugdawpoor roads. The leaders to be Enayet Ali Khan, Wuzeer Ali Khan. . . . Intizam-ood-dowlah is also requested to form a force for the taking of Shahjehanpoor and Pourayan, under the command of General Ismael Khan and Mohsun Ali Khan. Intizam-ood-dowlah will with the remaining troops and guns at his disposal, and the assistance of talookdars and zemindars, guard the Sookutta Nullah and when required reinforce the troops at Pilibheet and Shahjehanpoor and look to the provision of supplies for them. Mohomed Soorabz Khan. . . and Mahomed-ood-dowlah Bahadoor to proceed with troops under their command to the boundary of Pilibheet between the Dedah and to form an entrenchment at Billia Putwara. Enayet Khan, Amil of Sandee, Moulvie Fuzzul Huqq and Kashif Ali to be posted at Shahbad to interrupt the communication between Shahjehanpoor and Futtehghur. Mahomed Wallie Beg Khan, amil of Bangur, to stop the crossing of British troops over the Ganges from Moorwaa Ghat to Nanamow Ghat. Rajah Hurpershad Bahadoor to station his forces at Mohoriah Sewchuleea in the Baree Elaqua, for the collection of Khyrabad revenue and to check the advance of British troops from Bukshee Ki Talao and Mundeeaon. Mahomed Imad-ool-deen Khan Bahadur, Rajah Golab Sing Bahadoor, Rajah Narpat Sing Bahadoor to form 4 detachments under their respective commands to be detached to Sundeela and the other two in the direction of Mulliabad and Ruheemabad. Valait Ahmed Amil at Suffeepoor and Chowdhree amil of Russoolabad with the assistance of Talookdars and zemindars to form 2 parties, one to march towards Russoolabad and the other to Oonam. Rana Banee Madho Buksh Dilare Jung, and Mahomed Fuzl Azeem Khan Bahadoor with the aid of Talooqdars and troops at their disposal both foot and artillery to protect the borders of Oudh at the boundaries of Allahabad, Sooraon and Secundra sending half their force to reinforce the Nazim [of] Sooltanpur. Rugonath Sing Talookdar of Koree and Sindowlee, Rajah Dirg Bijah Sing Talookdar of Murarmow, Juggurnath Sing, Talookdar of Sihiree, the wife of Bussunt Sing Talookdar of Simerpaha and Rugver Sing Collector with half their force to watch the Ghats of the Ganges within the District of Cawnpore and prevent the crossing of British troops and with the remaining half meet British troops at Bunnee Bunthura and Lucknow. Mahomed Sultan Hossein Chuckladar of Hydergurh and the Talookdars and zemindars of Hydergurh, also Hidayit Ali amil of Goorshaiganj etc. to concentrate their forces and attack Lucknow from the direction of Mahomed Bagh. Syud Mahdu Hossein Khan Bahadur, Rajah Ali Buksh Khan Bahadur Talookdar of Rahona and Raja Madho Singh Bahadoor, Mahomed Hussun Khan Bahadur, Talookdar of Bijowgarh, Goolab Sing, Talookdar of Narwal, Rajah Hosein Ali Khan, Ramsurroup Talookdar of Khera Deeah to attack the troops at Sooltanpoor and to hold the district from Pertabghur and Tandah. Moo Kurrif-ood Dowlah Bahadur and Rajah Dabee Buksh Sing Bahadur. . . to attack Fyzabad and Amorodah and prevent the passage of troops within this respective boundaries. Hazim

Hossein Khan with the men he has collected and the assistance of Talookdars of Kawary and others will protect the Ghats of the Ghogra with one fourth of their men, half the entire force to cross and attack Durriabad. Mahomed Dara Khan, Marka Salar (chief of war) with his troops including artillery and Ahsan Ali Khan General and Goolam Abas, Naib Chukladar of Durriabad to attack Durriabad. Moosahib Ali Khan Bahadoor and Akher Alee with their respective troops including artillery, to attack the British at Nawabganj from the direction of Sutrick and Jalliapara. Rajah Dirgbejae Sing, Talookdar of Mahonah, Gholam Hosein Khan commanding Abassee Regiment, Hafiz Soorab Ali Tehseeldar to station their troops at Mahonah near Bakshi-ki-Talao and to hold the position for the purpose of interrupting the line of communication. Mahomed Yusuf Ali Khan Sipah Salar, General Mahomed Hamid Khan, Khoda Bukx Khan Bahadur, Rajah Goorbux Sing, Ghoolam Russool Karindah of Ameerood Dowlah, Ameer Hussein Khan Bahadoor, Mahomed Ali Khan Bahadoor, Collector Mahomed Abdool Malee, Collector, Reenut Sing, Talookdar of Thahanee to concentrate their forces and attack Nawabgunge Bara Bunkee. . .

SOURCE: Arrangement for a general attack on British troops throughout the protected country [Oudh] on 22 Suffur 1275 [1 Oct. 1858]. For. Dept. Secret Cons. 26 Nov. 1858, Cons. No. 38.

APPENDIX TO CHAPTER 5

Talukdars in Salon, Unao, Sultanpur, Faizabad and Dariabad and their conduct in the Revolt

	Name	Estate	Govt. Jama	Caste	Comments
	DISTRICT SALON				
1.	Thakurain Baijnath Koer Chatrapal Singh, her adopted son	Shumspur	40,465	Bissein	Chatrapal Singh at the commencement of the outbreak seized sixteen boats filled with government ammunition and plundered them. He furnished men and guns in support of the rebel nazim Fazl Azim. The nazim with the help of the Bisseins retained possession of the area for five months and fought two pitched battles against the British.
2.	Thakurain Sannath Koer, Jangbahadur Singh	Bhudri	77,114	Bissein	Supplied men and guns to Fazl Azim. But around the middle of 1858, according to Barrow, the talukdar was willing to become a 'good subject whenever the opportunity offers'.
3.	Sita Buksh and Shankar Buksh	Dhungurh	12,769	Bissein	Did not fight the British.
4.	Thakurain Kublas Koer	Powasi Dhegwers	45,542	Bissein	Did not fight the British.
5.	Dhowkuh Singh	Shekhpur Chowras	6,758	Bissein	Did not fight the British.

6.	Hanwant Singh Kalakankar	Rampur 97,320	Bissein	Fought against the British but committed no hostilities since the fall of Lucknow.
7.	Shevdutt Singh	Duhirjan 7,009	Bissein	About 600 rebel zamindars took refuge in his fort and supported by his men harrassed the British authorities across the border. They opposed any British troops sent against them and were supported by the other Bisseins of the neighbourhood.
8.	Jaganath Buksh Basant Singh Bhagwan Buksh	Nain 80,512	Kanhpuriah	Rebels from the beginning, fought against the British with both Beni Madho and Fazl Azim.
9.	Rana Beni Madho	Shankarpur 1,59,620	Bais	A rebel from the beginning. He fought in the seige of Lucknow, then again at Bailee Guard. Then was openly in arms against the British in southern Awadh. His brother, Jograj Singh, was appointed Collector by the Begum, and also went with a force to assist the Nana at Kanpur. Beni Madho was offered a free pardon and a settlement of his estate as in the King's time. He first accepted, then drew back and took to arms again.
10.	Rana Raghunath Singh	Khajurgaon 95,000	Bais	He attacked the steamer proceeding from Kanpur to Allahabad. Joined the rebel forces at Lucknow and fought at the Bailee Guard. He had 1,500 retainers but could collect three to four thousand men. His karinda attended the rebel Durbar. He accepted terms when the British entered the district.
11.	Wife of Bassant Singh	Simarpaha 45,000	Bais	Fought against the British at Bailee Guard but died of illness. Her conduct was good till the fall of Lucknow but after that Beni Madho probably prevailed upon her men to join the rebellion.
12.	Jagganath Buksh	Simri 28,645	Bais	His men assisted the rebels, the talukdar himself being a minor under his grandmother; sent a force to Lucknow and later joined Beni Madho and opposed Sir Hope Grant.

Appendix to Chapter 5

13.	Fateh Bahadur	Sitaon 27,133	Bais	Fought against the British at the Bailee Guard. Joined Beni Madho, although Beni Madho had once imprisoned him during the Nawabi rule.
14.	Thakur Buksh	Shisnapur 7,933	Bais	Did not oppose the British was willing to act for them.
15.	Zulfikar Khan	Puhramow 10,211	Pathan	Remained quiet during the rebellion but could not come into the British camp because of hostilities all around him.
16.	Chaudhuri Raghunath Singh	Jabrowli 15,660	Janwar	Was a bitter foe of Beni Madho in Nawabi times but the quarrel was made up by the raja of Daundiakhera and he fought for Beni Madho in the revolt.
17.	Bhopal Singh	Gourah Kooshti 37,270	Bais	Lost his entire estate in 1264; joined Beni Madho.
18.	Sirdar Singh	Chinameyan 21,000	Bais	A rebel from the beginning of the rebellion. He fought the British at Simri and joined Beni Madho.
19.	Ajodhia Buksh	Chunhar 15,000	Bais	Lost little under British rule but rebelled at the very beginning, firing on steamers even before rebel king proclaimed. Fought at Lucknow, a follower of Beni Madho.
20.	Bhoop Singh	Pahoo 9,492	Bais	Lost his entire ilaqa, fought at Lucknow and was a follower of Beni Madho.
21.	Jagmohan Singh Mardan Singh Koli Singh	Gurudaspur 6,432 Bheeturgaon 9,725	Bais Janwar	Fought at Lucknow, though small talukdars; Mardan Singh was Beni Madho's right hand man in all schemes.

22.	Digbijai Singh	Morarmow 34,737	Bais	One of the major chiefs of Baiswara. Saved European fugitives escaping from Babu Ram Buksh of Daundiakhera. Did not himself fight at Lucknow but was obliged to send men to the assistance of the rebels.
23.	Ramghulam Singh	Mustafabad 21,000	Kanhpuriah	Protected some *amlahs* of the British but soon joined the rebellion, opposed Havelock, fought at Lucknow and elsewhere and assisted Beni Madho and the raja of Amethi.
24.	Jugeshur Buksh	Kyeholah 13,000	Kanhpuriah	Remained quiet during the rebellion and was obliged to appear before the nazim. After the fall of Lucknow he joined Jograj brother of Beni Madho.
25.	Jugpal Singh	Tiloi 74,000	Kanhpuriah	Was loyal to the British, saved a Thanadar and Tahsildar and rescued 16,000 rupees Government Treasure from Mutineers and made it over to the British. He did not go to Lucknow and his villages were plundered because of his loyalty.
26.	Surjeet Singh	Tekasi 10,000	Kanhpuriah	Well-disposed to the British right through.
27.	Bisheshur Buksh	Illegible	Kanhpuriah	Well-disposed to the British right through.
28.	Sheodarshan Singh	Puhremau 45,000	Kanhpuriah	First of Salon talukdars to adopt the Begum's cause. Fought the British at the Bailee Guard. In the later stages of the rebellion joined the raja of Amethi.
29.	Arjun Singh	Rossi 5,655	Kanhpuriah	Lost his ilaqas. Was quiet in the beginning but later turned hostile.
30.	Surnam Singh	Gowrah 9,730	Kanhpuriah	Remained quiet throughout and presented himself to the British at the fall of Lucknow.

31.	Hanumanparshad	Bhuwan Shahpoor 6,279	Kaeth	Remained quiet during the rebellion, his village was plundered by the rebels.
32.	Mahipat Singh	Barrah 3,500	Gautam	Plundered the Mutineers who fled with Government treasure from Salon.
33.	Mouzam Khan	Illegible 28,537	Mewati	Behaved well enough to be settled with.
34.	Muzufur Hussein	Serai Saijun 5,196	Syud	Sided with the British and helped them.
35.	Dost Mohomed	Puriwan 2,603	Sheikh	Sided with the British and helped them; was plundered by the talukdar of Nain.
36.	Narpat Singh	Jagatpur	Bais	Follower of Beni Madho.
37.	Jograj Singh	Bheekh	Bais	Follower of Beni Madho.
38.	Sheombur Singh	Rajapur 4,547	Kanhpuriah	Was not a rebel. Rebels plundered all his property.
39.	Mardan Singh	Duargurh 6,000	Bais	A rebel from the beginning with Beni Madho.

DISTRICT SULTANPUR

40.	Babu Gulab Singh.	Tirowl 17,435	Sombansi	Refused shelter to European refugees, joined the nazim of Sultanpur, took possession of Soram, fought at Tirowl and at Sultanpur. In Sept. 1858 he was with Fazl Azim with 2,000 mutineers with him.

41.	Sultumat Bahadur	Berispur 9,515	Sombansi	He remained quiet at the beginning of the disturbances and assisted the refugees to Allahabad. When the nazim came to Partapgarh he joined him and took possession of pargana Nawabganj in Allahabad district. Fought at Nusrutpur, Tirowl and Sultanpur, but after the moving in of British troops in the later half of 1858 he crossed over to the British side.
42.	Hanuman Baksh	Domeepur 14,812	Sombansi	A rebel from the beginning, fought at Tirowl, Nusrutpur and Sultanpur. But by September 1858 he had retired into his fort and had sent a vakil to the British.
43.	Babu Sreejit Singh	Tejgurh 22,909	Sombansi	Remained quiet at the beginning but when the nazim came to Partapgarh he appeared before him and was with the nazim in the fight at Sultanpur. However, after the moving in of the British columns he sent in his vakil and furnished supplies to the British.
44.	Birji Bahadur Singh Deoli		Sombansi	He was very hostile during the mutinies; he took possession of a number of villages. His men joined Gulab Singh in the fight at Tirowl, he fought the British at Sultanpur with the nazim.
45.	Babu Bani Parshad	Pirthiganj 11,315	Sombansi	Joined the nazim and fought the British at Sultanpur. But was the first talukdar in Sultanpur to present himself to the British troops and officers when they entered the district.
46.	Balbahadur Singh	Soojakhur 24,482	Sombansi	Joined the nazim and fought the British at Sultanpur but later changed sides and provided supplies for British troops.
47.	Bhagwan Singh	Purabgaon 7,540	Sombansi	Fought with the nazim at Sultanpur. Did not present himself to the British till September 1858.

Appendix to Chapter 5 195

48.	Mahipal Singh	Umuree 2,500		Fought the British with the nazim and did not present himself to the British.
49.	Surbahadur Singh	Untoo 11,750		Fought the British at Sultanpur but later presented himself to the British.
50.	Madho Parshad	Deehrah 32,000	Bachgoti	He was a minor. His karinda was a rebel; he took possession of Mirzapur Churahree in the Allahabad district and murdered the zamindar of that place. He joined the nazim in every action that took place with the British.
51.	Lal Bhagwant Singh	Duriapur 12,000	Bachgoti	Though he presented himself to the nazim, he never actively fought the British.
52.	Raja Lal Madho Singh	Amethi 1,28,000	Bandhalgoti	An arch rebel from the beginning of the disturbances. He fought the British at Lucknow and at Banni, was chief of the Begum's force fighting at Alambagh; he resisted the Europeans between the Dilkhusha and Bailee Guard. He fought the Gurkhas at Sultanpur. After the fall of Lucknow he vacillated for some time and finally joined the rebels again. It was said that he could collect 10,000 fighting men in a few hours.
53.	Durga	Kunkwah	Bachgoti	A rebel from the very beginning. Was with Lal Madho, whose manager he was, at every disturbance that took place.
54.	Bhoop Singh	Kohrah 1,800	Bandhalgoti	A rebel from the beginning, a follower of Lal Madho.
55.	Hanawant Singh	Sutuha 1,500	Bandhalgoti	A rebel from the beginning, a follower of Lal Madho.

56.	Raja Ali Buksh	Muhownah 10,000		A rebel from the beginning to end. He fought the Nepal forces at Kundoo Nullah. The British officers described him as a 'very hostile and bad man'.
57.	Mohomed Hussain	Banigurh 10,000		A rebel from the beginning.
58.	Dalip Singh	Pindarah 10,000		He took part in the plunder of Tiloi.
59.	Gulab Khan	Kurjas 7,000	Khanzadah	He took part in the plunder of Tiloi.
60.	Kalka Buksh	Rampur 14,000	Bachgoti	Fought the Gurkhas at Chandah but later asked the Chief Commissioner's pardon.
61.	Sheokoer	Garahpur 7,000	Bachgoti	Was not a party to the rebellion.
62.	Ishraj Singh	Duhlah 16,000	Bachgoti	,,
63.	Birj Baksh	Pakuppur 16,000	Bachgoti	,,
64.	Ranjeet Singh	Koodwah 44,943	Bachgoti	Was not a party to the rebellion. Waited on the Chief Commissioner with Rustam Sah.
65.	Pirthipal Singh	Daodpur 38,844	Bachgoti	Was not a party to the rebellion.

Appendix to Chapter 5   197

66.	Deena Singh	Madhpur 17,000	Bachgoti	Was not a party to the rebellion.
67.	Ganesh Singh	Eespoor 16,000	Bachgoti	,,
68.	Sheomangal Singh	Udeyadesh 15,000	Bachgoti	,,
69.	Bishnath Singh	Bhadiyan 15,000	Bachgoti	The talukdar was very hostile to the British and died during the revolt.
70.	Jaganath Baksh	Jamoo 30,000	Kanhpuriah	Was not a party to the rebellion.
71.	Raja Hussain Ali Khan	Hussainpur 44,000	Khanzadah	Joined the nazim and fought General Frank's column at Sultanpur. Opposed the Gurkha forces at Kandu Nallah. Fought the British again at Sultanpur in August. His fort was the chief gun carriage factory. He was in communication with Fisher's Irregulars before the mutiny at Sultanpur.
72.	Bakhtawar Khan	Amihut	Khanzadah	Joined the raja of Hussainpur. A British officer noted 'The Khanzadahs have been our worst enemies'.
73.	Ramswarup	Khurpradeeh 30,000	Gangabani	Did not fight the British but joined Mehdie Hussain in the fight against Man Singh at Shahganj.
74.	Rustam Sah	Dera 40,000	Rajkumar	A well-known loyal subject.

75.	Raja Madho Partap Singh	Kondurar 70,000	Bachgoti	Simple rebellion.
76.	Partap Singh	Banermoud 6,000	Sombansi	Took no major part in the revolt.

DISTRICT UNAO

77.	Babu Ram Baksh	Daundiakhera 1,25,000	Bais	A rebel from the beginning to the end. Was a friend of the Nana. According to calculations he was worth eight or ten lakhs of rupees.
78.	Jaganath Baksh	Simri 42,000	Bais	He was a minor, his karindas — Dhowkul Singh and Zalim Singh — joined Beni Madho and fought against the British at Bailee Guard. Remained with Beni Madho till Campbell's campaign.
79.	Shewamber Singh	Banpur 4,000	Bais	Did not join the insurgents.
80.	Raja Hindpal Singh	Naraingarh 1,00,000	Bais	Was a rebel from the very beginning. Before the fall of Lucknow, he together with Hiralal Misser and Shewnath Bajpai (who were appointed chakladars of the district) interrupted the progress of the British. He fought at the Bailee Guard. After the fall of Lucknow he surrendered but later opened communications with the rebels, especially with Beni Madho and Musahib Ali. The British were not happy with his behaviour though it is difficult to know if he actively joined the rebels even after he had surrendered.
81.	Barjone Singh	Pacheeweaon 40,000	Bais	Went to Lucknow on the compulsion of Hindpal Singh but surrendered after the fall of that city.

Appendix to Chapter 5

82.	Babu Debi Baksh	Purwa 3,000	Bais	A rebel from the beginning of the disturbances. Sent his men to assist the Nana at Kanpur and his karinda was present in the fighting of Simri and at the Bailee Guard. He was a follower of Beni Madho.
83.	Thakur Baksh	Baldupur 12,000	Bais	Sent 100 men to fight at the Bailee Guard and at Simri. He remained a follower of Beni Madho.
84.	Chowdri Musahib Ali	Bhilwul 10,000		A rebel from beginning to end. Obstructed the British forces towards Lucknow, fought in the Bailee Guard with two or three thousand men, and at Alambagh. Also obstructed the Gurkha force. Remained a rebel.
85.	Doomca Singh	Mullownah 32,000	Bais	Sent men to assist the Nana. Fought at the Bailee Guard and at Simri. Joined Beni Madho and remained with him.
86.	Rajib Ali Beg	Mohiruddin-pur 10,000		A follower of Beni Madho.
87.	Ram Buksh		Gautam	"

DISTRICT FAIZABAD

88.	Ram Swarup Singh	Sidhipur 45,000	Gangabansi	Took no part in the revolt.
89.	Man Singh	Shahganj 2,25,000	Brahmin	In the beginning rendered assistance to the British; later joined and led the rebels in Lucknow. But with the advance of Campbell's troops towards Lucknow retired to his fort and surrendered at the first opportunity.
90.	Raja Abbas Ali	Tanda 15,000	Syed	A rebel from the beginning, he was naib to Mahomed Hussain, the nazim who commenced hostilities in Gorakhpur.

Awadh in Revolt

91.	Tuhdil Singh	Ghatinpur 2,000	Chauhan	A rebel from the beginning but did not go to Lucknow. He fought against Man Singh at Shahganj.
92.	Abhaidatt Singh	Pachimrath 50,000	Bachgoti	Did not participate in the rebellion.
93.	Raghunath Koer	Jelalpur 80,000	Gangabansi	A rebel from the beginning, fought the British at Lucknow and Man Singh at Shahganj.
94.	Jaidatt Singh	Bheeti 70,000	Bachgoti	Did not join the revolt.
95.	Udres Singh	Jhuwoorah 40,000	Rajkumar	A rebel from the beginning, fought the British forces at Chanda and invaded the Jaunpur district. But with the coming back of the British forces surrendered.

DISTRICT DARIABAD

96.	Shewumber Singh	Asah 6,000	Aintha	Furnished fifty men at Lucknow against the British but committed no other acts of rebellion.
97.	Daljit Singh	Shewgurh 40,000	Aintha	Fought at the Bailee Guard and joined Beni Madho.
98.	Sahajram Baksh	Roobunee 40,000	Aintha	This man and Lal Madho Singh were the commanding officers in the attack on Alambagh. Later joined Mosahib Ali and supplied provisions to rebel forces passing through his ilaqa.
99.	Bahadur Singh	Usadamow 6,374		Fought at the Bailee Guard and at Alambagh. Later sent in his *mukhtar*.

Appendix to Chapter 5

100.	Chandi Baksh	Ramnagar 6,123	Never personally came in to surrender to the British who stipulated his personal attendance as a condition for settlement.
101.	Shere Bahadur Singh	Hunyar 6,116	Remained loyal to the British.
102.	Azim Ali Chaudhuri	Jhoolwara 1,123	He was plundered by the insurgents for helping the British to collect revenue.
103.	Sarfaraz Ahmed Chaudhuri	Bilwal 13,243	—do—
104.	Ram Singh	Saifpur 2,415	Is actually the karinda of Chatterpat Singh whose estate he usurped. In the beginning of the revolt he helped British officers to escape but later joined the Begum and obtained khilat for recapturing Dariabad.
105.	Udham Singh and Balwant Singh	Thundwa 1,706	Remained rebellious even though his mukhtar came in to Lucknow to accept settlement.
106.	Hussain Ali	Kuthi 6,503	Opposed the British but surrendered.
107.	Avtar Singh	Hanapur 4,000	Fought at Lucknow and also against Hope Grant.
108.	Rani Talamund Koer	Mirzapur 41,266	Her karinda came and surrendered to the British but never provided the assistance he promised. Her relation Harinda Ram Rup was one of the leading rebels of the area. Her ilaqa was full of rebels and a large number of them were her villagers.

109. Nowrang Singh	Kyampur 2,200	His uncle Greptar Singh fought at the Bailee Guard. His peasants 'cordially assisted the Begum'. Both the uncle and the nephew refused to submit to the British and aided and abetted Ram Singh. But they finally submitted in September 1858.
110. Bhujring Singh	Nungrowoa 1,522	Was a very hostile rebel, hand in glove with Ram Singh. He had lost his estate in 1264 fasli.
111. Syed Rahamat Ali	Mustafabad 1,705	Did not himself participate in the rebellion but his ilaqa contained rebels in strength.
112. Wazir Ali	2,466	Was appointed a Collector by the Begum and was in constant rebellion. He fought in Lucknow and had a regiment of infantry with him at Dariabad.
113. Madkar Shah	Serorackpur 2,161	Was a rebel from the beginning who fought at Lucknow; in September 1858 it was reported that his whereabouts were not known.
114. Hanwant Singh	Bhudani 3,015	Did not participate in the revolt.
115. Mahomed Abid	Puraee 5,311	Was rebel leader who fought in Lucknow, he said he would submit but did not.
116. Sajad Hussain	Shazee 1,300	Was not a participant in the rebellion.
117. Sadiq Hussain	Gowtha 11,524	Fought against the British at Lucknow, fled from his estate at the approach of British troops.

Appendix to Chapter 5

118.	Partap Singh	Sukrowree 1,588	Was not a participant in the rebellion.
119.	Wajahutulah	Sydurpur 7,193	Was not a participant in the rebellion.
120.	Gurnparshad	Sisowna 2,000	He fought at the Bailee Guard, a lot of his peasants rebelled as well.
121.	Ram Parshad Singh	Khurjiri 10,000	Fought with Ram Singh.
122.	Thakur Ram Sahay	Sumrowlea 7,440	Remained friendly towards the British and was plundered for that reason.
123.	Babu Mahpal Singh	Solahabaree 2,695	His brother sought against the British in Lucknow. He was also in open rebellion in the district.
124.	Koonjal Singh	Newle 5,827	Was deprived of his estate in 1264 fasli; he ousted the holder in the revolt. Insurgents were in great numbers in his ilaqa.
125.	Bolaki Dube	Sidhour	Fought against the British at Bailee Guard and Alambagh and later joined Ram Singh in open rebellion.
126.	Raja Gurbux Singh	Ramnagar 1,597	'A thorough rebel and is always fighting'.

SOURCES:
1. Conduct of Salon Taukdars: BROG File No. 1037.
2. List of forts belonging to the Talukdars of Southern Awadh: BROG File No. 395.
3. List of Talukdars: BROG File No. 396.
4. Statement of Conduct of 41 Persons of the Principal Landholders of Zillah, Durryabad prior to and since the occupation of Head Quarter Station: BROG File No. 396, also available in Collection to Political Despatches 33 Part 2, Collection No. 23.
5. List of Parties Hostilely Disposed Towards the British Government. Ibid.

This list may not be absolutely complete. I should add a cautionary note, particularly to the Dariabad list. The items listed 4 and 5 in the above source show the disposition of landholders. From them I have picked up those that were mentioned to be talukdars or who seemed to be talukdars from the description given. However, the Salon, Unao, Sultanpur and Faizabad lists are fairly complete.

GLOSSARY

Amil	pre-British district revenue official
Asami	cultivator
Attah	flour; ground wheat
Badmash	wicked person
Badshah	king
Bania	Hindu trader, moneylender
Barkandaz	a soldier wielding a matchlock
Bigha	measure of land, in north India usually 3,025 square yards.
Biswa	a twentieth; a twentieth share of a village or estate
Chakladar	revenue official in charge of a fixed region (chakla) under the Nawabi administration
Chaukidar	watchman
Dak	post
Daroga	superintendent of a department
Diwan	chief officer of State; Finance Minister
Fakir	a Muslim mendicant
Firangi	a European
Fasli	of the fasl, or harvest; fasli year denotes the agricultural year, from the sowing of kharif through to the harvesting of rabi, approximately June to April-May
Golandaz	a gunner
Harkara	a postman, a runner
Havildar	a petty officer in the army
Hukumnamah/ Hukumnamajat	orders
Huzur Tahsil	system of revenue collection in which revenue is paid direct to the government treasury.
Ijara	a farm, let out for a fixed sum
Ilaqa	estate
Izzat	honour, prestige

Jama	aggregate revenue payable by a cultivator or estate
Jamabandi	detailed rent roll or revenue statement of a village or estate.
Jamadar	most junior commissioned officer in the Indian army
Kachari	a court of justice
Karinda	an agent or manager
Kutcha	built of mud; unripe, crude
Khalsa	land held immediately of Government, paying revenue direct to the State
Kharif	autumn harvest reaped in October-November
Khilat	a robe of honour
Khuda	God
Khudkasht	a proprietary cultivator, cultivating his own holding; leased-in land cultivated by a proprietor
Kist	instalments
Kurmi	a low-caste cultivator
Mafi	land held rent-free
Mahal	revenue-paying unit
Mahajan	a money lender or a village small town banker
Maulavi	a Muslim divine or learned man
Malguzar	one who pays revenue
Mohurs	gold coins
Mukhtar	agent
Munshi	scribe, writer
Naib	deputy
Najeeb	a militia man
Nankar	an assignment of revenue or land made as a reward for undertaking revenue-management rights
Nazim	head of a district
Nazrana	gifts, presents
Nazul	Crown or Government land
Nikasi	an account of the revenue assessed upon a estate; total net proceeds.
Pahikasht	holding cultivated by a non-resident cultivator
Paltan	a regiment or battalion of infantry

Pargana	administrative subdivision of a tahsil, consisting of a number of villages
Pattidari	system of tenure in which land is farmed in severalty but in which the revenue demand on the estate is apportioned by the kin group on ancestral shares
Poorbeeah	literally an easterner, a common name for the sepoys of Awadh
Quanungo	hereditary local revenue accountant of pargana or group of villages
Rabi	spring crops or harvest reaped in February-March
Rais (raes)	a man of position
Raiyat (ryot)	peasant, cultivator
Risala	a troop of horses
Risaldar	an officer of Indian infanty
Sarkar	government, state
Sir	lands cultivated by a landholder directly or with hired labour; home farm
Subah	province of a Kingdom
Tahsil	subdivision of a district
Tahsildar	officer in charge of a tahsil, collector of rent/revenue from a tahsil
Thakur	lord, master, Rajput title or respect
Vakil	representative

BIBLIOGRAPHY

I. ARCHIVAL SOURCES

Uttar Pradesh State Archives, Lucknow
1. Board of Revenue Oudh General
2. Board of Revenue District Files

National Archives of India, New Delhi
1. Foreign Department, Secret Consultations
2. Foreign Department, Political Consultations
3. Foreign Department, Political Proceedings
4. Foreign Department, Secret Proceedings
5. Military Department, Proceedings

India Office Library and Records, London
(i) *Records*
1. Home Miscellaneous Series
2. Collections to Political Despatches
3. Bengal Military Consultations
4. India Military Consultations
5. Bengal Commercial Reports
6. Bengal Board of Revenue (Miscellaneous) [only files marked Custom]
7. N.W.P. (Sudder) Board of Revenue (Customs) Proceedings.

(ii) *Private Papers*
1. Mutiny Papers of Havelock, Outram and Campbell
2. Private Papers of Sir Henry Lawrence
3. Private Papers of Philip Goldney

II. PRINTED SOURCES AND OFFICIAL PUBLICATIONS

Benett, W.C., *Report of the Final Settlement of the Gonda District* (Allahabad, 1878).

Benett, W.C., *Gazetteer of the Province of Oudh*, 3 vols. (Allahabad, 1877).
Ferrar, M.L., *The Regular Settlement and Revised Assessment of the District of Sitapur* (Lucknow, 1875).
Forbes, W.E., *Report on the Revenue Settlement of the Partabgarh District* (Lucknow, 1877).
Forrest, G.W., *Selections from Letters, Despatches and State Papers in the Military Department of the Government of India, 1857-58*, 4 vols. (Calcutta, 1893-1912).
General Report on the Administration of the province of Oudh, 1859.
King, R.M., *Report on the Land Revenue Settlement of the Partabgarh District* (Lucknow, 1869).
Macandrew, I.F., *Report of the Settlement of the Eleven Pergunnas in the District of Roy Bareilly* (Lucknow, 1867).
————*Report of the Settlement Operations of the Rae-Bareily District* (Lucknow, 1872).
————*Settlement of the Land Revenue of the Sultanpur District* (Lucknow, 1873).
Millet, A.F., *Report of the Land Revenue Settlement of Fyzabad District* (Allahabad, 1880).
Papers Relating to Indian Mutinies, 3 vols, (at the Indian Institute Library, Oxford).
Papers relating to Land Tenures, & Revenue Settlements in Oude, (Calcutta, 1865).
Parliamentary papers: 1856 XLV; 1857 XXX, 1857-8 XLIV (in 4 parts); 1859 V, VIII.
Reports on the Revenue Settlement of the North-Western Provinces of the Bengal Presidency, under Regulation IX of 1833 (Banaras, 1863).
Rizvi, S.A., and Bhargava, M.L., (eds.), *Freedom Struggle in Uttar Pradesh*, 6 vols., (Lucknow, 1957).
Selections from Revenue Records, North Western Provinces 1822-33, (Allahabad, 1872).
Selections from Revenue Records, North Western Provinces (Allahabad, 1873).

III. SECONDARY WORKS

Anderson, P., *Passages from Antiquity to Feudalism* (London, 1974).
Anon., 'The Physical Capabilities of Oude', *Calcutta Review*, vol. 26, June 1856.
————, *Dacoitee in Excelsis; or The Spoilation of Oude By the East India Company* (London, n.d.).
Arnold, E., *The Marquess of Dalhousie's Administration of British India*, 2 vols. (London, 1865).
Aston, T.H., (ed.), *Crisis in Europe* (London, 1965).

Baden-Powell, B.H., *Land Systems of British India*, 3 vols. (Oxford, 1892).
Baird, J.G.A., *Private Letters of the Marquess of Dalhousie* (Edinburgh, 1910).
Ball, C., *History of the Indian Mutiny*, 2 vols. (London, n.d.).
Barat, A., *The Bengal Native Infantry: its organization and discipline, 1796-1852* (Calcutta, 1962).
Barth, F., *Political Leadership among the Swat Pathans* (London, 1959).
Basu, P., *Oudh and the East India Company, 1785-1801* (Lucknow, 1943).
Bell, E., *Retrospects and Prospects of Indian Policy* (London, 1868).
Benett, W.C., *A Report on the Family History of Chief Clans of the Roy Bareilly District* (Lucknow, 1870).
Bhatnagar, G.D., 'The Annexation of Oudh', *Uttaara Bharati*, vol. 3 (1956).
Bloch, M., *Feudal Society*, 2 vols. (London, 1961).
―――, *French Rural History* (London 1966).
Brenner, R., 'Agrarian Class Structure and Economic Development in pre-Industrial Europe', *Past and Present*, No. 70, Feb., 1976.
Buckler, F.W., 'The Political Theory of the Indian Mutiny', *Royal Historical Society Transactions*, Series 4, vol. V, 1932.
Butler, S.H., *Oudh Policy: Considered Historically and with reference to the present political situation* (Allahabad, 1896).
Butter, D., *Outline of the Topography and Statistics of the Southern Districts of Oudh* (Calcutta, 1839).
Cardew, F.G., *Sketch of the Services of the Bengal Native Army to the year 1895* (Calcutta, 1903).
Carnegy, P., *Historical Sketch of Tahsil Fyzabad, Zillah Fyzabad* (Lucknow, 1870).
Chattopadhyaya, H.P., 'The Sepoy Army, its Strength, Composition and Recruitment', *Calcutta Review*, May, July, Aug., Sept., 1956.
Chaudhuri, S.B., *Civil Disturbances during British Rule in India* (Calcutta, 1955).
―――, *Civil Rebellion in the Indian Mutinies 1857-59* (Calcutta, 1957).
―――, *Theories of the Indian Mutiny 1857-1859* (Calcutta, 1965).
―――, *English Historical Writings on the Indian Mutiny, 1857-1859* (Calcutta, 1979).
Cobb, R., *The Police and the People: French Popular Protest* (Oxford, 1970).
Cohn, B.S., 'Political Systems in 18th Century India: the Banaras region' *The Journal of the American Oriental Society*, LXXXII, No. 3, July-Sept. 1962.
Crooke, W., *The Tribes and Castes of N.W.P. and Oudh*, 4 vols. (Calcutta, 1896).
―――, 'Songs about the King of Oudh', *Indian Antiquary*, vol. XL, 1911.

Darogha Haji Abbas Ali, *A Historical Album of the Rajas and Taluqdars of Oudh* (Lucknow, 1880).

Datta, K.K., 'Contemporary Account of the Indian movement of 1857', *Bihar Research Society Journal*, September-December 1950.

―――, *Biography of Kunwar Sing and Amar Sing* (Patna, 1957).

De, B., 'Some Implications of Political Tendencies and Social Factors in 18th Century India', in O.P. Bhatnagar (ed.), *Studies in Social History (Modern India)* (Allahabad, 1964).

Edwardes, H.B., and Merivale, H., *Life of Sir Henry Lawrence* 2 vols. (London, 1873).

Elliott, C.A., *The Chronicles of Oonao* (Allahabad, 1862).

Engels, F., *The Peasant War in Germany* (Moscow, various editions).

Fisher, M., 'The Imperial Court and the Province: A Social and Administrative History of pre-British Awadh (1775-1856)', (unpublished Ph.D. dissertation, University of Chicago, March 1978).

Forbes-Mitchell, W., *Reminiscences of the Great Mutiny 1857-59* (London, 1894).

Frykenberg, R.E., *Land Control and Social Structure in Indian History* (Wisconsin, 1969).

Gimlette, G.H.D., *A Postscript to the Records of the Indian Mutiny: an attempt to trace the subsequent careers and fate of the rebel Bengal regiments, 1857-58* (London, 1927).

Gouldner, A.W., *For Sociology* (Harmondsworth, 1976).

Gubbins, M.R., *An Account of the Mutinies in Oudh and the Siege of the Lucknow Residency* (London, 1858).

Guha, R., *Subaltern Studies I: Writings on South Asian History and Society* (Delhi, 1982).

Gupta S.C., *Agrarian Relations and Early British Rule in India* (London, 1963).

Habib, I., *The Agrarian System of Mughal India* (Bombay, 1964).

―――, 'Potentialities of Capitalistic Development in the Mughal Economy', *Enquiry*, Winter, 1971.

―――, 'The Colonialization of the Indian Economy, 1757-1900', *Social Scientist*, March 1975.

Hibbert, C., *The Great Mutiny: India 1857* (London, 1978).

Hill, C., *The World Turned Upside Down* (Harmondsworth, 1976).

Hilton, R., *The English Peasantry in the later Middle Ages* (Oxford, 1975).

―――, *Peasants, Knights and Heretics* (Cambridge, 1976).

―――, (ed.) *Transition from Feudalism to Capitalism*, (London, 1976).

―――, *Bond Men Made Free* (London, 1977 repr.).

Hobsbawm, E.J., *Primitive Rebels* (Manchester, 1959).

―――, *Bandits* (London, 1969).

―――, (with G. Rude) *Captain Swing* (Penguin University Books, 1973).

―――, 'The Revival of Narrative: Some Comments', *Past and Present*, No. 86, February 1980.

Husain, I., 'Lucknow between Annexation and the Mutiny', (mimeographed paper from Aligarh Muslim University).

Hutchinson, G., *Narrative of the Mutinies in Oude* (London, 1859).

Innes, McLeod, *Lucknow and Oudh in the Mutiny* (London, 1896).

―――, *The Sepoy War* (London, 1897).

Irwin, H.C., *The Garden of India; or Chapters in Oudh history and affairs*, (London, 1880).

James, M., *Lineage, Family and Civil Society* (Oxford, 1974).

―――, 'English Politics and the Concept of Honour', *Past and Present*, Supplement, 1976.

Joshi, P.C., *Rebellion, 1857: A Symposium* (Delhi, 1957).

Kaye, J.W., *History of the Sepoy War in India 1857-58*, 3 vols. (London, 1880).

Keen, M.H., *The Outlaws of Medieval England* (London, 1977 repr.).

Khan, M. Mohammed Masihuddin, *Oude: Its Princes and its Government Vindicated* (London, 1857).

Kiernan, V., *The Lords of the Human Kind* (London, 1969).

Ladendorf, J.M., *The Revolt in India, 1857-58: an annotated bibliography of English language materials* (Switzerland, 1966).

Lawrence, H.M., *Essays on the Indian Army and Oude* (Serampore, 1859).

Lee-Warner, W., *Life of the Marquess of Dalhousie* (London, 1904).

Lefebvre, G., 'Revolutionary Crowds', in J. Kaplow (ed.), *New Perspectives on the French Revolution* (New York, 1965).

―――, *The Great Fear of 1789; Rural Panic in Revolutionary France* (London, 1973).

Le Roy Ladurie, E., *Carnival: A People's Rising in Romans* (London, 1980).

Macandrew, I.F., *On Some Revenue Matters Chiefly in the Province of Oudh* (Calcutta, 1876).

MacLagan, M., *Clemency Canning* (London, 1962).

Majumdar, R.C., *The Sepoy Mutiny and the Revolt of 1857* (Calcutta, 1957).

Malleson, G.B., *A History of the Indian Mutiny* (London, 1878-80).

Martin, R.M., *The Indian Empire*, 2 vols. (London, n.d.).

Marx, K., *A Critique of Hegel's Philosophy of Right, Introduction*, in L. Colletti (ed.), *Marx: Early Writings* (Harmondsworth, 1975).

―――, and Engels, F., *Precapitalist Socio-Economic Formations* (Moscow, 1979).

―――, *The First War of Indian Independence* (Moscow, 1967 repr.).

Metcalf, T.R., *The Aftermath of Revolt: India 1857-1870* (Princeton, 1964).
───, *Land, Landlords and the British Raj: Northern India in the Nineteenth Century* (California, 1979).
Mukherjee R., 'The Azamgarh Proclamation and Some Questions on the Revolt of 1857 in the North-Western Provinces', *Essays in Honour of Prof. S.C. Sarkar* (Delhi, 1976).
───, 'Trade and Empire in Awadh 1765-1804', *Past and Present*, No. 94, February 1982.
Neale, W.C., 'Reciprocity and Redistribution in the Indian Village: sequel to some Notable Discussions', in K. Polanyi (ed.), *Trade and Market in the Early Empires* (Illinois, 1957).
───, *Economic Change in Rural India — Land Tenure and Reform in Uttar Pradesh, 1800-1955* (Yale, 1962).
Palmer, J.A.B., *The Mutiny Outbreak at Meerut in 1857* (Cambridge, 1966).
Pandey, G., *The Ascendancy of the Congress in Uttar Pradesh, 1926-34*, (Delhi, 1978).
───, 'A View of the Observable: A Positivist "Understanding" of Agrarian Society and Political Protest in Colonial India', *Journal of Peasant Studies*, vol. 7, No. 3, April 1980.
Pemble, J., *The Raj, the Indian Mutiny and the Kingdom of Oudh* (Sussex, 1977).
Prasad, S.N., *Paramountcy under Dalhousie* (Delhi, 1964).
Reeves, P.D. (ed.), *Sleeman in Oude* (Cambridge, 1971).
Rothermund, D., *Government, Landlord and Peasant in India, Agrarian Relations under British Rule, 1865-1935*, (Wiesbaden, 1978).
Rude, G., *The Crowd in the French Revolution* (Oxford, 1959).
───, *Paris and London in the 18th Century* (London, 1974 repr.).
───, *Ideology and Popular Protest* (London, 1980).
Russell, W.H., *My Indian Mutiny Diary*, ed. by M. Edwardes (London, 1957).
Sahlins, Marshall D. 'On the Sociology of Primitive Exchange', *The Relevance of Models for Social Anthropology*, A.S.A. Monographs I (London, 1965).
Sarkar, J.N., *Fall of the Mughal Empire*, 4 vols., (Calcutta, 1972 repr.).
Scott, J.C., *The Moral Economy of the Peasant: Rebellion and Subsistence in Southeast Asia* (Yale, 1976).
Sen, A., 'A Pre-British Economic Formation in India of the late 18th Century: Tipu Sultan's Mysore', in B. De (ed.), *Perspectives in Social Sciences I* (Calcutta, 1977).
Sen, S.N., *1857* (Delhi, 1958).
Sengupta, K.K., *Recent Writings on the Revolt of 1857: A Survey* (New Delhi, 1975).

Shadwell, L., *The Life of Colin Campbell, Lord Clyde*, 2 vols. (Edinburgh, 1881).
Sharar, A.H., *Lucknow: the Last Phase of an Oriental Culture*, translated and edited by E.S. Harcourt and F. Hussain (London, 1975).
Siddiqi, A., *Agrarian Change in a Northern Indian State, Uttar Pradesh 1818-1833* (Oxford, 1973).
Siddiqi, M.H., *Agrarian Unrest in North India: The United Provinces, 1918-22* (Delhi, 1978).
Sitaram, *From Sepoy to Subedar*, ed. by James Lunt, translated by Capt. Norgate (London, 1970).
Sleeman, W.H., *A Journey through the Kingdom of Oude in 1849-1850* (London, 1858).
Spear, T.G.P., *Twilight of the Mughals* (Cambridge, 1951).
Srinivasachari, C., *The Inwardness of British Annexations in India* (Madras, 1951).
Srivastava, A.L., *First Two Nawabs of Oudh* (Lucknow, 1933).
Stokes, E., *English Utilitarians and India* (Oxford, 1964).
―――, *The Peasant and the Raj: Studies in Agrarian Society and Peasant Rebellion in Colonial India* (Cambridge, 1978).
Stone, L., 'The Revival of Narrative: Reflections on a New Old History', *Past and Present*, No. 85, Nov. 1979.
Thompson, E.P., 'The Moral Economy of the English Crowd in the 18th Century', *Past and Present*, No. 50, 1971.
―――, 'Patrician Society, Plebian Culture', *Journal of Social History*, Summer, 1974.
―――, 'Eighteenth Century English Society: Class Struggle without Class', *Social History*, vol. 3, No. 2, May 1978.
Whitcombe, E., *Agrarian Conditions in Northern India, the United Provinces Under British Rule, 1860-1900* (London, 1972).
Wilson, H.H., *A Glossary of Judicial and Revenue Terms of British India* (London, 1875).

INDEX

(Italics indicate location in both text and footnote on the same page; 'n' indicates location in footnote only).

administration during revolt, 137-9, 140-4
Agaie Ali Khan, 9-10
Alambagh, 91, 92, 102, 104
Allahabad, 69, 70, 100
amani, 3, 9
Amethi, 46, 54, 129-30
annexation of Awadh: economic background and implications of, 33-5; strategic implication of, 35; impact of, 36-8; religious leaders in Lucknow after, 36; rise of prices after, 36; not accepted as a *fait accompli*, 37; discussed by sepoys, 74
Awadh Proclamation, 107-8; shift from, 117-18, 157
Azamgarh, 69, 70, 127, 129, 163; Proclamation, *153*

Bachgoti, 100, 167
Baden-Powell, H., *30*, 31n
Bahadur Shah, 65
Bahraich, 2, 3, 14, 26, 53, 99, 122, 125, 158, 165; extent of dispossession of talukdars in, 59; mutiny in, 69, 74
Baiswara, 1, 40, 12n, 134, 164, 165; Summary Settlement in parganas of, 48; recruitment area for sepoys, 77; preparation for resistance in, 122-3; final resistance in, 129-31
Ball, Charles, 86, 104n, 129, 161
Balrampur (raja of), 15, 80; threatened by rebels, 121, 161, 166-7
Barrow, 41, 54, 113, 160
Begum Hazrat Mahal, 91; perceptions of failure, 103; confiscates Man Singh's and Rustam Singh's estates, 118, 120; threatens Balrampur, 121; in Bahraich, 125-6; plans onslaught on British, 126; escapes to Nepal, 131; in controlling position, 155; challenged by Maulavi, 140-2; Proclamation of, 151-3, 154
Begums of Wajid Ali: give consent to crowning of Birjis Qadr, 135
Benares, 34, 69-70, 101
Benett, W. C., 12n, 13n, 14, 15n, 17n, 18n; description of grain-sharing, 20-2
Bengal: overassessment in, 42
Bird, 40
Birjis Qadr: crowned king, 135-6, 150; hailed as Krishna, 154, 155
Butter D., 1n, 2n, 25n, 77

Campbell, Sir Colin (Lord Clyde), 82, 88, 89, 90, 92, 95, 96, 102, 104, 123, 160, 161, 167; winter campaign of, 127-34; personally supervises campaign in Baiswara, 129; acknowledges strength of resistance in Awadh, 134
Canning, 69, 107, 134, 157, 159
chaklas (chakladar), 2, 3, 4, 5, 6; exactions of, 9-11
Chaudhuri, S. B., 65n, 83, 93n, 158
Chinhat, 82, 84
Cohn, B. S., *1*, 12
complementarity/interdependece of talukdar and peasant, 22-4, 165; area of, 27; affected by Summary Settlement, 51-3; disruption of 59-60; important as recruitment area, 78; area of—important in sending rebels to Lucknow, 95
cotton: cultivation of, 34
Dariabad: Summary Settlement in, 47, 99, 123, 158

Index

Dalhousie: reasons for annexing Awadh, 32-3
Delhi, 1, 65, 67, 79, 102
Directions for Settlement Officers, 40
Doab, 34, 102, 171, 172

Elliott, C.A. (*Chronicles of Oonao*), 2n, 12n, 13n, *15*, 40n, 162n
Etah, 65
Etawah, 65

Faizabad, 2n, 15n, 16, 26, 27, 51, 54, 89, 101, 102, 115, 121, 126, 158; operation of Summary Settlement in, 44; overall assessment in, 44; pargana-wise overassessment in, 44-5; extent of dispossession of talukdars in, 57; mutiny in, 69-70
Fateh Islam, 148, 153
Fazl Azim, 118, 120
Feroze Shah, 115, 128, 163, 172; Proclamation of, *148-50*, 154;
firearms: recovered or surrendered, 166

Gonda, 2, 26, 99, 102, 122, 125, 158, 165; extent of dispossession of talukdars in, 57; mutiny in, 69-70
Gorakhpur, 99, 101

Hanuman Ghari: communal clashes at, 33n, 36
Hanwant Singh, 23, 91, 122, 157, 160, 161, 164, 167, 168, 169; refuses to pay revenue, 39; losses in Summary Settlement, 54, 80-81; fires on steamer, 118; gives reasons for revolt's failure, 171-2
Hardoi, 2n, 127, *128*
Harprashad, 126, 127, 140
Havelock, 82, 86, 88, 102
Hindu-Muslim unity, 153-4
Holt Mackenzie, 40
huzur tahsil: Sleeman's description of, 3; merits of system, 4; chiefs of Baiswara under, 4n, declining revenue from land under, 5

indigo: cultivation of, 34
ijara (ijaradars), 3; consequences of in pargana Mohan, 6-8; Sleeman's description of, 8n; British suspicion of, 9, 11

jama (jamabandi), *see* Summary Settlement
Jaunpur, 69, 70, 100, 101
jumog lagana (jumogdar), 4-5

Kanhpuriahs: resistance of, 129
Kanpur, 26, 36, 79, 83, 85, 91, 96, 102, 125
Kaye (*Sepoy War*): on anti-talukdari policy, 38n; on tendency of overassessment on the part of British officers, 43; description of mutiny in terms of regions, *64-5*, 67, 163
Khairabad, 2; rebels at, 128, 140
Khalsa, 3; decline of in Bahraich and all over Awadh, 3
Khan Ali Khan, 84, 128
Khan Bahadur Khan: advises rebels to take up guerilla tactics, 90, 108-9, 128, 163
Kists, 38; trouble over, 39
Kunwar Singh, 79, *163*

Lawrence, Henry, 68, 71, 73, 85
Loni Singh, 112, 128, 160; losses in Summary Settlement, 55; refuses to obey imperial orders but acknowledges Birjis Qadr, 140
Lucknow, 1, 2, 27, 36, 37, 67, 68, 82, 83, 85, 86, 88, 99, 100, 102, 103, 104, 106, 111, 115-16, 121, 126, 127, 128, 133, 134, 135, 163; Summary Settlement in, 47-9, 51; mutiny in, 66; tension in, 66; focus of revolt, 82, *90-7*, *98*; rebels from Delhi come to, 91; fighting men in, 93-6; loot of Lucknow, 104-5; arrests in Lucknow, 105; rebels around Lucknow, 109-110

MacLagan, M., 106n, *107*
Mahmudabad, raja of: losses in

Index

Summary Settlement, 55; first to join rebels, 84, 139
Mainpuri, 65
Majumdar, R.C., 65n, 83
Man Singh, 38, 91, 92, 96, 101, 157, 160, 163, 165; losses in Summary Settlement, 54, 80; desertion of, 104; beseiged in his fort, 118-20
Marx, K., 25n, 105n, 106n
Maulavi Ahmadullah Shah, 36, 115; brief biography and rift with Begum, *140-2*
Meerut, 65, 68
Mehndi Hussain: chief organizer in southern Awadh, 99-100; pressurized by peasants, 101; submission of, 103, 115, 131, 161
Metcalf, T.R., 55, 160n, *161-2*, 167n
moral economy, 22-3, 59
Mughal Empire (*also* Mughals), *1*, 2, 3, 6, 12n; crop sharing in, 20; legitimizing role of, 136-7; revival of Mughal administrative model, 147; tradition of Hindu Muslim co-existence in, *153*
Muhamdi, 27, 125, 158; under rebels, 124
mutiny (*also see* sepoys) signal for, 68, 70; co-ordination in, 70-71; success of—seen as fall of Company rule, 67, 69; common pattern running through, 71-2; rumours and panic in, 72-6; and prophecy about end of British rule, 75; violence in, 71-72; areas of, 76-7

Nana Sahib, 79, 83, 121, 125, 163
Narpat Singh: resists Walpole, 111-112; 115, 123, 128
nazim, 2, 9, 11
Nepal, 26, 101, 127; rebels in, *131-3*
North-Western Provinces, 40, 158, 165; overassessment in, 42

Outram, 3, 4, 32, 87-8, 89, 96, 97, 102, 104, 107n, 157, 158-9, 165

Partapgarh, 1, 26, 27, 78, 121, 122, 123;
overassessment in, 50; extent of dispossession of talukdars in, 57
peasants: participation in grain-sharing, 20-2; loyalty to talukdars, 23-4; moral economy of, 22-3; well-cultivated lands of, 23-4; dominated by talukdars, 24-6; complementarity in relationship with talukdars, 24; fighting men of talukdars, 25, 27-8; areas of interdependece between talukdars and, 27; usufructuary rights of, 28; subordinate rights of, 30-1; Summary Settlement and, 53-9; voluntary return of land to talukdars by, 81; as excellent garrison troops, 86-7; refuse provisions, 89, 96-7; form fighting force in Lucknow, 95; form fighting force in districts, 100-1; pressurizing Mehndi Hussain, 101; active role of, 164-6; initiative of, 166-9; as sepoys, 167-8
'pooling', 20; implications of, 22

Rae Bareli, 2n, 26, 27, 78, 121; extent of dispossession of talukdars in, 57
Raja Drigbijai Singh, 111, 112, 124, 128, 147
Raja Jailal Singh, 84, 92, 135, *138*, 163
Raja Lal Madho Singh: overassessed in the Summary Settlement, 46; losses in Summary Settlement, 54, 80; sums up plight of loyal talukdars, 121; leads resistance in southern Awadh, 122-3; surrenders and implications of surrender, 91, 96, 118, 129-30, 157, 160, 167
Raj Jagdish, 55, 56
Rana Beni Madho: on peasants' loyalty, 23, 38; losses in Summary Settlement, 54; focus of resistance in southern Awadh, 112-*13*, 122; cut off by Hope Grant, 116-17; sends letter of allegiance, 118; threatening the British in Baiswara, 123; encounter with British at Purwa, 122, 126; chase of Beni Madho, 130-1; refers to English as 'heathens', 151; receives

support from peasantry, 91, 157, 160, 161, 162, 163, 164, 167, 168, 174
Residency, 82, 83, 85, 87-8
Rohilkhand, 90, 125, 126, 127, 128, 171, 172
Russell, W. H., 77, 104, 108, 130
Rustam Sah, 80, 120, 157

Saadat Khan, *1*, 17, 33
Salon, 1, 27, 54, 85, 118, 158; overall assessment during Summary Settlement, 49; overassessment in certain parganas, 49; mutiny in, 69
Sahlins, M. D.: on 'pooling', 22
Sen, S. N., 65n, 83
seer land: Baden-Powell's description of, 30; difficulties during Summary Settlement regarding, 41
sepoys, 64, 76; communication between mutinous regiments, 67-9; signal for mutiny of, 68, 70; ill-paid, 71; greed for money, 71; murders by, 71-72; refusal to touch *attah*, 73; common life style of, 74; annexation of Awadh discussed by, 74; recruitment area of, 77-9; lack of data about recruitment of, 78; implications of being recruited from one area, 78-9; mutinous regiments fighting in Awadh, 79; flee to Sitapur, 83-4; curse Man Singh, 104; keep control over administration, 136; payment of, 144-7; reasons of revolt given by, 150-1; as peasants, 167-8
Siddiqi, Majid, 55
Sitapur, 2n, 27, 68, 122, 125, 158; overassessment in parganas of, 43-4; overall assessment of, 44, 51; losses of talukdars in Summary Settlement, 55; mutiny in, 69; sepoys flee to, 83-4; resistance in, 128,
Sitaram, 78, 168
'slave ploughman': description of, 29-30
Sleeman, W.H. (*A Journey through the Kingdom of Oude*), 3n; description of *jumog lagana*, 4-5; in conversation with Beni Madho, 23, 164; report on Awadh, 32; on importance of Awadh as a market, 35n; on anti-talukdari bias of British policy, 37; on recruitment of sepoys, 77
Stokes, Eric, 160n, 162
subsidiary alliance: effects of, 33
'subsistence ethic', *22*, 62
Sultanpur, 1, 26, 78, 99, 100, 102, 121, 122-3, 127, 158; overall assessment in, 46; parganawise overassessment in, 46-7; extent of dispossession of talukdars in, 57; mutiny in, 69
Summary Settlement: trouble over *kists* during, 38-9, instructions for, 39-40; N.W.P. and Awadh similar for purposes of, 40; difficulties in execution of, 41; process of trial and error in, 41; operation of, 41-2; tendency to overassess in, 42-3; overassessment in, 43-53 (*also see* under individual districts); computation of assessment in, 50-1; implications of assessment, 51; areas of overassessment, 51-3; disposal of rights in, 53-9; losses of talukdars in Sitapur by, 55; overall impact of, 59-63
symbiosis: of talukdars and peasants, 24n
talukdars: evolution of rights, 12-16; distinction between 'auction' and hereditary, *15*; land-grabbing instincts of, *15*; rajas and, *17*; dues collected by, 18-20; process of surplus extraction (*also see* 'pooling'), 20-2; importance of custom in estates of, 22-4; mutual co-operation between peasants and, 22-4; peasants' loyalty to, 23-4; domination of, 24-6; complementarity in relationship with peasants, 24; 'beneficence' of, 24; area controlled by, 26-7; revenue paid by, 27; areas of interdependence between peasant and, 27; and kinsmen, 27-8; rights below, 27-31; apprehension after

annexation among, 37; forts of, 37-8; seen as opponents of the British, 38; Summary Settlement and, 53-9; role of talukdars while mutinies taking place, 80-1; help to the British, 80; and their men fighting in Lucknow, 91; desertions by, 103; retire to their forts, 106-7; loyal, *107*, 158; willing to respond to Proclamation, 116-18; duplicity of, 118; estates of loyal — plundered, 120-1; imperial orders to, 139-40; grievances of — emphasized in various Proclamations, 155-7; role of, 157-64; as *rakhwars, 169*

thanas: number of — established by British, 113-15

Thomason, 40, 53

Tilism, 36-37n

Tiloi (raja of): well-cultivated lands under, 24n; attacked by rebels, 120; tries to make Beni Madho submit, 130

Unao, 2n, 27, 85, 121, 123, 158; common people resisting the British in, 86; under rebel control, 112

Wajid Ali, 33n, 161; followed by his subjects to Kanpur, 36

Wellesley, 1; promises London 'a supper of Oudh', 32n, 164